A Study Companion to
Introduction to World Religions

A Study Companion to
Introduction to World Religions

Compiled and edited by

BETH WRIGHT

Fortress Press
Minneapolis

A STUDY COMPANION TO INTRODUCTION TO WORLD RELIGIONS

Cover image: DIPTENDU DUTTA/AFP/Getty Images
Cover design: Laurie Ingram
Book design: PerfecType, Nashville, TN

Library of Congress Cataloging-in-Publication Data is availble
Print ISBN: 978-1-4514-6468-9
eBook ISBN: 978-1-4514-6515-0

The paper used in this publication meets the minimum requirements of American National Standard for Information Sciences — Permanence of Paper for Printed Library Materials, ANSI Z329.48-1984.

Manufactured in the U.S.A.

CONTENTS

FOR THE INSTRUCTOR: HOW TO USE THE STUDY COMPANION

This study companion provides many resources to supplement the rich material offered by the textbook *Introduction to World Religions*. Instructors may find the following features particularly helpful:

▶ The *Chapter Summaries* for each part provide an overview that highlights key themes and concepts. Encourage your students to read them before they read the section in the textbook and to prepare for quizzes and exams.

▶ *Key Personalities* are significant historical figures from the tradition; a brief biographical sketch is included for each. Additional materials are often also provided, such as quotations from primary sources or scholarly analysis of the figure's work or significance. Students can review these before or after reading a section and may find them helpful for pre-exam review or when searching for a paper topic. (Note: In chapter 3, "Indigenous Religions," *A Brief Survey of Traditions* replaces the Key Personalities section. In addition the *Annotated Bibliography* offers further resources related to the topics of the chapter's case studies.)

▶ *Primary Source Readings* offer students further historical context and content related to the religion under discussion. You may wish to use the materials as the source of exam questions that ask the students to analyze the text in light of what they know of the faith tradition.

▶ *Key Terms* are important concepts and vocabulary words from the tradition, accompanied by definitions. Students should be encouraged to familiarize themselves with these terms in preparation for quizzes and exams.

▶ *Questions for Study and Discussion* and *Questions for Reflection* offer students the chance to test their comprehension of the topic and key concepts. They may serve as a source for homework assignments (students write their answers and turn them in), class discussion (students write their answers before coming to class), or preparation for tests (students write their responses below the questions and review them for the exam).

▶ *Additional Online Resources* offer a taste of online information about the topics discussed in the section. Encourage students to use the links as starting places on the web that may lead them to essay or research paper topics.

If your course requires students to write a research paper, direct them to the guide at the end of this book. It provides a step-by-step process of writing a research paper, including deciding on a topic and developing a thesis, note taking, outlining, writing and revising a draft, ensuring proper bibliographic style (examples are included), and polishing the final paper. Also included are helpful bibliographies of online and print reference works and style manuals.

We hope this study companion provides useful material to supplement the textbook and assists you in your effort to expand students' understanding of world religions.

FOR THE STUDENT: HOW TO USE THE STUDY COMPANION

This study companion is intended to help you get the most out of *Introduction to World Religions*—to further your understanding of each of the faiths discussed in the textbook and to spark your critical thinking about a religion's structures, values, and relationships with other social forces. The companion is organized like the textbook: each chapter corresponds to a part in the book and typically includes chapter summaries, key personalities, excerpts from related primary source material, key terms with definitions, questions for discussion and reflection, and selected online resources.

Before you begin reading a section of the textbook, or after reading it to ensure you understood the main ideas, read the *Chapter Summaries*. You will notice that the chapters focusing on a single religion or closely related group of religious traditions (e.g., Indigenous Religions) have a fairly consistent structure, with some variations: typical subsections include a historical overview, beliefs, sacred writings, worship and festivals, and the religion in the modern world. The summaries feature a brief look at the principle beliefs and practices, history and development, and contemporary concerns of each religion.

Also before you read a section, it might be useful to note the *Key Personalities* and *Key Terms*. The Key Personalities list a selection of significant historical figures from the tradition, a brief biography for each, an excerpt from the person's own work or a scholar's insights into the figure's significance, and in some cases related resources available online. Key Terms are a selected list of concepts particular to a religion or study of a religion, names of important institutions or movements, and so forth and their definitions. You will want to be at least familiar with these personalities and terms by the time you have finished reading the section.

(In chapter 3, "Indigenous Religions," *A Brief Survey of Traditions* and an *Annotated Bibliography* replaces the Key Personalities section found in the other chapters. The information listed in these sections is related to the topics of the chapter's case studies.)

The *Primary Source Readings* appearing in each part of this guide are intended to provide additional context for and insight into the faith tradition discussed in the textbook. After you read a section in the textbook, these materials can help further your understanding of the topic or act as touchstones for class discussion or essays.

Immediately after you have read a chapter in the book, you might wish to go through the related *Questions for Study and Discussion* and *Questions for Reflection*. On your own you can use these questions to test your knowledge of the basic concepts and values of the religion, while also reflecting back on the text and thinking critically about the tradition. Some of the questions are intended to focus on reading comprehension—asking you to demonstrate your understanding by using your own words to define terms, describe ideas, and summarize key points. Other questions encourage you to make comparisons, analyze the deeper meanings of a text, and return to the book to consider the illustrations, personal essays ("I am . . ."), and sidebars and what they tell you about a religion's core beliefs and values. The questions can also be used in a class discussion group or as the basis for essay or research paper topics.

A short list follows under the heading *Selected Online Resources*. The websites included in this guide are simply a sample of online resources related to world religions and the study of religion. Online museum exhibits, academic research sites, the texts of sacred writings, personal testimonies or perspectives on religion, and historical data are all available on the web. Use the sites offered here as a jumping-off point; when your interest is caught by a particular topic or individual mentioned in a section, you can do quick research on the web to learn more before heading to the library shelves.

Following the pre-test and the thirteen chapters corresponding to the textbook is a guide to writing research papers on topics in world religion. It includes bibliographies of reference works in print and electronic media, as well as online sources related to world religions. You can also learn useful research methods and tips on writing effective papers, as well as see examples of proper footnote and bibliographic citation form.

One final note: Many of the key terms and personalities listed in this guide, along with other vocabulary, are included in the "Rapid Fact-Finder" (located at the back of the book, before the index), a detailed, alphabetically organized glossary. Be sure to check out this additional resource to assist you in your understanding and further exploration of world religions.

Part One: Understanding Religion

Chapter Summaries

1. What Is Religion?

Scholars in the past and today have focused on the personal expression of faith and the organized institution as two major aspects of religion apparent across cultures. Essentialists define the essence of religion (faith, belief) as nonempirical and focus on the outward behavior reflected by that essence. Functionalists study religion's societal roles through a variety of lenses, including psychology, sociology, and politics. A third approach looks at the wide variety of religions as part of a family whose members share certain traits.

2. Phenomenology and the Study of Religion

Phenomenology is one historical approach to the study of religion, involving a classification of the various aspects of religion, including objects, rituals, and teachings. Some scholars go a step further and define religions by their a priori sense of the holy. This philosophical approach raises the question of objectivity in the study of religion; one must ask how an outsider (a nonbeliever) can understand a religion in the way an insider, or believer, does. A common approach in contemporary scholarship is to acknowledge the inherent cultural biases of the person studying a religion and to use rigorous, critical analysis, or metatheory, to engage with and critique the scholar's own assumptions.

3. The Anthropology of Religion

An anthropological approach to religion focuses on the cultural aspects. Emile Durkheim's view that religion is a projection of society's values and Mary Douglas's studies of symbols and classifications have been influential in the field. Myths and symbols offer another doorway to understanding religion; while myths highlight significant issues and values of a given culture, symbols help believers find personal meaning within a religious tradition.

4. The Sociology of Religion

Contemporary sociological study of religion focuses on the social construction of religion and, in particular, the connections between beliefs and practices. Max Weber, a major influence on the field, established what is now called "meaning theory," which emphasizes the way religion gives meaning to human life and society. More recent areas of study within the field are secularization and new religious movements.

5. The Psychology of Religion

William James attempted to promote a scientific view of religion, while Sigmund Freud considered religious belief to be based on an illusion. Carl Jung had a more positive approach than Freud in his psychological studies, focusing on the role the image of God plays in the psyche as part of an individual's development. Contemporary scholarship has developed in a number of areas, including children's religious development, connections between mental health and religious belief, and the study of charismatic religion.

6. Theological Approaches to the Study of Religion

A theological study of a religion seeks to understand what it means to its believers and how it functions as a worldview. Some scholars may focus on an emic or etic approach—a believer's viewpoint or an external observer's. Other scholars subscribe to the insider/outsider concept in which they are always outsiders studying the insiders, or believers. The question of objectivity is always in play, so that a theological approach must acknowledge the observer's cultural biases whether from inside or outside the religious tradition. Comparative religious study has offered insights into how religions influence each other and therefore the scholarship developed about them.

7. Critical Theory and Religion

Critical theory about religion developed in Western thought as part of a general trend that questioned notions of truth and certainty of knowledge. The most influential thinkers in this area are Karl Marx, Friedrich Nietzsche, and Sigmund Freud. While the Frankfurt School followed Marx and Freud in seeing religion and culture as being manipulated by those in power, post-structuralists like Michel Foucault and Jacques Derrida focused on the historical nature of ideas and the instability of language that lead to questioning all assertions about knowledge.

8. Ritual and Performance

Depending on a scholar's methodology, rituals may be analyzed for their specific roles within a religious tradition or their value within a given culture. Catherine Bell has created categories of rituals based on what they do, like serving as rites of passage or commemorating an event. Mircea Eliade discussed ritual as reenacting myth, bringing the past into the present. Arnold van Gennep noted the underlying pattern beneath rituals of separation, transition, and reintegration. Bruce Lincoln has studied female initiation and points to the different pattern involved: enclosure, metamorphosis or magnification, and emergence.

Religious Adherents of Major Traditions in the World

Source: J. Gordon Melton, Martin Baumann, eds., *Religions of the World: A Comprehensive Encyclopedia of Beliefs and Practices*, 2nd ed. (Santa Barbara, CA: ABC-CLIO, 2010), lix

Religion	Followers in 1970	Followers in 2010	% of Population	Annual % growth 2000–2010	Followers in 2025	Followers in 2050
Christians	1,234,969,000	2,292,454,000	33.2	1.44	2,708,029,000	3,220,348,000
Roman Catholics	665,895,000	1,155,627,000	16.7	0.88	1,323,840,000	1,522,294,000
Protestants	210,986,000	419,316,000	6.1	1.85	530,485,000	671,148,000
Independents	86,018,000	369,156,000	5.3	2.69	502,211,000	655,556,000
Muslims	579,875,000	1,549,444,000	22.4	1.86	1,962,881,000	2,494,229,000
Hindus	458,845,000	948,507,000	13.7	1.53	1,098,680,000	1,241,133,000
Agnostics	542,318,000	639,852,000	9.3	-0.58	625,648,000	556,416,000
Chinese folk	231,814,000	458,316,000	6.6	0.87	504,695,000	525,183,000
Buddhists	234,028,000	468,736,000	6.8	1.46	542,372,000	570,283,000
Ethnoreligionists	165,687,000	261,429,000	3.8	1.31	267,440,000	272,450,000
Atheists	165,301,000	138,532,000	2.0	-0.11	133,320,000	132,671,000
New religionists	39,332,000	64,443,000	0.9	0.52	66,677,000	63,657,000
Sikhs	10,677,000	24,591,000	0.4	1.69	29,517,000	34,258,000
Jews	15,100,000	14,641,000	0.2	0.62	15,521,000	16,973,000
Spiritists	4,657,000	13,978,000	0.2	1.10	15,664,000	17,080,000
Daoists	1,734,000	9,017,000	0.1	3.02	13,194,000	15,018,000
Confucianists	4,759,000	6,461,000	0.1	0.22	6,698,000	6,014,000
Baha'is	2,657,000	7,447,000	0.1	1.80	10,491,000	15,113,000
Jains	2,629,000	5,749,000	0.1	1.65	6,845,000	7,943,000
Shintoists	4,175,000	2,782,000	0.0	0.16	2,674,000	2,355,000
Zoroastrians	125,000	181,000	0.0	0.05	166,000	170,000
Total population	3,698,683,000	6,906,560,000	100.0	1.24	8,010,511,000	9,191,294,000

Key Personalities

Karl Marx (1818–83)

German intellectual who critiqued capitalism and the function of religion in society.

"The philosopher, social scientist, historian and revolutionary, Karl Marx, is without a doubt the most influential socialist thinker to emerge in the 19th century. Although he was largely ignored by scholars in his own lifetime, his social, economic and political ideas gained rapid acceptance in the socialist movement after his death in 1883."

(Steven Kreis, "Karl Marx, 1818-1883," 2000, The History Guide: Lectures on Modern European Intellectual History, http://www.historyguide.org/intellect/marx.html)

"Marx published *A Contribution to the Critique of Political Economy* in 1859. . . . Marx argued that the superstructure of law, politics, religion, art and philosophy was determined by economic forces. 'It is not,' he wrote, 'the consciousness of men that determines their existence, but their social existence that determines their consciousness.' This is what Friedrich Engels later called 'false consciousness.'"

(John Simkin, "Karl Marx: Biography," Spartacus Educational, n.d., http://www.spartacus.schoolnet.co.uk/TUmarx.htm)

ADDITIONAL RESOURCES

▸ *Capital: A Critique of Political Economy*, vol. 1 (English translation of *Das Kapital*) http://www.marxists.org/archive/marx/works/1867-c1/
▸ Text of *The Communist Manifesto* (downloadable text file) http://www.indepthinfo.com/communist-manifesto/text.shtml

Émile Durkheim (1858–1917)

French scholar considered the father of sociology.

"[Since his] grandfather and great-grandfather had also been rabbis, [he] appeared destined for the rabbinate, and a part of his early education was spent in a rabbinical school. This early ambition was dismissed while he was still a schoolboy, and soon after his arrival in Paris, Durkheim would break with Judaism altogether. But he always remained the product of close-knit, orthodox Jewish family, as well as that long-established Jewish community of Alsace-Lorraine that had been occupied by Prussian troops in 1870, and suffered the consequent anti-Semitism of the French citizenry. Later, Durkheim would argue that the hostility of Christianity toward Judaism had created an unusual sense of solidarity among the Jews."

(Robert Alun Jones, *Emile Durkheim: An Introduction to Four Major Works* [Beverly Hills: Sage, 1986], http://durkheim.uchicago.edu/Biography.html)

"In 1912, Durkheim published his fourth major work, *Les Formes élémentaires de la vie religieuse* (The Elementary Forms of the Religious Life). . . . His scientific approach to every social phenomenon had not only managed to draw the ire of the Catholic Church, some philosophers, and the Right Wing, but he had also gained quite a fair bit of power in the world of academia; his lecture courses were required curriculum for all philosophy, literature, and history students."

("Emile Durkheim Biography," 2002, http://www.emile-durkheim.com/emile_durkheim_bio_002.htm)

ADDITIONAL RESOURCES

▸ *The Elementary Forms of the Religious Life* (1915 edition available for online viewing or in downloadable forms) http://www.archive.org/details/elementaryformso00durk
▸ *The Rules of Sociological Method and Selected Texts on Sociology and Its Method* (portions of text available on Google Books) http://books.google.com/books?id=dM01B9O6s8YC

Mircea Eliade (1907–86)

A Romanian-born philosopher and historian of religion who served thirty years as chair of the history of religions department at the University of Chicago.

"Eliade contends that the perception of time as an homogenous, linear, and unrepeatable medium is a peculiarity of modern and non-religious humanity. Archaic or religious humanity (*homo religiosus*), in comparison, perceives time as heterogeneous; that is, as divided between profane time (linear), and sacred time (cyclical and reactualizable). By means of myths and rituals which give access to this sacred time religious humanity protects itself against the 'terror of history,' a condition of helplessness before the absolute data of historical time, a form of existential anxiety."

(Bryan Rennie, "Mircea Eliade (1907-1986)," n.d., http://www.westminster.edu/staff/brennie/eliade/mebio.htm)

"Eliade started to write *The Myth of the Eternal Return* in 1945, in the aftermath of World War II, when Europe was in ruins, and Communism was conquering Eastern European countries. The essay dealt with mankind's experience of history and time, especially the conceptions of being and reality. According to Eliade, in modern times people have lost their contact with natural cycles, known in traditional societies. Eliade saw that for human beings their inner, unhistorical world, and its meanings, were crucial. Behind historical processes are archaic symbols. Belief in a linear progress of history is typical for the Christian worldview, which counters the tyranny of history with the idea of God, but in the archaic world of archetypes and repetition the tyranny of history is accepted. . . . Eliade contrasts the Western linear view of time with the Eastern cyclical world view."

(Petri Liukkonen and Ari Pesonen, "Mircea Eliade (1908-1986)," 2008, http://www.kirjasto.sci.fi/eliade.htm)

ADDITIONAL RESOURCES

▸ *The Sacred and the Profane* (the text of the book viewable online and in downloadable form)
http://www.scribd.com/doc/312238/Mircea-Eliade-The-Sacred-The-Profane
▸ "Mircea Eliade" (an essay exploring the nature of Eliade's association with Heidegger and right-wing politics during the Nazi era and how it affected his philosophy of religion)
http://www.friesian.com/eliade.htm

Emmanuel Levinas (1906–95)

Lithuanian-born philosopher, ethicist, and Talmudic commentator who influenced postmodern thinkers such as Derrida.

"Levinas' philosophy is directly related to his experiences during World War II. His family died in the Holocaust, and, as a French citizen and soldier, Levinas himself became a prisoner of war in Germany. . . . This experience, coupled with Heidegger's affiliation to National Socialism during the war, clearly and understandably led to a profound crisis in Levinas' enthusiasm for Heidegger. . . . At the same time, Levinas felt that Heidegger could not simply be forgotten, but must be gotten beyond. If Heidegger is concerned with Being, Levinas is concerned with ethics, and ethics, for Levinas, is beyond being—Otherwise than Being."

(Bren Dean Robbins, "Emmanuel Levinas," Mythos & Logos, 2000, http://mythosandlogos.com/Levinas.html)

"Levinas's second magnum opus, *Otherwise Than Being or Beyond Essence* (1974), an immensely challenging and sophisticated work that seeks to push philosophical intelligibility to the limit in an effort to lessen the inevitable concessions made to ontology and the tradition . . . is generally considered Levinas's most important contribution to the contemporary debate surrounding the closure of metaphysical discourse, much commented upon by Jacques Derrida, for example."

(Peter Atterton, "The Emmanuel Levinas Web Page," n.d., http://www.levinas.sdsu.edu/)

ADDITIONAL RESOURCES

▸ "Emmanuel Levinas," *Stanford Encyclopedia of Philosophy* (essay discussing Levinas's philosophy; includes biographical outline)
http://plato.stanford.edu/entries/levinas/

▶ *Basic Philosophical Writings* (portions of text available on Google Books) http://books.google.com/books?id =dmHH1Xie8Q0C

Claude Lévi-Strauss (1908–2009)

French scholar who pioneered structural anthropology.

"The basis of the structural anthropology of Lévi-Strauss is the idea that the human brain systematically processes organised, that is to say structured, units of information that combine and recombine to create models that sometimes explain the world we live in, sometimes suggest imaginary alternatives, and sometimes give tools with which to operate in it. The task of the anthropologist, for Lévi-Strauss, is not to account for why a culture takes a particular form, but to understand and illustrate the principles of organisation that underlie the onward process of transformation that occurs as carriers of the culture solve problems that are either practical or purely intellectual."

(Maurice Bloch, "Claude Lévi-Strauss Obituary," *Guardian* [London], November 3, 2009, http://www.guardian.co .uk/science/2009/nov/03/claude-levi-strauss-obituary)

"'Mythologiques,' his four-volume work about the structure of native mythology in the Americas, attempts nothing less than an interpretation of the world of culture and custom, shaped by analysis of several hundred myths of little-known tribes and traditions. . . . In his analysis of myth and culture, Mr. Lévi-Strauss might contrast imagery of monkeys and jaguars; consider the differences in meaning of roasted and boiled food (cannibals, he suggested, tended to boil their friends and roast their enemies); and establish connections between weird mythological tales and ornate laws of marriage and kinship."

(Edward Rothstein, "Claude Lévi-Strauss, 100, Dies; Altered Western Views of the 'Primitive,'" *New York Times*, November 4, 2009, http://www.nytimes.com/2009/11/04 /world/europe/04levistrauss.html)

ADDITIONAL RESOURCES

▶ "Library Man: On Claude Lévi-Strauss" (an in-depth review of Patrick Wilcken's biography of Lévi-Strauss) http://www.thenation.com/article/157879 /library-man-claude-levi-strauss
▶ *The Raw and the Cooked* (vol. 1 of *Mythologiques*, portions of text available on Google Books) http://books.google.com/books?id =BmkKavks2P4C

Max Weber (1864–1920)

German sociologist who used historical and economic tools to analyze capitalism and its role in society.

"Weber may have 'spent his life having a posthumous dialogue with the ghost of Karl Marx' (Cuff, p. 97). This dialogue concerned (i) economic determinism or the extent to which developments are rooted in the material base, and (ii) the extent to which economic factors alone can be considered at the root of social structure. . . . Many contemporary sociologists think of Weber as complementing Marx, examining issues that Marx thought less important, providing a way of thinking about the individual within a structural approach, and laying out a sociological methodology. Weber's writing had an influence on structural functionalism, critical theory, some of the social interaction approaches, and much contemporary sociological theory, including some Marxist approaches that use ideas from Weber."

(Paul Gingrich, "Notes on Max Weber," Introduction to Social Theory, Sociology 250, University of Regina, September 30, 1999, http://uregina.ca/~gingrich/s30f99.htm)

"Weber suggested two sets of ethical virtues that a proper political education should teach—the ethic of conviction (Gesinnungsethik) and the ethic of responsibility (Verantwortungsethik). According to the ethic of responsibility, on the one hand, an action is given meaning only as a cause of an effect, that is, only in terms of its causal relationship to the empirical world. The virtue lies in an objective understanding of the possible causal effect of an action and the calculated reorientation of the elements of an action in such a way as to achieve a desired consequence. An ethical question is thereby reduced to a question of technically correct procedure, and free action consists of choosing the correct means.... According to the ethic of conviction, on the other hand, a free agent should be able to choose autonomously not only the means, but also the end.... In this respect, Weber's problem arises from the recognition that the kind of rationality applied in choosing a means cannot be used in choosing an end. These two kinds of reasoning represent categorically distinct modes of rationality, a boundary further reinforced by modern value fragmentation."

(Sung Ho Kim, "Max Weber," *Stanford Encyclopedia of Philosophy*, August 24, 2007, http://plato.stanford.edu /entries/weber/)

ADDITIONAL RESOURCES

▶ "Max Weber's View of Objectivity in Social Science" (essay by Steve Hoenisch) http://www.criticism.com/md/weber1.html

▶ *The Protestant Ethic and the Spirit of Capitalism* (text of the book) http://xroads.virginia.edu/~HYPER/WEBER /cover.html

William James (1842–1910)

American scholar trained in medicine who wrote on philosophy, psychology, and religion.

"In his later writings, James argued that children should be unfettered, allowed to indulge their natural impulses. Childhood, for him, was a time of 'divine rapture' and 'magical light.' The dictates of religion, which he saw as an 'outrage to nature,' would repress children and 'draw a pall over the lovely outlying world of sense.' More important, religion asked children to defer to an inviolable authority, a cruel and hateful God, who wanted to deny the child expression of his individuality.... In perpetual battle with this hostile force, James said that, as a child, he could never feel pleasure or happiness without an underlying sense of fear that God would strike in retribution."

(From Linda Simon, *Genuine Reality: A Life of William James* [Chicago: University of Chicago Press, 1999], http:// www.uky.edu/~eushe2/Pajares/jamesreal.html)

"James oscillated between thinking that a 'study in human nature' such as Varieties [*of Religious Experience*] could contribute to a 'Science of Religion' and the belief that religious experience involves an altogether supernatural domain, somehow inaccessible to science but accessible to the individual human subject.... In 'A Pluralistic Universe' he defends the mystical and anti-pragmatic view that concepts distort rather than reveal reality, and in his influential Pragmatism (1907), he presents systematically a set of views about truth, knowledge, reality, religion, and philosophy that permeate his writings from the late 1870s onwards."

(Russell Goodman, "William James," *Stanford Encyclopedia of Philosophy*, October 23, 2009, http://plato.stanford .edu/entries/james/)

ADDITIONAL RESOURCES

▶ William James (extensive collection of resources related to James's life and work) http://www.uky.edu/~eushe2/Pajares/james .html

▶ *The Varieties of Religious Experience* (the entire text available on Google Books) http://books.google.com/books?id =uX9gc4-YW9AC

Carl Jung (1875–1961)

Swiss psychiatrist who developed the theory of the "collective unconscious" and founded the field of analytical psychology.

"The contents of the collective unconscious are called *archetypes*. Jung also called them dominants, imagos, mythological or primordial images, and a few other names, but archetypes seems to have won out over these. An archetype is an unlearned tendency to experience things in a certain way.... The mother archetype is symbolized by the primordial mother or 'earth mother' of mythology, by Eve and Mary in western traditions, and by less personal symbols such as the church, the nation, a forest, or the ocean. According to Jung, someone whose own mother failed to satisfy the demands of the archetype may well be one that spends his or her life seeking comfort in the church, or in identification with 'the motherland,' or in meditating upon the figure of Mary, or in a life at sea."

(C. George Boeree, "Carl Jung: 1875-1961," Personality Theories, 2006, http://webspace.ship.edu/cgboer/jung.html

"Jung saw myth and its meaning within the individual psyche. In spite of myths and their components being shared by all members of a society—and essentially by all mankind—their workings are strictly personal. According to Jung, man is on a quest towards self-realization, and myths serve as clues to this process. Although every person has this quest, fulfilling it in various degrees, it is a solo venture, each man for himself."

(Stefan Stenudd, "Psychoanalysis of Myth: Freud's and Jung's Theories on Myth and Its Origin," 2006, http://www.stenudd.com/myth/freudjung/jung.htm)

ADDITIONAL RESOURCES

▶ The Jung Page (essays, book and film reviews, lexicon, and other resources for Jungian scholarship)
http://www.cgjungpage.org/index.php
▶ "Carl Gustav Jung (1875-1961)" (an essay comparing Jung's approach to religion to the approach of philosophers like Immanuel Kant)
http://www.friesian.com/jung.htm

Jacques Derrida (1930–2004)

Algerian-born French philosopher who proposed the theory of deconstruction.

"Derrida was famous for deconstruction, the claim that texts subtly undermine their ostensible meanings. Texts (all discourse altogether, from a transient remark to the most pondered philosophy) are open to repeated interpretation. . . . Our understanding of a word depends on other words—on an endless chain of signifiers, pointing to nothing beyond themselves and developing out a history of usage entirely lost to us. In short, language depends on

nothing, no fundamental ground of logic, science or society. . . . There is no end to interpretation, and no escaping it, says Derrida. All we can do is point to its workings."

(C. John Holcombe, "Jacques Derrida," Text Etc., 2007, http://www.textetc.com/theory/derrida.html)

"He drew critically on the work of Emmanuel Levinas in order to insist on the Other as one to whom an incalculable responsibility is owed, one who could never fully be 'captured' through social categories or designative names, one to whom a certain response is owed. This conception became the basis of his strenuous critique of apartheid in South Africa, his vigilant opposition to totalitarian regimes and forms of intellectual censorship, his theorisation of the nation-state beyond the hold of territoriality, his opposition to European racism, and his criticism of the discourse of 'terror' as it worked to increase governmental powers that undermine basic human rights. This political ethic can be seen at work in his defence of animal rights, in his opposition to the death penalty, and even in his queries about 'being' Jewish and what it means to offer hospitality to those of differing origins and language."

(Judith Butler, "Jacques Derrida," *London Review of Books*, November 4, 2004, http://www.lrb.co.uk/v26/n21/judith-butler/jacques-derrida)

ADDITIONAL RESOURCES

▶ "Jacques Derrida" (an essay on Derrida's theories, with bibliography)
http://plato.stanford.edu/entries/derrida/
▶ "Jacques Derrida: Defining Deconstruction" (short excerpt from the film *Derrida* 2004)
http://www.youtube.com/watch?v=vgwOjjoYtco

Mary Douglas (1921–2007)

An English anthropologist who focused on classification systems in societies and their associated use of symbols.

"The celebrated anthropologist Mary Douglas (1921–2007) devoted her career to explaining, in terms generous enough to include all peoples and refined enough to be meaningful, what humans do. What indeed are we doing? Billions of us, running around, busying ourselves about billions of tasks, weaving in and out of harmony with our world and with each other? What we think and do is sometimes called culture. Cultural anthropology traditionally has been absorbed in describing the specific cultures of specific social groups in certain times and places: the important work of data-gathering. Douglas' special contribution was to greatly further the fundamental discussion of why and how human beings do culture at all. Drawing on data from specific groups, she explored the shared journey of being human. She suggests that human beings, in all their variety, essentially are busying themselves about two tasks: trying to make meaningful sense of the world and trying to coordinate their lives with the people around them."

(John Clay, "Anthropology and Accountability: An Interview with Mary Douglas," 2001, updated 2008, http:// www.bhag.net/int/intdougm/intdougm_inte.html)

"In 1966, Douglas published her most celebrated work, Purity and Danger: An Analysis of Concepts of Pollution and Taboo. This book is best remembered for its stylish demonstration of the ways in which all schemes of classification produce anomalies: whether the pangolin for the Lele, or the God incarnate of Catholic theology. Some of this classificatory 'matter out of place'—from humble house dust in her Highgate house to the abominations of Leviticus for the Hebrews—was polluting, but other breaches of routine classification had the capacity to renew the world symbolically."

(Richard Fardon, "Dame Mary Douglas (Obituary)," *Guardian* [London], May 18, 2007, http://www.guardian .co.uk/news/2007/may/18/guardianobituaries.obituaries)

ADDITIONAL RESOURCES

▶ "I Think We Won: Mary Douglas Interview" (video)
  http://fourcultures.com/2009/05/08/i-think -we-won-mary-douglas-interview/

▶ "Purity and Danger: A Report on the Book" (summary and key points from Douglas's book *Purity and Danger*)
  http://ihome.ust.hk/~lbcaplan/mphil/purity.html

Victor Turner (1920–83)

Scottish anthropologist who studied cultural symbols, especially rituals, in various societies.

"For Turner, liminality is one of the three cultural manifestations of communitas—it is one of the most visible expressions of anti-structure in society. Yet even as it is the antithesis of structure, dissolving structure and being perceived as dangerous by those in charge of maintaining structure, it is also the source of structure. Just as chaos is the source of order, liminality represents the unlimited possibilities from which social structure emerges. While in the liminal state, human beings are stripped of anything that might differentiate them from their fellow human beings—they are in between the social structure, temporarily fallen through the cracks, so to speak, and it is in these cracks, in the interstices of social structure, that they are most aware of themselves. Yet liminality is a midpoint between a starting point and an ending point, and as such it is a temporary state that ends when the initiate is reincorporated into the social structure."

(Charles La Shure, "Turner and Liminality," October 18, 2005, http://www.liminality.org/about/whatisliminality/)

"In rites of passage, liminal entities have no sure footing in community, and are socially without power, and are generally subjected to all kinds of taunts and torments. . . . Others may embrace liminality by rejecting a culture's values, voluntarily giving up social structure in favor of a raw structure-less communitas. . . . Communitas is characterized by spontaneity, rather than goals and decisions. Communitas exists between periods of structure, and is revealed in liminality. It is beneath structure, and in that sense is marginal and inferior to it. At the same time, because it exists where structure does not, it has a transcendental and 'holy' quality. Outside of structural states, communitas produces deep and powerful experiences."

(Calvin Ashmore, "Victor Turner: The Ritual Process," Icosilune, February 12, 2009, http://www.icosilune.com /2009/02/victor-turner-the-ritual-process)

Additional Resources

- ▶ "Victor Turner" (an essay discussing Turner's influence on the field of anthropology) http://www.indiana.edu/~wanthro/turner.htm
- ▶ "Ritual, Anti-Structure, and Religion: A Discussion of Victor Turner's Processual Symbolic Analysis" (article from *Journal for the Scientific Study of Religion*) http://www.cas.sc.edu/socy/faculty/deflem /zturn.htm

Primary Source Readings

The following excerpted readings represent some of the important primary sources mentioned in the main text. Additional primary sources are available both in print and online, and students are encouraged to contact their instructors for further information.

I.1   Wilfrid Cantwell Smith, The Meaning and End of Religion (Minneapolis: Fortress Press, 1990), 1–14, 193–94.

What is religion? What is religious faith? Such questions, asked either from the outside or from within, must nowadays be set in a wide context, and a rather exacting one. The modern student may look upon religion as something that other people do, or he may see and feel it as something in which also he himself is involved. . . . Many considerations, then, must be taken into account in any analysis that is to satisfy a serious modern inquirer. We may enumerate four or five as among the more weighty. First, of course, there is science. . . . It is relevant . . . in so far as particular studies of psychology, sociology, economic history . . . have seemed to illuminate the

ostensibly religious behavior of man. . . . Second, there is the multiplicity of religious traditions. . . . Any adequate interpretation of a Christian's faith, for instance, must make room for the fact that other intelligent, devout, and moral men, including perhaps his own friends, are Buddhists, Hindus, or Muslims. . . . [Third] is the further fact of diversity within each tradition. . . . Next [fourth] may be noted that sheer fact of change. The world is in flux, and we know it. Like other aspects of human life, the religious aspect too is seen to be historical, evolving, in process. Any modern endeavor to clarify what religion is, must now include a question as to what at various stages of development religion has been. . . . Finally, we would mention the vitality of faith.

. . . For a time some thought that the onslaught of science, comparative religion, uncertainty, and the rest—in a word, the onslaught of modernity—meant or would mean the gradual decline and disappearance of the religious tradition. This no longer seems obvious. . . . This much at least is clear: that the amalgam of inner piety and outer institution that at a certain stage in their dynamic development was intellectually reified under the term "religion" and "religions" was conceived thus because some people fell into the habit of doing so. Once he has become aware of what has happened, man cannot escape choosing between whether or not he will continue to use these particular concepts. To me . . . they seem now clearly inadequate.

The proposal that I am putting forward can, at one level, be formulated quite simply. It is that what men have tended to conceive as religion and especially as a religion, can more rewardingly, more truly, be conceived in terms of two factors, different in kind, both dynamic: an historical 'cumulative tradition,' and the personal faith of men and women. On the verbal plane, I seriously suggest that terms such as Christianity, Buddhism, and the like must be dropped, as clearly untenable once challenged. . . . We could rehabilitate perhaps the venerable term "piety."

I.2 Mircea Eliade, The Sacred and the Profane: The Nature of Religion (New York: Harcourt Books, 1987), 62–65.

We have taken our examples from different cultures and periods, in order to present at least the most important mythological constructions and ritual scenarios that are based on sacred space. For in the course of history, religious man has given different valorizations to the same fundamental experience. We need only compare the conception of the sacred space (and hence of the cosmos) discernible among the Australian Achilpa with the corresponding conceptions of the Kwakiutl, the Altaic peoples, or the Mesopotamians, to realize the differences among them. There is no need to dwell on the truism that, since the religious life of humanity is realized in history, its expressions are inevitably conditioned by the variety of historical moments and cultural styles. But for our purpose it is not the infinite variety of the religious experiences of space that concern us but, on the contrary, their elements of unity. Pointing out the contrast between the behavior of nonreligious man with respect to the space in which he lives and the behavior of religious man in respect to sacred space is enough to make the difference in structure between the two attitudes clearly apparent.

If we should attempt to summarize the result of the descriptions that have been presented in this chapter, we could say that the experience of sacred space makes possible the "founding of the world": where the sacred manifests itself in space, *the real unveils itself*, the world comes into existence. But the irruption of the sacred does not only project a fixed point into the formless fluidity of profane space, a center into chaos; it also effects a break in plane, that is, it opens communication between the cosmic planes (between earth and heaven) and makes possible ontological passage from one mode of being to another. . . . Hence the manifestation of the sacred in space has a cosmological valence. . . . The first conclusion we might draw would be: *the world becomes*

apprehensible as world, as cosmos, in the measure in which it reveals itself as a sacred world.

. . . Religious man can live only in a sacred world, because it is only in such a world that he participates in being, that he has a *real existence*. . . . Religious man thirsts for *being*. His terror of the chaos that surrounds his inhabited world corresponds to his terror of nothingness. The unknown space that extends beyond his world, for religious man, this profane space represents absolute nonbeing. If, by some evil chance, he strays into it, he feels emptied of his ontic substance, as if he were dissolving into Chaos, and he finally dies.

. . . The experience of sacred time will make it possible for religious man periodically to experience the cosmos as it was *in principio*, that is, at the mythical moment of creation.

I.3 Rudolf Otto, The Idea of the Holy, trans. John W. Harvey (New York: Oxford University Press, 1958), 5–11.

Holiness—the holy—is a category of interpretation and valuation peculiar to the sphere of religion. It is, indeed, applied by transference to another sphere—that of ethics—but it is not itself derived from this. . . . The fact is we have come to use the words 'holy,' "sacred" in an entirely derivative sense, quite different from that which they originally bore. We generally take "holy" as meaning "completely good"; it is the absolute moral attribute, denoting the consummation of moral goodness. . . . We may speak of the holiness or sanctity of duty or law, meaning merely that they are imperative upon conduct and universally obligatory.

But this common usage of the term is inaccurate. It is true that all this moral significance is contained in the word "holy," but it includes in addition a clear overplus of meaning, and this is now our task to isolate. . . . It will be our endeavor to suggest this unnamed Something to the reader as far as we may, so that he may himself feel it. There is no religion in which it does not live as the real innermost core, and without it no religion would be worthy of the name. To find a word to stand for this element in isolation, this "extra" in the meaning of "holy" above and beyond the meaning of goodness, . . . I adopt a word coined from the Latin *numen*. . . . It may perhaps help . . . if I cite a well-known example, in which the precise 'moment' or element of religious feeling of which we are speaking is most actively present. When Abraham ventures to plead with God for the men of Sodom, he says: "Behold now, I have taken upon me to speak unto the Lord, which am but dust and ashes." (Gen 18:27) There you have a self-confessed "feeling of dependence," which is yet at the same time far more than, and something other than, *merely* a feeling of dependence.

I.4   *Sigmund Freud,* The Future of an Illusion *(Harmondsworth: Penguin Books, 1992), 199–200.*

The more autonomous nature became and the more the gods withdrew from it, the more earnestly were all expectations directed to the third function of the gods—the more did morality become their true domain. It now becomes the task of the gods to even out the defects and evils of civilization, to attend to the sufferings which men inflict on one another in their life together and to watch over the fulfillment of the precepts of civilization, which men obey so imperfectly. Those precepts themselves were credited with a divine origin; they were elevated beyond human society and were extended to nature and the universe.

And thus a store of ideas is created, born from man's need to make his helplessness tolerable and built up from material of memories of the helplessness of his own childhood and the childhood of the human race. It can clearly be seen that the possession of these ideas protects him in two directions—against the dangers of nature and Fate, and against the injuries that threaten him from human society itself. Here is the gist of the matter. Life in this world serves a higher purpose; no doubt it is not easy to guess what that purpose is, but it certainly signifies a perfecting of man's nature. It is probably the spiritual part of man, the soul, which in the course of time has so slowly and unwillingly detached itself from the body, that is the object of this elevation and exaltation. Everything that happens in this world is an expression of the intentions of an intelligence superior to us, which in the end, though its ways and byways are difficult to follow, orders everything for the best—that is, to make it enjoyable for us. Over each one of us there watches a benevolent Providence which is only seemingly stern and which will not suffer us to become a plaything of the overmighty and pitiless forces of nature. Death itself is not extinction, is not a return to inorganic lifelessness, but the beginning of a new kind of existence which lies on the path of development to something higher. And, looking in the other direction, this view announces that the same moral laws which our civilizations have set up govern the whole universe as well, except that they are maintained by a supreme court of justice with incomparably more power and consistency. In the end all good is rewarded and all evil punished, if not actually in this form of life then in the later existences that begin after death. In this way all the terrors, the sufferings and hardships of life are destined to be obliterated.

. . . Of the one divine being into which all the gods of antiquity have been condensed, . . . this was a return to the historical beginnings of the idea of God. Now that God was a single person, man's relations to him could recover the intimacy and intensity of the child's relation to his father. But if one had done so much for one's father, one wanted to have a reward, or at least to be his only beloved child, his Chosen People. . . . [These religious ideas] are prized as the most precious possession of civilization, as the most precious thing it has to offer its participants. It is far more highly prized than all the devices for winning treasures from the earth or providing men with sustenance or preventing their illnesses, and so forth. People feel that life would not be tolerable if they did not attach to these ideas the value that is claimed for them.

Key Terms

critical theory   The view that religious knowledge, like all forms of truth claims, can be questioned; it attempts to question all assumptions about religions and their uniqueness.

emic perspective   The study of religion from within the cultural world of the believer.

essentialist   One who believes that the essence of religion is real and nonempirical, that it must be experienced firsthand to be understood, and that the institutions and worldly trappings of religion are secondary to this essence.

etic perspective   The study of religion from the outside.

family resemblance definition   An approach associated with the philosopher Ludwig Wittgenstein that assumes nothing is defined by only one essence or function; therefore, what we call religions are defined by a set of traits that they share to one degree or another.

functionalist   One who seeks to determine the social, psychological, or political role played by forces that are called "religious."

meaning theory   The theory that religion gives meaning to human existence and reality, helping to make sense of what might appear senseless.

phenomenology   The attempt to classify and describe religions in terms of their objects, rituals, teachings, etc.

post-structuralism   A reaction to the concept of structuralism, that is, the idea that there is a limited number of structures in myth, language, and the world; it denies that these structures are given or unchanging and focuses on the influence of culture and power in society.

rational choice theory   The theory that religions are like products in a global marketplace.

ritual   Religious ceremonial performed according to a set pattern of words, movements and symbolic actions. Rituals may involve the dramatic re-enactment of ancient myths featuring gods and heroes, performed to ensure the welfare of the community.

Questions for Study and Discussion

1. Explain the difference between the essentialist perspective and the functionalist perspective on religion.
2. What is phenomenology? How is Rudolf Otto's theory of the holy an example of the lack of objectivity that is possible in phenomenological approaches to religion?
3. Gavin Flood wrote that in studying religion the significant distinction is between "the critical and the non-critical" (see p. 26). Explain what he means and how it relates to critical theories of religion such as post-structuralism.
4. Give an example of a performance that is also a ritual that you have witnessed or read about. What marked it as a ritual rather than theater?
5. Jeremy Carrette writes, "After critical theory the study of religion becomes a political activity" (see p. 46). Do you agree or disagree? Explain.

Questions for Reflection

Write your personal reflections to each of these questions in the space provided.

1. Describe how religion may have an essence. (See p. 20.)

2. How does ritual express religion? (See pp. 47–48.)

3. Think about the importance of being "methodologically agnostic," and describe its advantages. (See p. 33.)

4. Do the theorists of religion in chapter 7, "Critical Theory and Religion" (pp. 43–46), address how *you* see religion and politics?

5. What is meant by "insiders" and "outsiders" in the study of religion? (See pp. 41–42.)

6. What theory or methodology related to the study of religion and mentioned in Part 1 appeals most to you? Why?

Selected Online Resources

▶ World Religions Photo Library
   http://www.worldreligions.co.uk
▶ Sacred Texts Timeline—a detailed timeline of the sacred texts of major world religions
   http://www.sacred-texts.com/time/timeline.htm
▶ "Anthropology of Religion"—A brief essay on the anthropology of religion, including a history of the field and a bibliography
   http://www.indiana.edu/~wanthro/religion.htm

Part 2: Religions of Antiquity

Chapter Summaries

9. Religion Before History

Because of the absence of written sources, research into prehistoric religion must depend on other evidence, typically from archeological digs. While burial places, drawings, and temple ruins provide some clues to the earliest religious practices and beliefs, we must still admit to the tentativeness of any theories. So when we find goddess figures from a society based on hunting, we may theorize that they represented a hope for protection during pregnancy and childbirth. Cave paintings depicting animals can be interpreted as part of hunting ritual and magic. Megalithic structures probably had astronomical functions.

10. Land of the Aztecs and Incas

The origins of formalized religions in both Mexico and Peru have been traced back as early as 1200 BCE. The Olmecs are known for their use of jaguar images on pavements and sarcophagi. The Maya had an elaborate religion based on ceremonial centers and temples; the contemporary Mayan religion, like the ancient one, focuses on the contract between the people and their gods. The Aztecs believed in two primordial beings that created the gods, who in turn created the earth. The Incas' religion focused on ritual and organization; Incas worshiped a creator-god as well as other gods and participated in a sun cult and an ancestor cult.

11. The Ancient Near East: Cradle of Civilization

Mesopotamia is the heart of the Near East, famed for its fertile land and long history of settlements and cities. The Sumerians' religion is the earliest we know of from the area; it was based on worship of Anu, the supreme god, and Inanna, the mother goddess of love and war. Sumerian myths answered fundamental questions like why the world and human beings exist. The Gilgamesh Epic, based on Sumerian stories but written in Akkadian, is about the adventures of a king who sought immortality. Canaanite religion featured animal sacrifice, statues of gods and goddesses, and divination. The Hittites, based in what is now Turkey, believed in the power of sacrifices to support their gods. The king was high priest and responsible for performing rituals to protect the land.

12. Ancient Egypt: Land of the Priest-King

We know little about ancient Egyptian religious beliefs, since there are no extant studies from the period. Based on archeological evidence, we can say that Egyptians worshipped a variety of gods, some of which resemble animals, and natural forces like the sun. During the rule of the pharaoh Amenophis IV, a monotheistic belief system developed, based on the worship of the god Aten. Egyptian cult and funerary temples show a focus on the rituals held within them; purity was maintained by architectural features as well as sacrifices. The fragments of books of wisdom that have been recovered offer practical advice as well as spiritual guidance for living a life worthy of a reward in the afterlife.

13. Zoroastrianism: A Historical Overview

The religion of the ancient Indo-Iranians, who settled in Persia around 1500 BCE, is a forerunner of Zoroastrianism; it featured no temples but household ritual offerings and a naturalistic view of the divine. Zarathushtra (or Zoroaster in the West) was a prophet and priest of ancient Persia. He emphasized a personal spiritual practice based on a free-will choice between good and evil. God is the wholly good creator of all things; the world is essentially good but threatened by evil. Zoroastrianism was spread though the Babylonian Empire after it was conquered by Cyrus in 539 BCE. During the Islamic conquest of Persia in the seventh century CE, Zoroastrians were denied legal rights and attacked by Muslims. Today they are a small community mostly concentrated in Tehran in modern-day Iran, with a worldwide population of about 115,000.

14. Zoroastrian Beliefs

Because God (Ohrmazd) created the world to aid him in battle against the Devil (Ahriman), the material world is not evil but good. Any evil that exists is attributable to Ahriman. Human nature has two sides: physical and spiritual. After death an individual is judged and rewarded or punished in both aspects. The person's primary duty in life is to make their body a dwelling place of the Bounteous Immortals. Zoroastrians believe that having children and growing food are both part of caring for God's creation. In the fire temple, worshippers pray individually, and priests perform higher ceremonies on behalf of laypeople.

15. The Ancient Religions of Greece and Rome

The Minoan temple at Crete provides evidence of the worship of bulls as well as a belief in snakes as house guardians sacred to the household goddess. The epic poetry of Homer gives us some insights into ancient Greek beliefs: gods are portrayed as essentially immortal humans with the power to affect people's lives but not their ultimate destiny, death. The fifth century BCE was a crucial time for human civilization—with significant contributions by philosophers and writers like Herodotus, Socrates, Sophocles, and Euripedes. Aristotle's treatise *Metaphysics* delves into the nature of God as the "Unmoved Mover" and First Cause. Meanwhile, Hellenization under Alexander the Great led rulers to call themselves divine and mystery cults to spread.

In Roman religion each god had a specific function or office, to be worshipped accordingly. Romans incorporated gods and mythologies from other cultures, including Greek and Etruscan. Ritual was the dominant concern, although the intellectual elite debated that nature of the divine and the world. The imperial cult promoted the emperor as the head of the state religion and thereby empowered by divine as well as political office. Based on excavations at Pompeii, we know that family cults were the heart of everyday life in the Roman Empire, with household shrines devoted to gods and ancestors.

16. The Religion of the Celts: The Old Gods

Based on inscriptions from the northwestern provinces of the Roman Empire, we can deduce that Druidic religious belief there was intensely local, with every place and tribe having its own deity or deities. A few gods and goddesses were more widespread, including some nature gods. Worship was likely held in groves, and bodies of water were considered sacred. Animal sacrifice was a regular practice, and human sacrifice was also likely.

17. The Religions of Scandinavia: The Norse Gods

Iceland provides the most helpful sources on pre-Christian indigenous religions in Scandinavia. These are poems that allude to gods, goddesses, and rituals of Norse myths. While some gods were worshipped over limited areas, others, like Thor, were part of religion throughout the region. Norse myths also feature the trickster god Loki and the Valkyries, women who bring the souls of dead warriors to Valhalla. Religious life was marked by festivals determined by the sun; these involved human and animal sacrifice and communal meals.

18. Nomads of the Steppes

The Mongol Empire was at its peak during the fourteenth century CE. Mongols worshipped the god Tengri, both a supreme god and the name for all that was "heavenly." Powerful rulers like Genghis Khan were often conflated with Tengri. Tribal leaders were also shamans, who acted as healers as well as divined hidden knowledge.

In Russia before the ninth century Perun was worshipped as Supreme Being and god of thunder and lightning. Other gods represented elements like sun and fire. Vampires and werewolves also feature in ancient Slavic religion. Western Slavic gods were warlike and all-knowing. In Baltic religion goddesses were prominent; Laima and Mara were the goddesses of fate and guardians of humans.

Key Personalities

Quetzalcoatl

A mythological figure in Maya and Aztec religion and also the name give to Aztec high priests. He may have been a king of a pre-Aztec civilization. He is associated with the rediscovery of the complex Mayan calendar. His name derives from the sacred Quetzal bird. In mythology he is a god of the air who descended to earth and taught humanity the arts of civilization. He opposed the practice of human sacrifice. His activities aroused the wrath of another deity, and he fled in a boat made of serpent skin. He is often symbolized by a feathered serpent.

"It is entirely correct to think of the Aztec legend Quetzalcoatl in three contexts—as historical personality, as divinity and as literary subject. In the first incarnation he is a 10th century priest-king; in the second a deity associated with progress and human-ity; in the third an object of intense interest to both ancient Aztec and more contemporary European scholars.

"The historical Quetzalcoatl was probably born around AD 947. His father, Mixcoatl, was ruler of the Toltecs. . . . Quetzalcoatl proved to be a wise and progressive ruler. . . . [He] abolished human sacrifice and decreed that henceforth sacrificial objects be limited to snakes, flowers and small birds."

(Jim Tuck, "The Quetzalcoatl 'Trinity,'" Mexconnect, 2008, http://www.mexconnect.com/articles/269-the-quetzal coatl-trinity)

Akhenaten

The name adopted by Amenophis IV (also called Amenhotep IV), king of Egypt 1353–1335 BCE, in honor of Aten ("the sun disc"), whose cult he pro-moted to the exclusion of all others in a short-lived reform of Egyptian religion. He built a magnificent new capital at el-Amarna.

"The nature of Akhenaten's revolution is well estab-lished—he overthrew Egyptian polytheism in favor of the worship of a single god, Aten—but the reason behind it is still unknown. Many people have offered theories. . . . According to John Tuthill, a professor at the University of Guam, Akhenaten's reasons for his religious reform were political. By the time of Akhenaten's reign, the god Amen had risen to such a high status that the priests of Amen had become even more wealthy and powerful than the pharaohs. However, Barbara Mertz argued that Akhenaten and his courtiers would not have easily perceived this. . . . The reasons for Akhenaten's revolution still remain a mystery."

(Megaera Lorenz, "Akhenaten," Heptune, 2000, http://www.heptune.com/Akhnaten.html)

Homer

The author of the Greek epics the *Iliad* and the *Odyssey*, which date from between the tenth and eighth centuries BCE. According to the historian Herodotus, Homer was the first to detail the char-acters and functions of the gods of Mount Olympos.

"The gods of Homer, it has often been noted, are magnified men; but why are they so very big and so very boisterous? Simply because they are, in part, Northerners. Vastness, formlessness, fantastic excess are not 'Greek' in the classical sense. Very northern are the almost Berserker rages of Zeus himself and the roughness of his divine vengeance. To wave his ambrosial locks and shake Olympus by the nod-ding of his brows, may be both Greek and godlike, but how about such manners as 'pushing the other gods from their seats,' 'tossing them about the hall'; hurling his son by the foot over the battlements of Olympus; beating his wife and hanging her up with anvils to her feet, suggesting that she 'would like to eat Priam raw'? There is such magic in the words of Homer that we are apt to forget that these are not the ways of Greek gods, however primitive, but the rude pranks of irresponsible giants. The old *theoi* have been, indeed, considerably 'tossed about' and are none the better for the process."

(Jane Harrison, *Myths of Greece and Rome* [Garden City, NY: Doubleday, 1928], 8–9, http://www.sacred-texts.com /cla/mgr/mgr03.htm)

ADDITIONAL RESOURCE

▶ *The Iliad* by Homer (the epic as translated by Samuel Butler, available online or as a downloadable text file) http://classics.mit.edu/Homer/iliad.html

Zarathushtra (aka Zardusht, Zoroaster) (about seventh to sixth centuries BCE)

Prophet and founder of Zoroastrianism. He lived in Persia, either in the tenth and ninth centuries BCE, or, more likely, in the seventh and sixth. At the age of thirty he had a revelation of Ahura Mazda, which drove him to preach against polytheism. According to tradition he died performing the fire sacrifice, which was the central ceremony of the new faith.

"When he was twenty years old, he departed against his parents' will, leaving his home. . . . He came to a group of people who were famed locally for great knowledge. And he questioned them: 'What greatly advantages the soul?' And they said: 'To feed the poor, to give fodder to cattle, to carry wood to fire, to make the hom-libation to water, and to worship many devs with the Word, the Word which is called religion.' Then Zardusht fed the poor, and gave fodder to cattle, and carried wood to fire, and prepared the hom-libation for water. But never did Zardusht worship any dev whatsoever with the Word."

(*Textual Sources for the Study of Zoroastrianism*, ed. and trans. Mary Boyce [Chicago: University of Chicago Press, 1984], 75)

"Zoroaster saw humanity divided into two opposing parties: the truth-followers (*ashavant*), who were just and god-fearing; and the evil-followers (*dregvant*), among whom were classed all evil rulers, evil-doers, evil-speakers, those of evil conscience, and evil-thinkers (Yasna 49.11). But this basic dualism that Zoroaster saw here and now on earth he projected to the whole cosmos. He came to see that this fundamental tension existed both in the material as well as in the spiritual spheres. Over against a transcendental good mind stood the evil mind; over against the good spirit stood the evil spirit; and so on. Yet, on every level, a choice had to be made. This insistence on freedom of choice was the marked characteristic of Zoroaster's teaching."

(S. A. Nigosian, *The Zoroastrian Faith: Tradition and Modern Research* [Montreal, Quebec: McGill-Queen's University Press, 1993], 21)

Magi

Priests of the people of Medes who came to power in western Persia in the seventh century BCE and helped spread Zoroastrianism.

"As Zoroastrianism swept westward, it encountered the Magi, a priestly tribe of Medes. The Magi had long held the secrets of priestly ritual for the Median people. They were also the keepers of medical lore and of the knowledge of astronomy. Sometime around the eighth century, they adopted Zoroastrianism and claimed Zarathushtra as one of their own. They brought additional ritual practices to the religion. . . . It was the Magi who first presented the teachings of Zarathushtra to the Greeks. Christians recognize the Zoroastrian priests as the Magi, the "Three Wise Men" who followed a star to Bethlehem to see the infant Jesus."

(Paula R. Hartz, *Zoroastrianism: World Religions* [New York: Facts on File, 1999], 35–36)

Socrates (469–399 BCE)

Greek philosopher and teacher and mentor of Plato. He taught by a method of question and answer which sought to elicit a consistent and rational response and hence to arrive at a universally agreed truth. He was executed in Athens for corrupting the youth and introducing strange gods.

"Socrates remains . . . an enigma, an inscrutable individual who, despite having written nothing, is considered one of the handful of philosophers who forever changed how philosophy itself was to be conceived. All our information about him is second-hand and most of it vigorously disputed, but his trial and death at the hands of the Athenian democracy is nevertheless the founding myth of the academic discipline of philosophy, and his influence has been felt far beyond philosophy itself, and in every age. . . . Socrates has been encumbered with the admiration and emulation normally reserved for founders of religious sects—Jesus or Buddha—strange for someone who tried so hard to make others do their own thinking, and for someone convicted and executed on the charge of irreverence toward the gods."

(Debra Nails, "Socrates," *Stanford Encyclopedia of Philosophy*, November 7, 2009, http://plato.stanford.edu/entries /socrates/)

ADDITIONAL RESOURCE

▶ The Socrates Project (an extensive database of theses and arguments ascribed to Socrates, as well as critiques and interpretations from various commentators) http://www.archelogos.com/socrates/

Augustine of Hippo (354–430 CE)

Bishop of Hippo in North Africa who was converted to Christianity from the teaching of the Manichaeans. He stressed the absolute grace of God in men and women's salvation and the depravity of human beings through original sin.

"I heard the voice as of a boy or girl, I know not which, coming from a neighbouring house, chanting, and oft repeating, 'Take up and read; take up and read.' . . . I rose up, interpreting it no other way than as a command to me from Heaven to open the book, and to read the first chapter I should light upon. . . . So quickly I returned to the place where . . . I [had] put down the volume of the apostles. . . . I grasped, opened, and in silence read that paragraph on which my eyes first fell—'Not in rioting and drunkenness, not in chambering and wantonness, not in strife and envying; but put on the Lord Jesus Christ, and make not provision for the flesh, to fulfil the lusts thereof.' No further would I read, nor did I need; for instantly, as the sentence ended—by a light, as it were, of security infused into my heart—all the gloom of doubt vanished away."

(Augustine, *Confessions*, Book 8, http://www.newadvent .org/fathers/110108.htm)

ADDITIONAL RESOURCE

▶ Augustine of Hippo (extensive collection of scholarly articles, primary source materials, images and other resources for the study of Augustine)
  http://www9.georgetown.edu/faculty/jod /augustine/

Genghis Khan (died 1227 CE)

The ruler of the Mongols; he was believed by his people to be of heavenly descent.

"Genghis Khan . . . created a body of law that he was to work on throughout his life. . . . He made it law that there was to be no kidnapping of women. He declared all children legitimate, whomever the mother. He made it law that no woman would be sold into marriage. . . . Genghis Khan regulated hunting—a winter activity—improving the availability of meat for everyone. He introduced record keeping. . . . He created a supreme officer of the law, who was to collect and preserve all judicial decisions, to oversee the trials of all those charged with wrongdoing and to have the power to issue death sentences. He created order in his realm that strengthened it and his ability to expand."

(Frank E. Smitha, "Genghis Khan and the Great Mongol Empire," MacroHistory and World Report, n.d., http:// www.fsmitha.com/h3/h11mon.htm)

ADDITIONAL RESOURCE

▶ "Genghis Khan" (1996 photo essay from *National Geographic*)
  http://ngm.nationalgeographic.com/1996/12 /genghis-khan/edwards-text

Primary Source Readings

The following excerpted readings represent some of the important primary sources mentioned in the main text. Additional primary sources are available both in print and online, and students are encouraged to contact their instructors for further information.

II.1 From the Epic of Gilgamish (Gilgamesh): The Babylonian Legend of the Deluge

Source: http://www.sacred-texts.com/ane/eog/index.htm

1. Gilgamish said unto him, to Uta-Napishtim the remote:
2. "I am looking at thee, Uta-Napishtim.
3. Thy person is not altered; even as am I so art thou.
4. Verily, nothing about thee is changed; even as am I so art thou.
5. A heart to do battle doth make thee complete,
6. Yet at rest [?] thou dost lie upon thy back.
7. How then hast thou stood the company of the gods and sought life?"

Thereupon Uta-Napishtim related to Gilgamish the Story of the Deluge, and the Eleventh Tablet continues thus

8. Uta-Napishtim said unto him, to Gilgamish:
9. "I will reveal unto thee, O Gilgamish, a hidden mystery,
10. And a secret matter of the gods I will declare unto thee.
11. Shurippak, a city which thou thyself knowest,
12. On [the bank] of the river Puratti (Euphrates) is situated,
13. That city is old; and the gods [dwelling] within it
14. Their hearts induced the great gods to make a windstorm (*a-bu-bi*),
15. There was their father Anu,
16. Their counsellor, the warrior Enlil,
17. Their messenger En-urta [and]
18. Their prince Ennugi.
19. Nin-igi-ku, Ea, was with them [in council] and
20. reported their word to a house of reeds."

FIRST SPEECH OF EA TO UTA-NAPISHTIM, WHO IS SLEEPING IN A REED HUT.

21. O House of reeds, O House of reeds! O Wall. O Wall!
22. O House of reeds, hear! O Wall, understand!
23. O man of Shurippak, son of Ubar-Tutu,
24. Throw down the house, build a ship,
25. Forsake wealth, seek after life,
26. Hate possessions, save thy life,
27. Bring all seed of life into the ship.
28. The ship which thou shalt build,
29. The dimensions thereof shall be measured,
30. The breadth and the length thereof shall be the same.
31. Then launch it upon the ocean.

UTA-NAPISHTIM'S ANSWER TO EA.

32. I understood and I said unto Ea, my lord:
33. See, my lord, that which thou hast ordered,
34. I regard with reverence, and will perform it,
35. But what shall I say to the town, to the multitude, and to the elders?

SECOND SPEECH OF EA.

36. Ea opened his mouth and spake
37. And said unto his servant, myself,
38. Thus, man, shalt thou say unto them:
39. Ill-will hath the god Enlil formed against me,
40. Therefore I can no longer dwell in your city,
41. And never more will I turn my countenance upon-the soil of Enlil.
42. I will descend into the ocean to dwell with my lord Ea.
43. But upon you he will rain riches
44. A catch of birds, a catch of fish
45. . . .an [abundant] harvest,
46. . . .the sender of . . .
47. . . .shall make hail [to fall upon you]. . . .

THE LOADING OF THE SHIP.

81. With everything that I possessed I loaded it [i.e., the ship].
82. With everything that I possessed of silver I loaded it.
83. With everything that I possessed of gold I loaded it.
84. With all that I possessed of all the seed of life I loaded it.
85. I made to go up into the ship all my family and kinsfolk,
86. The cattle of the field, the beasts of the field, all handicraftsmen I made them go up into it.
87. The god Shamash had appointed me a time [saying]
88. The sender of . . . will at eventide make a hail to fall;
89. Then enter into the ship and shut thy door.
90. The appointed time drew nigh;
91. The sender of . . . made a hail to fall at eventide.
92. I watched the aspect of the [approaching] storm,
93. Terror possessed me to look upon it,
94. I went into the ship and shut my door.
95. To the pilot of the ship, Puzur-Enlil the sailor
96. I committed the great house [i.e., ship], together with the contents thereof.

THE ABUBU (CYCLONE) AND ITS EFFECTS DESCRIBED.

97. As soon as something of dawn shone in the sky

98. A black cloud from the foundation of heaven came up.

99. Inside it the god Adad thundered,

100. The gods Nabû and Sharru (*i.e.*, Marduk) went before,

101. Marching as messengers over high land and plain,

102. Irragal (Nergal) tore out the post of the ship,

103. En-urta went on, he made the storm to descend.

104. The Anunnaki brandished their torches,

105. With their glare they lighted up the land.

106. The whirlwind (or, cyclone) of Adad swept up to heaven.

107. Every gleam of light was turned into darkness.

108. . . .the land . . .as if had laid it waste.

109. A whole day long [the flood descended] . . .

110. Swiftly it mounted up . . . [the water] reached to the mountains

111. [The water] attacked the people like a battle.

112. Brother saw not brother.

113. Men could not be known [or: recognized] in heaven.

114. The gods were terrified at the cyclone.

115. They shrank back and went up into the heaven of Anu.

116. The gods crouched like a dog and cowered by the wall.

117. The goddess Ishtar cried out like a woman in travail.

118. The Lady of the Gods lamented with a sweet voice [saying]:

ISHTAR'S LAMENT.

119. May that former day be turned into mud,

120. Because I commanded evil among the company of the gods.

121. How could I command evil among the company of the gods,

122. Command battle for the destruction of my people?

123. Did I of myself bring forth my people

124. That they might fill the sea like little fishes?

UTA-NAPISHTIM'S STORY CONTINUED.

125. The gods, the Anunnaki wailed with her.

126. The gods bowed themselves, and sat down weeping.

127. Their lips were shut tight (in distress) . . .

128. For six days and nights

129. The wind, the storm raged, and the cyclone overwhelmed the land.

THE ABATING OF THE STORM.

130. When the seventh day came the cyclone ceased, the storm and battle

131. which had fought like an army.

132. The sea became quiet, the grievous wind went down, the cyclone ceased.

133. I looked on the day and voices were stilled,

134. And all mankind were turned into mud,

135. The land had been laid flat like a terrace.

136. I opened the air-hole and the light fell upon my cheek,

137. I bowed myself, I sat down, I cried,

138. My tears poured down over my cheeks.

139. I looked over the quarters of the world, (to] the limits of ocean.

140. At twelve points islands appeared.

141. The ship grounded on the mountain of Nisir.

142. The mountain of Nisir held the ship, it let it not move.

143. The first day, the second day, the mountain of Nisir held the ship and let it not move.

144. The third day, the fourth day, the mountain of Nisir held the ship and let it not move.

145. The fifth day, the sixth day, the mountain of Nisir held the ship and let it not move.

146. When the seventh day had come

147. I brought out a dove and let her go free.

148. The dove flew away and [then] came back;

149. Because she had no place to alight on she came back.

150. I brought out a swallow and let her go free.

151. The swallow flew away and [then] came back;

152. Because she had no place to alight on she came back.

153. 1 brought out a raven and let her go free.

154. The raven flew away, she saw the sinking waters.

155. She ate, she waded [?], she rose [?], she came not back.

UTA-NAPISHTIM LEAVES THE SHIP.

156. Then I brought out [everything] to the four winds and made a sacrifice;

157. I set out an offering on the peak of the mountain.

158. Seven by seven I set out the vessels,

159. Under them I piled reeds, cedarwood and myrtle (?).

160. The gods smelt the savour,

161. The gods smelt the sweet savour.

162. The gods gathered together like flies over him that sacrificed. . . .

ENLIL DEIFIES UTA-NAPISHTIM AND HIS WIFE.

198. Then the god Enlil went up into the ship,

199. He seized me by the hand and brought me forth.

200. He brought forth my wife and made her to kneel by my side.

201. He touched our brows, he stood between us, he blessed us [saving],

202. Formerly Uta-Napishtim was a man merely,

203. But now let Uta-Napishtim and his wife be like unto us gods.

204. Uta-Napishtim shall dwell afar off, at the mouth of the rivers.

II.2 Maya Creation Myth

The Popol Vuh, Book I, from Lewis Spence, *The Popol Vuh, the Mythic and Heroic Sagas of the Kiches of Central America* (London: David Nutt, 1908).

Source: http://www.sacred-texts.com/nam/pvuheng.htm

Over a universe wrapped in the gloom of a dense and primeval night passed the god Hurakan, the mighty wind. He called out 'earth,' and the solid land appeared. The chief gods too counsel; they were Hurakan, Gucumatz, the serpent covered with green feathers, and Xpiyacoc and Xmucane, the mother and father gods. As the result of their deliberations animals were created. But as yet man was not. To supply the deficiency the divine beings resolved to create manikins carved out of wood. But these soon incurred the displeasure of the gods, who, irritated by their lack of reverence, resolved to destroy them. Then by the will of Hurakan, the Heart of Heaven, the waters were swollen, and a great flood came upon the manikins of wood. They were drowned and a thick resin fell from heaven. The bird Xecotcovach tore out their eyes; the bird Camulatz cut off their heads; the bird Cotzbalam devoured their flesh; the bird Tecumbalam broke their bones and sinews and ground them into powder. Because they had not thought on Hurakan, therefore the face of the earth grew dark, and a pouring rain commenced, raining by day and by night. Then all sorts of beings, great and small, gathered together to abuse the men to their faces. The very household utensils and animals jeered at them, their mill-stones, their plates, their cups, their dogs, their hens. Said the dogs and hens, "Very badly have you treated us, and you have bitten us. Now we bite you in turn." Said the mill-stones, "Very much were we tormented by you, and daily, daily, night and day, it was *squeak, screech, screech,* for your sake. Now you will feel our strength, and we will grind your flesh and make meal of your bodies." . . . Then ran the manikins hither and thither in despair. They climbed to the roofs of the houses, but the houses crumbled under their feet; they tried to mount to the tops of the trees, but the trees hurled them from them; they sought refuge in the caverns, but the caverns closed before them. Thus was accomplished the ruin of this race, destined to be overthrown. And it is said that their posterity are the little monkeys who live in the woods.

II.3 *Enuma Elish*

"The Enuma Elish," the epic of creation, trans. L. W. King (from *The Seven Tablets of Creation*, London, 1902).

Source: http://www.sacred-texts.com/ane/enuma.htm

THE FIRST TABLET

When in the height heaven was not named,
And the earth beneath did not yet bear a name,
And the primeval Apsu, who begat them,
And chaos, Tiamut, the mother of them both
Their waters were mingled together,
And no field was formed, no marsh was to be seen;
When of the gods none had been called into being,
And none bore a name, and no destinies were
    ordained;
Then were created the gods in the midst of heaven,
Lahmu and Lahamu were called into being,
Ages increased,
Then Ansar and Kisar were created, and over them.
Long were the days, then there came forth
Anu, their son,
Ansar and Anu
And the god Anu
Nudimmud, whom his fathers, his begetters . . .
Abounding in all wisdom,
He was exceeding strong,
He had no rival.
Thus were established and were the great gods.
But Tiamat and Apsu were still in confusion.
They were troubled and in disorder.
Apru was not diminished in might
And Tiamat roared.
She smote, and their deeds,
Their way was evil.
Then Apsu, the begetter of the great gods,
Cried unto Mummu, his minister, and said unto
    him:

"O Mummu, thou minister that rejoicest my spirit,
Come, unto Tiamut let us go!"
So they went and before Tiamat they lay down,
They consulted on a plan with regard to the gods,
    their sons.

Apsu opened his mouth and spake,
And unto Tiamut, the glistening one, he addressed
    the word:
"By day I cannot rest, by night I cannot lie down in
    peace.
But I will destroy their way.
Let there be lamentation, and let us lie down again
    in peace."

When Tiamat heard these words,
She raged and cried aloud
She uttered a curse, and unto Apsu she spake:

"What then shall we do?
Let their way be made difficult, and let us lie down
    again in peace."

Mummu answered, and gave counsel unto Apsu,
and hostile to the gods was the counsel Mummu
    gave:

"Come, their way is strong, but thou shalt destroy it;
Then by day shalt thou have rest, by night shalt thou
    lie down in peace."

Apsu harkened unto him and his countenance grew
    bright,
Since he [Mummu] planned evil against the gods his
    sons.
He was afraid,
His knees became weak; they gave way beneath him,
Because of the evil which their first-born had
    planned.

Then Ea, who knoweth all that is, went up and he
    beheld their muttering.

And Tiamat harkened unto the word of the bright
    god, and said:

"Let us wage war!"

They banded themselves together and at the side of
    Tiamat they advanced;
They were furious; they devised mischief without
    resting night and day.
They prepared for battle, fuming and raging;
They joined their forces and made war,
Ummu-Hubur [Tiamat] who formed all things,

Made in addition weapons invincible; she spawned
monster-serpents,
Sharp of tooth, and merciless of fang;
With poison, instead of blood, she filled their bodies.
Fierce monster-vipers she clothed with terror,
With splendor she decked them, she made them of
lofty stature.
Whoever beheld them, terror overcame him,
Their bodies reared up and none could withstand
their attack.

She set up vipers and dragons, and the monster
Lahamu,
And hurricanes, and raging hounds, and
scorpion-men,
And mighty tempests, and fish-men, and rams;
They bore cruel weapons, without fear of the fight.
Her commands were mighty, none could resist them;
After this fashion, huge of stature, she made eleven
[kinds of] monsters.
Among the gods who were her sons, inasmuch as he
had given her support,
She exalted Kingu; in their midst she raised him to
power.
To march before the forces, to lead the host,
To give the battle-signal, to advance to the attack,
To direct the battle, to control the fight,
Unto him she entrusted; in costly raiment she made
him sit, saying:

"I have uttered thy spell, in the assembly of the gods
I have raised thee to power.
The dominion over all the gods have I entrusted
unto him.
Be thou exalted, thou my chosen spouse,
May they magnify thy name over all of them the
Anunnaki."

She gave him the Tablets of Destiny, on his breast she
laid them, saying:

"Thy command shall not be without avail, and the
word of thy mouth shall be established."

Now Kingu, thus exalted, having received the power
of Anu,
Decreed the fate among the gods his sons, saying:

"Let the opening of your mouth quench the Fire-god;
Whoso is exalted in the battle, let him display his
might!"

THE SECOND TABLET

Tiamat made weighty her handiwork,
Evil she wrought against the gods her children.
To avenge Apsu, Tiamat planned evil,
But how she had collected her forces, the god unto
Ea divulged.
Ea harkened to this thing, and
He was grievously afflicted and he sat in sorrow.
The days went by, and his anger was appeased,
And to the place of Ansar his father he took his way.

He went and, standing before Ansar, the father who
begat him,
All that Tiamat had plotted he repeated unto him,
Saying,

"Tiamat our mother hath conceived a hatred for us,
With all her force she rageth, full of wrath.
All the gods have turned to her,
With those, whom ye created, they go at her side.
They are banded together and at the side of Tiamat
they advance;
They are furious, they devise mischief without rest-
ing night and day.
They prepare for battle, fuming and raging;
They have joined their forces and are making
war. . . ."

When Ansar heard how Tiamat was mightily in
revolt,
he bit his lips, his mind was not at peace,
Ansar unto his son addressed the word:

" . . . my mighty hero,
Whose strength is great and whose onslaught can
not be withstood,
Go and stand before Tiamat,
That her spirit may be appeased, that her heart may
be merciful.
But if she will not harken unto thy word,
Our word shalt thou speak unto her, that she may
be pacified."

He heard the word of his father Ansar
And he directed his path to her, toward her he took
    the way.
Anu drew nigh, he beheld the muttering of Tiamat,
But he could not withstand her, and he turned back.

Ansar, he spake unto him:

"Thou art my son, who maketh merciful his heart.
to the battle shalt thou draw nigh,
he that shall behold thee shall have peace."

And the lord rejoiced at the word of his father,
And he drew nigh and stood before Ansar.
Ansar beheld him and his heart was filled with joy,
He kissed him on the lips and his fear departed from
    him. . . .

The lord rejoiced at the word of his father,
His heart exulted, and unto his father he spake:

"O Lord of the gods, Destiny of the great gods,
If I, your avenger,
Conquer Tiamat and give you life,
Appoint an assembly, make my fate preeminent and
    proclaim it.
In Upsukkinaku seat yourself joyfully together,
With my word in place of you will I decree fate.
May whatsoever I do remain unaltered,
May the word of my lips never be chanced nor made
    of no avail." . . .

THE FOURTH TABLET

They prepared for him a lordly chamber,
Before his fathers as prince he took his place.
"Thou art chiefest among the great gods,
Thy fate is unequaled, thy word is Anu!
O Marduk, thou art chiefest among the great gods,
Thy fate is unequaled, thy word is Anu! . . .
O Marduk, thou art our avenger! . . ."
They give him an invincible weapon which over-
    whelmeth the foe.
"Go, and cut off the life of Tiamat,
And let the wind carry her blood into secret places."
After the gods his fathers had decreed for the lord
    his fate,

They caused him to set out on a path of prosperity
    and success.
He made ready the bow, he chose his weapon,
He slung a spear upon him and fastened it . . .
He raised the club, in his right hand he grasped it,
The bow and the quiver he hung at his side.
He set the lightning in front of him,
With burning flame he filled his body. . . .
Tiamat uttered wild, piercing cries,
She trembled and shook to her very foundations.
She recited an incantation, she pronounced her spell,
And the gods of the battle cried out for their
    weapons.
Then advanced Tiamat and Marduk, the counselor
    of the gods;
To the fight they came on, to the battle they drew
    nigh.
The lord spread out his net and caught her,
And the evil wind that was behind him he let loose
    in her face.
As Tiamat opened her mouth to its full extent,
He drove in the evil wind, while as yet she had not
    shut her lips.
The terrible winds filled her belly,
And her courage was taken from her, and her mouth
    she opened wide.
He seized the spear and burst her belly,
He severed her inward parts, he pierced her heart.
He overcame her and cut off her life;
He cast down her body and stood upon it.
When he had slain Tiamat, the leader,
Her might was broken, her host was scattered.
And the gods her helpers, who marched by her side,
Trembled, and were afraid, and turned back.
They took to flight to save their lives;
But they were surrounded, so that they could not
    escape.
He took them captive, he broke their weapons;
In the net they were caught and in the snare they sat
    down. . . .

THE FIFTH TABLET

He [Marduk] made the stations for the great gods;

The stars, their images, as the stars of the Zodiac,
    he fixed.
He ordained the year and into sections he divided it;
For the twelve months he fixed three stars.
After he had . . . the days of the year . . . images,
He founded the station of Nibir [the planet Jupiter]
    to determine their bounds;
That none might err or go astray,
He set the station of Bel and Ea along with him.
He opened great gates on both sides,
He made strong the bolt on the left and on the right.
In the midst thereof he fixed the zenith;
The Moon-god he caused to shine forth, the night he
    entrusted to him. . . .

THE SIXTH TABLET

When Marduk heard the word of the gods,
His heart prompted him and he devised a cunning
    plan.
He opened his mouth and unto Ea he spake
That which he had conceived in his heart he imparted
    unto him:
"My blood will I take and bone will I fashion . . .
I will create man who shall inhabit the earth,
That the service of the gods may be established, and
    that their shrines may be built.
But I will alter the ways of the gods, and I will change
    their paths. . . .

EPILOGUE

Let them [i.e., the names of Marduk] be held in
    remembrances and let the first man proclaim
    them;
Let the wise and the understanding consider them
    together!
Let the father repeat them and teach them to his son;
Let them be in the ears of the pastor and the
    shepherd!
Let a man rejoice in Marduk, the Lord of the gods,
That he may cause his land to be fruitful, and that he
    himself may have prosperity!
His word standeth fast, his command is unaltered;
The utterance of his mouth hath no god ever
    annulled.

He gazed in his anger, he turned not his neck;
When he is wroth, no god can withstand his
    indignation.
Wide is his heart, broad is his compassion. . . .

II.4 The Gathas

Source: http://www.sacred-texts.com/zor/toz/toz05.htm

CONFESSION OF FAITH

"The good, righteous, right religion which the Lord
has sent to the creatures is that which Zarathustra has
brought. The religion is the religion of Zarathustra,
the religion of Ahura-Mazda, given to Zarathustra."

THE CREED

"I praise the well-thought, well-spoken, well-per-
    formed thoughts, words, and works.
"I lay hold on all good thoughts, words, and works.
"I abandon all evil thoughts, words, and works. I
    bring to you, O Amĕsha-çpĕntas,
"Praise and adoration,
"With thoughts, words, and works, with heavenly
    mind, the vital strength of my own body.
. . .
"I drive away the Daêvas, I profess myself a Zarath-
    rustrian, an expeller of the Daêvas, a follower of
    the teachings of Ahura.
"A hymn-singer of the Amĕsha-çpĕntas, a praiser of
    the Amĕsha-çpĕntas.
"To Ahura-Mazda, the good, endued with good wis-
    dom, I offer all good."

GOD AS THE KING, THE LIFE, THE REWARDER

"Praises, and songs, and adorations do we offer to
Ahura-Mazda, and to Righteousness the Best; yea,
we offer and we ascribe them, and proclaim them.

"And to Thy good kingdom, O Ahura-Mazda! may
we attain for ever, and a good King be Thou over us;
and let each man of us, and so each woman, thus
abide, O Thou most beneficent of beings, and for
both the worlds!

. . .

"So mayst Thou be to us our life, and our body's vigour, O Thou most beneficent of beings, and that for both the worlds!

"Aye, let us win and conquer long life, O Ahura-Mazda! in Thy grace, and through Thy will may we be powerful. Mayst Thou lay hold on us to help, . . . and with salvation, O Thou most beneficent of beings!

. . .

"What reward most meet for our deserving Thou hast appointed for the souls, O Ahura-Mazda! of that do Thou bestow on us for this life, and for that of mind. Of that reward do Thou Thyself grant this advantage, that we may come under Thy protecting guardianship, and that of Righteousness for ever."

On Loan

"He who does not restore (a thing lent) when it is asked for back again, steals the thing; he robs the man. So he does every day, every night, as long as he keeps in his house his neighbour's property, as though it were his own."

On Waste

"Ahura-Mazda, indeed, does not allow us to waste anything of value that we may have, not even so much as an Asperena's weight of thread, not even so much as a maid lets fall in spinning."

Temperance

"Regarding wine, it is evident that it is possible for good and bad temper to come to manifestation through wine.

. . .

"It is not requisite for investigation, because he who is a good-tempered man, when he drinks wine, is such-like as a gold or silver cup which, however much more they burn it, becomes purer and brighter. It also keeps his thoughts, words, and deeds more virtuous; and he becomes gentler and pleasanter unto wife and child, companions and friends, and is more diligent in every duty and good work.

"And he who is a bad-tempered man, when he drinks wine, thinks and considers himself more than ordinary: He carries on a quarrel with companions, displays insolence, makes ridicule and mockery, and acts arrogantly to a good person. He distresses his own wife and child, slave and servant; and dissipates the joy of the good, carries off peace, and brings in discord.

"But every one must be cautious as to the moderate drinking of wine. Because, from the moderate drinking of wine, thus much benefit happens to him: since it digests the food, kindles the vital fire, increases the understanding and intellect, and blood, removes vexation, and inflames the complexion.

"It causes recollection of things forgotten, and goodness takes a place in the mind. It likewise increases the sight of the eye, the hearing of the ear, and the speaking of the tongue; and work, which it is necessary to do and expedite, becomes more progressive. He also sleeps pleasantly and rises light.

"And in him who drinks wine more than moderately, . . . himself, wife, and child, friend and kindred, are distressed and unhappy, and the superintendent of troubles and the enemy are glad. The sacred beings, also, are not pleased with him; and infamy comes to his body, and even wickedness to his soul.

"And even he who gives wine authorizedly unto any one, and he is thereby intoxicated by it, is equally guilty of every sin which that drunkard commits owing to that drunkenness."

II.5 Cicero, On the Nature of the Gods

Source: http://thriceholy.net/Texts/Cicero.html

I. There are many things in philosophy, my dear Brutus, which are not as yet fully explained to us, and particularly (as you very well know) that most obscure and difficult question concerning the Nature of the Gods, so extremely necessary both towards a knowledge of the human mind and the practice of true religion: concerning which the opinions of men are so various, and so different from each other, as to lead strongly to the inference that ignorance is the cause, or origin, of philosophy, and that the Academic philosophers have been prudent in refusing their assent to things uncertain: for what is more unbecoming to a wise man than to judge rashly? or what rashness is so unworthy of the gravity and stability of a philosopher as either to maintain false opinions, or, without the least hesitation, to support and defend what he has not thoroughly examined and does not clearly comprehend?

In the question now before us, the greater part of mankind have united to acknowledge that which is most probable, and which we are all by nature led to suppose, namely, that there are Gods. Protagoras doubted whether there were any. Diagoras the Melian and Theodorus of Cyrene entirely believed there were no such beings. But they who have affirmed that there are Gods, have expressed such a variety of sentiments on the subject, and the disagreement between them is so great, that it would be tiresome to enumerate their opinions; for they give us many statements respecting the forms of the Gods, and their places of abode, and the employment of their lives. And these are matters on which the philosophers differ with the most exceeding earnestness. But the most considerable part of the dispute is, whether they are wholly inactive, totally unemployed, and free from all care and administration of affairs; or, on the contrary, whether all things were made and constituted by them from the beginning; and whether they will continue to be actuated and governed by them to eternity. This is one of the greatest points in debate; and unless this is decided, mankind must necessarily remain in the greatest of errors, and ignorant of what is most important to be known.

II. For there are some philosophers, both ancient and modern, who have conceived that the Gods take not the least cognizance of human affairs. But if their doctrine be true, of what avail is piety, sanctity, or religion? for these are feelings and marks of devotion which are offered to the Gods by men with uprightness and holiness, on the ground that men are the objects of the attention of the Gods, and that many

benefits are conferred by the immortal Gods on the human race. But if the Gods have neither the power nor the inclination to help us; if they take no care of us, and pay no regard to our actions; and if there is no single advantage which can possibly accrue to the life of man; then what reason can we have to pay any adoration, or any honors, or to prefer any prayers to them? Piety, like the other virtues, cannot have any connection with vain show or dissimulation; and without piety, neither sanctity nor religion can be supported; the total subversion of which must be attended with great confusion and disturbance in life.

I do not even know, if we cast off piety towards the Gods, but that faith, and all the associations of human life, and that most excellent of all virtues, justice, may perish with it.

There are other philosophers, and those, too, very great and illustrious men, who conceive the whole world to be directed and governed by the will and wisdom of the Gods; nor do they stop here, but conceive likewise that the Deities consult and provide for the preservation of mankind. For they think that the fruits, and the produce of the earth, and the seasons, and the variety of weather, and the change of climates, by which all the productions of the earth are brought to maturity, are designed by the immortal Gods for the use of man. They instance many other things, which shall be related in these books; and which would almost induce us to believe that the immortal Gods had made them all expressly and solely for the benefit and advantage of men. Against these opinions Carneades has advanced so much that what he has said should excite a desire in men who are not naturally slothful to search after truth; for there is no subject on which the learned as well as the unlearned differ so strenuously as in this; and since their opinions are so various, and so repugnant one to another, it is possible that none of them may be, and absolutely impossible that more than one should be, right.

VI. Now, to free myself from the reproach of partiality, I propose to lay before you the opinions of various philosophers concerning the nature of the Gods, by which means all men may judge which of them are consistent with truth; and if all agree together, or if any one shall be found to have discovered what may be absolutely called truth, I will then give up the Academy as vain and arrogant. . . .

X. They who affirm the world to be an animated and intelligent being have by no means discovered the nature of the mind, nor are able to conceive in what form that essence can exist; but of that I shall speak more hereafter. At present I must express my surprise at the weakness of those who endeavor to make it out to be not only animated and immortal, but likewise happy, and round, because Plato says that is the most beautiful form; whereas I think a cylinder, a square, a cone, or a pyramid more beautiful. But what life do they attribute to that round Deity? Truly it is a being whirled about with a celerity to which nothing can be even conceived by the imagination as equal; nor can I imagine how a settled mind and happy life can consist in such motion, the least degree of which would be troublesome to us. Why, therefore, should it not be considered troublesome also to the Deity? For the earth itself, as it is part of the world, is part also of the Deity. We see vast tracts of land barren and uninhabitable; some, because they are scorched by the too near approach of the sun; others, because they are bound up with frost and snow, through the great distance which the sun is from them. Therefore, if the world is a Deity, as these are parts of the world, some of the Deity's limbs must be said to be scorched, and some frozen.

These are your doctrines, Lucilius; but what those of others are I will endeavor to ascertain by tracing them back from the earliest of ancient philosophers. Thales the Milesian, who first inquired after such subjects, asserted water to be the origin of things, and that God was that mind which formed all things from water. If the Gods can exist without corporeal sense, and if there can be a mind without a body, why did he annex a mind to water?

It was Anaximander's opinion that the Gods were born; that after a great length of time they died; and

that they are innumerable worlds. But what conception can we possibly have of a Deity who is not eternal?

Anaximenes, after him, taught that the air is God, and that he was generated, and that he is immense, infinite, and always in motion; as if air, which has no form, could possibly be God; for the Deity must necessarily be not only of some form or other, but of the most beautiful form. Besides, is not everything that had a beginning subject to mortality?

XI. Anaxagoras, who received his learning from Anaximenes, was the first who affirmed the system and disposition of all things to be contrived and perfected by the power and reason of an infinite mind; in which infinity he did not perceive that there could be no conjunction of sense and motion, nor any sense in the least degree, where nature herself could feel no impulse. If he would have this mind to be a sort of animal, then there must be some more internal principle from whence that animal should receive its appellation. But what can be more internal than the mind? Let it, therefore, be clothed with an external body. But this is not agreeable to his doctrine; but we are utterly unable to conceive how a pure simple mind can exist without any substance annexed to it.

Alcmaeon of Crotona, in attributing a divinity to the sun, the moon, and the rest of the stars, and also to the mind, did not perceive that he was ascribing immortality to mortal beings. . . .

Then Xenophanes, who said that everything in the world which had any existence, with the addition of intellect, was God, is as liable to exception as the rest, especially in relation to the infinity of it, in which there can be nothing sentient, nothing composite. . . .

XII. Empedocles, who erred in many things, is most grossly mistaken in his notion of the Gods. He lays down four natures as divine, from which he thinks that all things were made. Yet it is evident that they have a beginning, that they decay, and that they are void of all sense. . . .

It would be tedious to show the uncertainty of Plato's opinion; for, in his Timaeus, he denies the propriety of asserting that there is one great father or creator of the world; and, in his book of Laws, he thinks we ought not to make too strict an inquiry into the nature of the Deity. And as for his statement when he asserts that God is a being without any body— what the Greeks call 'asomatos'—it is certainly quite unintelligible how that theory can possibly be true; for such a God must then necessarily be destitute of sense, prudence, and pleasure; all which things are comprehended in our notion of the Gods. He likewise asserts in his Timaeus, and in his Laws, that the world, the heavens, the stars, the mind, and those Gods which are delivered down to us from our ancestors, constitute the Deity. These opinions, taken separately, are apparently false; and, together, are directly inconsistent with each other. . . .

XIII. . . . Aristotle, in his third book of Philosophy, confounds many things together, as the rest have done; but he does not differ from his master Plato. At one time he attributes all divinity to the mind, at another he asserts that the world is God. Soon afterward he makes some other essence preside over the world, and gives it those faculties by which, with certain revolutions, he may govern and preserve the motion of it. Then he asserts the heat of the firmament to be God; not perceiving the firmament to be part of the world, which in another place he had described as God. How can that divine sense of the firmament be preserved in so rapid a motion? And where do the multitude of Gods dwell, if heaven itself is a Deity? But when this philosopher says that God is without a body, he makes him an irrational and insensible being. Besides, how can the world move itself, if it wants a body? Or how, if it is in perpetual self-motion, can it be easy and happy? . . .

XVII. Here, then, you see the foundation of this question clearly laid; for since it is the constant and universal opinion of mankind, independent of education, custom, or law, that there are Gods, it must necessarily follow that this knowledge is implanted in our minds, or, rather, innate in us. That opinion respecting which there is a general agreement in universal nature must infallibly be true; therefore it must be allowed that there are Gods; for in this we have the concurrence, not only of almost all philosophers, but likewise of the ignorant and illiterate. It must be also confessed that the point is established that we have naturally this idea, as I said before, or prenotion, of the existence of the Gods. As new things require new names, so that prenotion was called 'prolepsis' by Epicurus; an appellation never used before. On the same principle of reasoning, we think that the Gods are happy and immortal; for that nature which hath assured us that there are Gods has likewise imprinted in our minds the knowledge of their immortality and felicity; and if so, what Epicurus hath declared in these words is true: "That which is eternally happy cannot be burdened with any labor itself, nor can it impose any labor on another; nor can it be influenced by resentment or favor: because things which are liable to such feelings must be weak and frail." We have said enough to prove that we should worship the Gods with piety, and without superstition, if that were the only question. . . .

XIX. Surely the mighty power of the Infinite Being is most worthy our great and earnest contemplation; the nature of which we must necessarily understand to be such that everything in it is made to correspond completely to some other answering part. This is called by Epicurus 'isonomia'; that is to say, an equal distribution or even disposition of things. From hence he draws this inference, that, as there is such a vast multitude of mortals, there cannot be a less number of immortals; and if those which perish are innumerable, those which are preserved ought also to be countless. Your sect, Balbus, frequently ask us how the Gods live, and how they pass their time? Their life is the most happy, and the most abounding with all kinds of blessings, which can be conceived. They do nothing. They are embarrassed with no business; nor do they perform any work. They rejoice in the possession of their own wisdom and virtue. They are satisfied that they shall ever enjoy the fullness of eternal pleasures.

XX. . . . Or let us suppose a Deity residing in the world, who directs and governs it, who preserves the courses of the stars, the changes of the seasons, and the vicissitudes and orders of things, surveying the earth and the sea, and accommodating them to the advantage and necessities of man. Truly this Deity is embarrassed with a very troublesome and laborious office. We make a happy life to consist in a tranquility of mind, a perfect freedom from care, and an exemption from all employment. The philosopher from whom we received all our knowledge has taught us that the world was made by nature; that there was no occasion for a workhouse to frame it in; and that, though you deny the possibility of such a work without divine skill, it is so easy to her, that she has made, does make, and will make innumerable worlds. But, because you do not conceive that nature is able to produce such effects without some rational aid, you are forced, like the tragic poets, when you cannot wind up your argument in any other way, to have recourse to a Deity, whose assistance you would not seek, if you could view that vast and unbounded magnitude of regions in all parts; where the mind, extending and spreading itself, travels so far and wide that it can find no end, no extremity to stop at. In this immensity of breadth, length, and height, a most boundless company of innumerable atoms are fluttering about, which, notwithstanding the interposition of a void space, meet and cohere, and continue clinging to one another; and by this union these modifications and forms of things arise, which, in your opinions, could not possibly be made without the help of bellows and anvils. Thus you have imposed on us an eternal master, whom we must dread day and night. For who can be free from fear of a Deity who foresees, regards, and takes notice of everything; one who thinks all things his own; a curious, ever-busy God?

Key Terms

Avesta   The scriptures of Zoroastrianism. They include the *Gathas*, a series of poems reminiscent of the hymns of the Vedas that may go back to Zoroaster himself. They may have been used as a liturgy to ward off Angra Mainyu and his evil spirits.

dakhma   A circular, stone tower open to the sky, called "Tower of Silence," used in Zoroastrian funeral rites to house the dead.

divination   Telling the future by reading the signs of nature in the weather, stars, or flight of birds or by the manipulation of objects such as bones or cards.

Hellenism   The adoption of the Greek language, culture, philosophy and ideas, particularly around the Mediterranean, from the time of Alexander the Great (356–323 BCE). It was the dominant cultural influence during the rise of Christianity.

megaliths   Large stone monuments dating from the late Neolithic period. Their original function is uncertain but they mark burial mounds and temples and they may have served as a calendar of times and seasons.

the mystery religions   Cults based on ancient myths which flourished in Greece, in Rome and throughout the Roman empire. Initiates went through a dramatic and secret ceremony in which they identified with the divinity at the center of the myth and experienced salvation and the assurance of immortality.

Neolithic period   The New Stone Age, from about 10,000 BCE until the Early Bronze Age.

Paleolithic period   The Old Stone Age, before 10,000 BCE in Europe and the Middle East.

prehistoric   Dating from the period before the development of writing; in the Middle East, before about 3000
    BCE.

shaman   (1) An ecstatic priest-magician among the Tungu people of Siberia. (2) By extension, a similar figure
    in other indigenous religions and ancient religions. Shamans induce a trance experience in which they are
    believed to leave the body and visit other worlds. The shaman's role is to convey sacrifices to the gods, to
    escort the dead to their destination and to return with divine prophecies.

Questions for Study and Discussion

1.   Prehistoric religion seems to emphasize what aspects of life?
2.   Briefly summarize the epic of Gilgamesh and explain its significance to the study of religion of the
      ancient Near East.
3.   Describe some common elements of the religions of the Ancient Near East, Greece, etc. (e.g. the flood
      story).
4.   How does the design of Egyptian temples reflect their purpose?
5.   Explain how, according to Zoroastrianism, "human beings are literally at one with their environment" (p.
      97). How does this belief affect principles and practices of the religion?
6.   Describe the relationship between the emperors and the gods in ancient Rome after Augustus.
7.   What role has human sacrifice played in ancient religions? Can you identify common themes or purposes
      across continents, historical periods, and cultures?

Questions for Reflection

Write your personal reflections on each of these questions in the space provided.

1.   How would you describe the art of the prehistoric period? (See pp. 60–65.)

2.   Why do you think so many ancient religions—in the Near East, Africa, Central America, Scandinavia—
      connected their gods and goddesses to natural forces and elements? (Think across the chapter.)

3.   What are the significances of holy places and sacred calendars? (See p. 66.)

4. Compare the architectures of the various ancient sacred places, and reflect on how symbolism is used. (Think across the examples in the chapter—Aztec, Egypt, Greece.)

5. Explain the dualism of Zoroastrianism. (See pp. 93–94.)

6. Are there any "constants" of belief and practice that span one civilization to another? (Think across the chapter.)

Selected Online Resources

▸ Ancient Mexico—essay and photos of artifacts related to Aztecs, Olmecs, and other peoples of ancient Mesoamerica
http://ancientweb.org/index.php/explore/country/Mexico

▸ "Hatshepsut"—article with accompanying photos about the female pharaoh, originally published in *National Geographic*, April 2009
http://ngm.nationalgeographic.com/2009/04/hatshepsut/brown-text

▸ Encyclopedia Mythica—articles and images related to mythology, folklore, and religion organized by culture and geographical region
http://www.pantheon.org/

▸ Celtic Art and Cultures—extensive information on the Celts, including timelines, maps, and photographs
http://www.unc.edu/celtic/index.html

▸ Avesta: Zoroastrian Archives—an extensive listing of informational web resources, including sacred texts, prayers, and historical information
http://www.avesta.org/avesta.html

▸ "Prehistoric Rock Paintings of Bhimabetaka"—author's personal experience viewing prehistoric rock paintings in India, with photographs
http://www.kamat.com/kalranga/rockpain/betaka.htm

Part 3: Indigenous Religions

Chapter Summaries

19. Understanding Indigenous Religions

Indigenous religions are the majority of the world's religions, despite the fact that many were destroyed in the past by the influx of other religions like Christianity. While indigenous cultures are so diverse as to be very difficult to generalize about, we can discern some common religious themes, such as respect for elders. The concept of the person can encompass spirits, natural phenomena, and ancestors. Gift exchange can be a sign of support and a way to maintain relationships as well as incur obligation. Shamans and witches can be significant community leaders as well as powerful religious figures.

20. Indigenous Religions in Asia

The key to understanding indigenous Asian religious is the role of the relationship between the person and gods, spirits, other humans, and nature. Male and female shamans enter trances that help them learn how to restore harmony between the people and their world. Taboo is often a significant force that requires specific ritual observances. One group, the Kondhs of India, sacrifice buffalo to ensure fertility of land, people, and animals; their other rituals include seeking the blessing of ancestors and guarding against ritual impurity.

21. The Foe of Papua New Guinea

The Foe's religion centers on a being called Siruwage and a chief spirit as well as three groups of spirits who live in fixed places. Some spirits wander from place to place and can be harmful to humans; the most feared spirits are those of the dead. Sorcery is another powerful component, typically involving rituals that cause someone to sicken and die.

22. Australian Aboriginal Religions

Aboriginal religions center on stories of the people's relationship to the land. The core concept of what Westerners have called Dreamtime is a nonlinear, ever-present concept encompassing life and death.

Different Aboriginal groups believe in variations of this concept. People access the Dreaming through song, dance, ritual, and other methods. Each Dreaming story has multiple layers of meaning, including sacred and secret meanings. Christian influence is apparent in some contemporary indigenous practice, as is the experience of European colonization.

23. Melanesia

Melanesians do not distinguish between sacred and secular or natural and supernatural. The center of life is the community of people and spirits, which link each person and their clan or family to a piece of land, give them an identity, and provide a path to the future. Sacred knowledge is restricted to initiated elders. Not all Melanesians believe in a powerful god or gods; many do believe in various spirits, including demons. Magic is important in most Melanesian communities, and certain people have special ritual responsibilities. Sacred places include both natural and human-made structures.

24. South American Indigenous Religions

Indigenous religions in South America reflect the enormous diversity of peoples and cultures on that continent. Many peoples view the cosmos as being divided into overlapping tiers, usually involving a heavenly realm and a world below where humans reside. Supernatural beings include uncreated gods, lesser deities related to natural phenomena, and spirits of animals, plants, and elementals. Shamans are the mediators of human-supernatural interaction. They help those attacked by spirits, heal the sick, and oversee rites of passage.

25. Native North Americans

Despite the near-genocide of indigenous people on the North American continent, Native peoples survived and retained their cultures, including their religions, to the present day. Although the belief systems are as varied as the indigenous nations themselves, some commonalities can be identified. One Great Spirit is at the heart of belief and ritual, based on the fundamental elements of nature and the Earth. The four powers of the world are made one in the circle that is life itself. The mystery of sevens appears in many Native cultures, including the seven sacred rites of the Sioux and the seven prophecies of the Ojibwa.

26. Inuit

The Inuit have typically lived in a delicate balance with the natural world: the extreme climate means they had to depend on their hunting and fishing skills to survive. Animals were believed to have souls; spirits could inhabit tools or influence the weather. The shaman helped the people communicate with the spirit world. Despite centuries of suppression, Inuit religion has survived and is even experiencing a revival today.

27. Norse Shamanism

Shamanism is practiced in small-scale societies dependent on hunting and farming for subsistence. The trance allows the shaman to cure the sick, bring the souls of the dead to the underworld, foretell the future, and transcend boundaries between the living and the dead. *Seidr* forms, including rocks and human-made objects, are important tools for the shaman, serving as channels to another world as well as altars for sacrifice.

28. African Indigenous Religions

The religions of Africa change along with the societies they are part of; historic encounters with Islam and Western colonial powers have left their mark. Common themes include ancestors as key figures in the belief systems; the secular not easily divided from the sacred; rituals intended to promote material well-being; and the adoption of ideas, beliefs, and practices from other religions. Centers of power are found in natural phenomena, animals, and humans. Family and community relationships are at the heart of religious belief and practice; all ritual is directed toward improving these relationships and therefore the well-being of the entire community. Spirit mediums, or diviners, are concerned with using their powers to bring healing, good health, and general prosperity to the people.

29. The Bangwa

This community in Cameroon worships spirits that are both gods and ancestors. They create special structures for their household gods where they make offerings on behalf of their families. They believe that everyone has a witch animal or spirit in their body that powerful people can use to transform themselves when needing to fight an enemy. Many are also Christian and bring their traditional worldview into their Christian practice and vice versa.

30. The Zulu

Because of contact with Christian missionaries, Zulu people worship a Lord-of-the-Sky, who is the source of both good and evil. He can only be approached on special occasions with proper preparation. The shades are the center of Zulu belief: they brood over their people in times of crisis, bringing transformation. Shades tend to be opposite in behavior and viewpoint from humans.

A Brief Survey of Traditions

Aboriginal Religion

"Australian Aboriginal cosmology centers on a concept that has been translated as the Dreaming, or Dream-time, which refers both to a founding drama of how the Ancestors rose up from beneath the earth to shape and mold an already existing, yet amorphous world, and to an eternal, atemporal metaphysical reality. . . . Although Dreaming does not adequately convey the full significance of the complex aspect Aboriginal cosmology, it does suggest the mystery of the connection of Aboriginal people to land, spirituality, and all that exists. . . . When the Ancestors rose up from beneath the earth, they journeyed from place to place, imbuing all things with their own essence, power, or energy and establishing a set of laws for all to follow. As the Ancestors traveled, they left tangible expressions of themselves in the landscape: here a rocky outcrop, there a tree or waterhole, metamorphosing a part of their own essence into some feature of the environment, or imprinting themselves onto cave walls or ritual objects. When they had completed their journeys, they went back under the earth from whence they had come. . . . The land is a vast web of sacredness. Land, spirit, and humans are inextricably interwoven. Aborigines say they are caretakers of the land rather than owners."

(Lynne Hume, "Aboriginal Religions," in *Religions of the World: A Comprehensive Encyclopedia of Beliefs and Practices*, ed. J. Gordon Melton, 2nd ed. [Santa Barbara, CA: ABC-CLIO, 2010], 8–10)

The Lakota

"The Lakota people fled their homeland in the eastern woodlands of the present-day United States in the winter of 1776 under attack by the Ojibwa, who called them "Sioux," a derogatory name that suggested they were less than human. . . .The Lakota soon became masters of the Midwestern plains and followed the plentiful buffalo herds for sustenance. [Despite being granted] 60 million acres of land in the Dakotas [in 1851], . . . the westward expansion of European Americans . . . whittled away this territory. Even the most sacred Black Hills were soon confiscated. Despite one decisive victory against General George Armstrong Custer (1839–1876), the Lakota could not stand against the brutal force of the U.S. Cavalry, whose most notorious act was the massacre of more than 300 Lakota people at Wounded Knee Creek in 1890.

"The center of Lakota religion is the sacred pipe, which is an essential part of every ceremony. According to the most fundamental of the Lakota sacred stories, the pipe was given to them generations ago by White Buffalo Woman. A sacred being, White Buffalo approached two young hunters in the form of an extraordinarily beautiful woman. When the older hunter reached out to possess her, he immediately dissolved into a pile of bones. Selfishness, manifested here as lust and greed, killed him. The younger hunter listened carefully as the sacred woman told him to return to his encampment, where his people were starving, and to tell them to prepare to receive her. The next day she presented the gift of the sacred pipe and instructed the people in its use.

"Although the pipe is smoked in many ritual situations, it is the predominant feature of the Inipi, a sweat bath, and the sweat bath is the first stage of almost every ritual undertaking. The sweat house is a small circular enclosure that represents the entire universe. . . . As the Lakota strip off their clothing and enter the Inipi, they strip away all bad thoughts and animosities.

(Thomas V. Peterson, "The Lakota," in Melton, J. Gordon, *Religions of the World, Second Edition: A Comprehensive Encyclopedia of Beliefs and Practices.* Santa Barbara, CA: ABC-CLIO, 2010, pp. 1675-1677.)

The Ojibwa

The Ojibwa (Ojibwe) and Ottawa Indians are members of a longstanding alliance also including the Potawatomi tribe. Called the Council of Three Fires, this alliance was a powerful one which clashed with the mighty Iroquois Confederacy and the Sioux. The Ojibwa people were less devastated by European epidemics than their densely-populated Algonquian cousins to the east, and they resisted conflict with white men much better than other tribes. Most of their lands were appropriated by the Americans and Canadians, a fate shared by all native peoples of North America, but plans to deport the Ojibwa to Kansas and Oklahoma never succeeded, and today nearly all Ojibwa reservations are within their original territory.

(Derived from http://www.native-languages.org/chippewa.htm)

The Yoruba

"The Yoruban people of Nigeria emerged out of prehistory with the founding of Ife, a city in southwestern Nigeria, which has been their center for a millennium. Yoruban towns are traditionally headed by a chief (*oba*) who is invested with authority by the chief in Ife. Although they are an agricultural people, everyday life is centered in the villages that are placed in the center of the local farmland.

"The Yorubans divide the cosmos into Orun, the sky, and Aiye, the Earth. In the sky dwells Olorun, the High God, a number of associated deities (the Orissa), and the ancestors. Olorun is seen as somewhat remote and difficult to approach; hence he is not the object of shrines, rituals, or prayers. He is seen as the source of all and the creator of the first 16 human beings. However, it is Orisa-nla who is credited with creating the Earth and transferring the first humans to their new home. It is also believed that Orisa-nla began his acts of creation at Ife. Hence Ife is the center of all religious and spiritual power.

"There are between 5 and 10 million Yorubans, most of whom reside in western Nigeria. There is a great variety in the practice associated with the widespread Yoruban system, not only in Nigeria and neighboring countries but also in its New World incarnations in Cuba and Brazil (where it developed an overlay of Christianity and is known variously as Santeria or Macumba). Both Christianity and Islam have come into Yoruban lands, resulting in a situation in which syncretistic religions have emerged."

(J. Gordon Melton, "Yoruban Religion/Spirituality," in *Religions of the World: A Comprehensive Encyclopedia of Beliefs and Practices*, ed. J. Gordon Melton, 2nd ed. [Santa Barbara, CA: ABC-CLIO, 2010], 3168–70)

Zulu Religion

"The Zulu people are one of the Bantu groups that migrated into what is now South Africa at some unknown point in the last two millennia. They date their own origin myth from a chief named Malandela, who had a son named Zulu who became the head of his own clan. He brought his clan to the Mfolosi Valley, north of the Thuleka River in present-day Natal. The Zulu people then entered into history with the emergence generations later of Shaka (1785–1828). A remarkable leader, Shaka reorganized the Zulus and turned them into a notable military force. His kingdom eventually covered some 11,000 square miles of territory. The British attacked the Zulu kingdom in 1879 . . . and the Zulu were pushed into a small "reserve" while most of their land was settled by whites.

"The Zulu trace their ancestry to Inkosi Yezulu, the Sky God, also known as Umvelingqangi. The male Sky God and his female counterpart, Earth, brought forth the people, Abuntu, though the exact process of creation is not clear. Also important to the Zulu are the ancestral spirits, especially those of outstanding chiefs, local village headmen, and men, in that order. The departed souls of the ancestors are known collectively as the *amalozi* or *amathinga*, and are pictured as residing in the earth but still having an active role in the life of their present progeny.

"Less formally active in Zulu religion are the sorcerers, often herbalists who also have a knowledge of magic, though anyone may be a sorcerer. The sorcerer uses magic to redress a grievance. Finally, there is the witch, a person, usually believed to be female, who is thought to be living a concealed existence in the village. The witch is one who uses magic for evil and inappropriate ends. The witch is judged to be present by the manifest evil consequences of her actions.

"Ritual activity for the Zulu happens most frequently in the circular villages called *kraals*, typically built on the side of a hill with the entrance facing down the slope. In the center of the kraal are the very important cattle herds. . . .Most Zulu ritual is about power (*amandla*), its use (and misuse). Power is derived from the Sky God, the ancestors, and medicine. Ritual connects with the source of the power that sustains life and creates order. Witches, of course, pervert the power.

"Today's 4 million (some estimate as many as 6 million) Zulu live across South Africa, but they are concentrated in Kwazulu, the name of the old reserve. The royal house originally established by Shaka still exists, and the Zulu nation's current king is Zwelithini Goodwill KaCyprian Bhekuzulu."

(J. Gordon Melton, "Zulu Religion," in *Religions of the World: A Comprehensive Encyclopedia of Beliefs and Practices*, ed. J. Gordon Melton, 2nd ed. [Santa Barbara, CA: ABC-CLIO, 2010], 3198–99)

Primary Source Readings

The following excerpted readings represent some of the important primary sources mentioned in the main text. Additional primary sources are available both in print and online, and students are encouraged to contact their instructors for further information.

III.1 Religious Rites of the Maori

Source: Edward Shortland, *Maori Religion and Mythology* (London: Longmans, Green, 1882), http://www.sacred-texts.com/pac/mrm/index.htm

The religious rites and ceremonies of the *Maori* . . . are immediately connected with certain laws relating to things *tapu*, or things sacred and prohibited, the breach of which laws by anyone is a crime displeasing to the *Atua* of his family. Anything *tapu* must not be allowed to come in contact with any vessel or place where food is kept. This law is absolute. Should such contact take place, the food, the vessel, or place, become *tapu*, and only a few very sacred persons, themselves *tapu*, dare to touch these things.

The idea in which this law originated appears to have been that a portion of the sacred essence of an *Atua*, or of a sacred person, was directly communicable to objects which they touched, and also that the sacredness so communicated to any object could afterwards be more or less retransmitted to anything else brought into contact with it. It was therefore necessary that anything containing the sacred essence of an *Atua* should be made *tapu* to protect it from being polluted by the contact of food designed to be cat; for the act of eating food which had touched anything *tapu*, involved the necessity of eating the sacredness of the *Atua*, from whom it derived its sacredness.

It seems that the practice of cannibalism must have had a close connexion with such a system of belief. To eat an enemy was the greatest degradation to which he could be subjected, and so it must have been regarded as akin to blasphemy to eat anything containing a particle of divine essence.

Everything not included under the class *tapu* was called *noa*, meaning free or common. Things and persons *tapu* could, however, be made *noa* by means of certain ceremonies, the object of which was to extract the *tapu* essence, and restore it to the source

whence it originally came. It has been already stated that every tribe and every family has its own especial *Atua*. The *Ariki*, or head of a family, in both male and female lines, are regarded by their own family with a veneration almost equal to that of their *Atua*. They form, as it were, the connecting links, between the living and the spirits of the dead; and the ceremonies required for releasing anything from the *tapu* state cannot be perfected without their intervention.

On arriving one evening at a *Maori* settlement, I found that a ceremony, in which everyone appeared to take deep interest, was to take place in the morning. The inhabitants were mostly professing Christians, and the old sacred place of the settlement was, from the increase of their numbers, inconveniently near their houses; a part of it was, therefore, required to be added to the *Pa*. I was curious to see in what way the land required would be made *noa*. In the morning when I went to the place I found a numerous assembly, while in the centre of the space was a large native oven, from which women were removing the earth and mat-coverings. When opened it was seen to contain only *kumara*, or sweet potato. One of these was offered to each person present, which was held in the hand while the usual morning service was read, concluding with a short prayer that God's blessing might rest on the place. After this each person ate his *kumara*, and the place was declared to be *noa*. I could not but think that the native teacher had done wisely in thus adopting so much of old ceremonial as to satisfy the scruples of those of little faith. In this case, every one present, by eating food cooked on the *tapu* ground, equally incurred the risk of offending the *Atua* of the family, which risk was believed to be removed by the Christian *karakia*.

By neglecting the laws of *tapu*, *Ariki*, chiefs, and other sacred persons are especially liable to the displeasure of their *Atua*, and are therefore afraid to do a great many ordinary acts necessary in private life. For this reason a person of the sacred class was obliged to eat his meals in the open air, at a little distance from his sacred dwelling, and from the place which he and his friends usually occupied; and if he could not eat all that had been placed before him he kept the remainder for his own sole use, in a sacred place appropriated for that purpose: for no one dared to eat what so sacred a person had touched.

The term *karakia* is applicable to all forms of prayer to the *Atua*: but there are a variety of names or titles to denote *karakia* having special objects. The translations of those now presented to the reader will, it is believed, speak for themselves as to the nature of *Maori* worship, and carry with them a more clear and full conviction as to what it really was than any mere statements however faithful. It will be seen that a *karakia* is in some cases very like a prayer, in other cases for the most part an invocation of spirits of ancestors in genealogical order, in other cases a combination of prayer and invocation.

THE KARAKIA OF HINETEIWAIWA

Said to have been used at the birth of her son Tuhuruhuru. It is of great antiquity, dating from a time long anterior to the migration to New Zealand.

Weave, weave the mat,
Couch for my unborn child,
Qui lectus aquâ inundabitur:
Rupe, et manumea inundabuntur:
Lectus meus, et mei fetûs inundabitur:
Inundabor aquâ, inundabor;
Maritus meus inundabitur.
Now I step upon (the mat).
The *Matitikura* to Rupe above,
* * * Toroa *
* * * Takapu *
* * * to cause to be born,
My child now one with myself.
Stand firm *turuturu* of Hine-rauwharangi,
* * * Hine-teiwaiwa,
Stand by your *tia*, Ihuwareware,
Stand by your *kona*, Ihuatamai,
Chide me not in my trouble,
Me Hine-teiwaiwa, O Rupe.
Release from above your hair
Your head, your shoulders,
Your breast, your liver,

Your knees, your feet,
Let them come forth.
The old lady with night-dark visage,
She will make you stretch,
She will make you rise up.
Let go *ewe*, let go take,
Let go *parapara*. Come forth.

CEREMONIES FOR THE DEAD

When a man dies his body is placed in a sitting posture, and is bound to a stake to keep it in a good position. It is seated with its face towards the sun as it rises from its cave. Then every one comes near to lament. The women in front, the men behind them. Their clothes are girded about their loins. In their hands they hold green leaves and boughs, then the song called *keka* commences thus:—

Tohunga chants	It is not a man,
All [2]	It is Rangi now consigned to earth, Alas! my friend.
Tohunga [2]	My evil omen,
All [2]	The lightning glancing on the mountain peak All Te Waharoa doomed to death.

After the *keka*, the *uhunga* or lament commences. The clothes in which the corpse should be dressed are the *kahuwaero*, the *huru*, the *topuni*, and the *tatata*. The lament ended, presents are spread to view, greenstone ornaments, and other offerings for the dead chief. A carved chest, ornamented with feathers, is also made, and a carved canoe, a small one resembling a large canoe, which is painted with *kokowai* (= red-ochre); also a stick bent at the top is set up by the way-side, in order that persons passing by may see it, and know that a chief has died. This is called a *hara*. The carved chest is called a *whare-rangi*. The corpse only is buried, the clothes are placed in the carved chest which is preserved by the family and descendants as a sacred relic.

On the morning following the burial, some men go to kill a small bird of the swamps called *kokata*, and to pluck up some reeds of *wiwi*. They return and come near the grave. The *tohunga* then asks "Whence come you?" The men reply, "From the seeking, from the searching." The *tohunga* again asks "Ah! what have you got? ah! what have you gained?" Thereon the men throw on the ground the *kotata* [*sic*] and the *wiwi*. Then the *tohunga* selects a stalk of *toetoe* or *rarauhe*, and places it near the grave in a direction pointing towards Hawaiki to be a pathway for the spirit, that it may go in the straight path to those who died before him. This is named a *Tiri*, and is also placed near where he died, in order that his spirit may return as an *Atua* for his living relations. The person to whom this *Atua* appears is called the *kaupapa* or *waka-atua*. Whenever the spirit appears to the *kaupapa* the men of the family assemble to hear its words. Hear the *karakia* of the *kaupapa* to prevail on the spirit to climb the path of the *Tiri*.

This is your path, the path of Tawaki
By it he climbed up to Rangi,
By it he mounted to your many,
To your Thousands;
By it you approached,
By it you clung,
By it your spirit arrived safely
To your ancestors.
I now am here sighing,
Lamenting for your departed spirit,
Come, come to me in form of a moth,
Come to me your *kaupapa*,
Whom you loved,
For whom you lamented.
Here is the *Tiri* for you,
The *Tiri* of your ancestors,
The *Tiri* of your Pukenga,
Of your *Wananga*,
Of me this *Tauira*.

The Reinga or Hades

When the spirit leaves the body it goes on its way northward, till it arrives at two hills. The first of these hills is a place on which to lament with wailings and cuttings. There also the spirit strips off its clothes. The name of this hill is Wai-hokimai. The name of the other hill is Wai-otioti: there the spirit turns its back on the land of life, and goes on to the Rerenga-wairua (Spirit's-leap). There are two long straight roots, the lower extremities of which are concealed in the sea, while the upper ends cling to a *pohutu-kawa* tree. The spirit stands by the upper end of these roots, awaiting an opening in the sea weed floating on the water. The moment an opening is seen, it flies down to the Reinga. Reaching the Reinga, there is a river and a sandy beach. The spirit crosses the river. The name of the newcomer is shouted out. He is welcomed, and food is set before him. If he eats the food he can never return to life.

III.2 Yoruba Legends

Source: M. I. Ogumefu, *Yoruba Legends* (London: Sheldon Press, 1929), http://www.sacred-texts.com/afr/yl/index.htm

The Kingdom of the Yorubas

The ancient King Oduduwa had a great many grandchildren, and on his death he divided among them all his possessions. But his youngest grandson, Oranyan, was at that time away hunting, and when he returned home he learnt that his brothers and cousins had inherited the old King's money, cattle, beads, native cloths, and crowns, but that to himself nothing was left but twenty-one pieces of iron, a cock, and some soil tied up in a rag.

At that time the whole earth was covered with water, on the surface of which the people lived.

The resourceful Oranyan spread upon the water his pieces of iron, and upon the iron he placed the scrap of cloth, and upon the cloth the soil, and on the soil the cock. The cock scratched with his feet and scattered the soil far and wide, so that the ocean was partly filled up and islands appeared everywhere. The pieces of iron became the mineral wealth hidden under the ground.

Now Oranyan's brothers and cousins all desired to live on the land, and Oranyan allowed them to do so on payment of tribute. He thus became King of all the Yorubas, and was rich and prosperous through his grandfather's inheritance.

AKITI THE HUNTER

A famous hunter and wrestler named Akiti boasted that he was stronger than any other man or animal. He had easily overcome a giant, a leopard, a lion, a wolf, and a boa-constrictor, and as nobody else opposed his claim, he called himself "the King of the forest."

Wherever he went, he sang his triumphant wrestling-song, and everyone feared and respected him. But he had forgotten the Elephant, who is a very wise animal and knows many charms. One day the Elephant challenged him and declared that he had no right to call himself "King," as the Elephant himself was the monarch of the forest and could not be defeated.

Akiti thereupon flung his spear at his enemy, but because of the Elephant's charm, the weapon glanced off his hide and did him no harm. Akiti next tried his bow and poisoned arrows, and his hunting-knife, but still without effect.

However, the hunter also possessed a charm, and by using it, he changed himself into a lion and flew at the Elephant, but the Elephant flung him off. Next he became a serpent, but he could not succeed in crushing the Elephant to death.

At last he changed himself into a fly, and flew into the Elephant's large flapping ear. He went right down inside until he came to the heart, and then he changed himself into a man again and cut up the heart with his hunting-knife. At last the Elephant fell dead, and Akiti stepped out of his body in triumph, for he was now without question "the King of the forest."

WHY WOMEN HAVE LONG HAIR

Two women quarreled, and one of them went out secretly at night and dug a deep pit in the middle of the path leading from her enemy's house to the village well.

Early next morning, when all were going to the well for water with jars balanced on their heads, this woman fell into the pit and cried loudly for help.

Her friends ran to her and, seizing her by the hair, began to pull her out of the pit. To their surprise, her hair stretched as they pulled, and by the time she was safely on the path, her hair was as long as a man's arm.

This made her very much ashamed, and she ran away and hid herself.

But after a while she realized that her long hair was beautiful, and then she felt very proud and scorned all the short-haired women, jeering at them. When they saw this, they were consumed with jealousy, and began to be ashamed of their short hair. "We have men's hair," they said to one another. "How beautiful it would be to have long hair!"

So one by one they jumped into the pit, and their friends pulled them out by the hair.

And in this way they, and all women after them, had long hair.

THE BAT

The Bat is half a bird and half a rodent, and lives partly on the earth and partly in the air, but both rats and birds shun him, and this is why:

The rats, his cousins, were once fighting a great battle with the birds, and Bat fought in their midst.

But when he saw that the birds were likely to be victorious, he left the rats and flew up into the air to fight on the side of the birds.

Both the rats and the birds were disgusted at this cowardly action, so they ceased from fighting one another and all combined to attack the Bat.

Since that day he has been forced to hide in dark places all day, and only comes out in the evening when his enemies cannot see him.

THE ANTS AND THE TREASURE

There once was a poor man who was very kind to animals and birds. However little he had, he always spared a few grains of corn, or a few beans, for his parrot, and he was in the habit of spreading on the ground every morning some titbits for the industrious ants, hoping that they would be satisfied with the corn and leave his few possessions untouched.

And for this the ants were grateful.

In the same village there lived a miser who had by crafty and dishonest means collected a large store of gold, which he kept securely tied up in the corner of a small hut. He sat outside this hut all day and all night, so that nobody could steal his treasure.

When he saw any bird, he threw a stone at it, and he crushed any ant which he found walking on the ground, for he detested every living creature and loved nothing but his gold.

As might be expected, the ants had no love for this miser, and when he had killed a great many of their number, they began to think how they might punish him for his cruelty.

"What a pity it is," said the King of the ants, "that our friend is a poor man, while our enemy is so rich!"

This gave the ants an idea. They decided to transfer the miser's treasure to the poor man's house. To do this they dug a great tunnel under the ground. One end of the tunnel was in the poor man's house, and the other end was in the hut of the miser.

On the night that the tunnel was completed, a great swarm of ants began carrying the miser's treasure into the poor man's house, and when morning came and the poor man saw the gold lying in heaps on the floor, he was overjoyed, thinking that the gods had sent him a reward for his years of humble toil.

He put all the gold in a corner of his hut and covered it up with native cloths.

Meanwhile the miser had discovered that his treasure was greatly decreased. He was alarmed and could not think how the gold could have disappeared, for he had kept watch all the time outside the hut.

The next night the ants again carried a great portion of the miser's gold down the tunnel, and again the poor man rejoiced and the miser was furious to discover his loss.

On the third night the ants laboured long and succeeded in removing all the rest of the treasure.

"The gods have indeed sent me much gold!" cried the poor man, as he put away his treasure.

But the miser called together his neighbours and related that in three consecutive nights his hard-won treasure had vanished away. He declared that nobody had entered the hut but himself, and therefore the gold must have been removed by witchcraft.

However, when the hut was searched, a hole was found in the ground, and they saw that this hole was the opening of a tunnel. It seemed clear that the treasure had been carried down the tunnel, and everyone began hunting for the other end of the tunnel. At last it was discovered in the poor man's hut! Under the native cloths in the corner they found the missing treasure.

The poor man protested in vain that he could not possibly have crept down such a small tunnel, and he declared that he had no notion how the gold had got into his hut. But the rest said that be must have some charm by which he made himself very small and crept down the tunnel at night into the miser's hut.

For this offence they shut him up in a hut and tightly closed the entrance. On the next day he was to be burnt alive.

When the ants saw what had come of their plan to help him, they were sorely perplexed and wondered how they could save their poor friend from such a painful death

There seemed nothing for them to do but to eat up the whole of the hut where the prisoner was confined. This they accomplished after some hours, and the poor man was astonished to find himself standing in an open space. He ran away into the forest and never came back.

In the morning the people saw that the ants had been at work, for a few stumps of the hut remained. They said: "The gods have taken the punishment out of our hands! The ants have devoured both the hut and the prisoner!"

And only the ants knew that this was not true.

THE HEAD

There is a certain country where the inhabitants have heads but no bodies. The Heads move about by jumping along the ground, but they never go very far.

One of the Heads desired to see the world, so he set out one morning secretly. When he had gone some distance, he saw an old woman looking out of the door of a hut, and he asked her if she would kindly lend him a body.

The old woman willingly lent him the body of her slave, and the Head thanked her and went on his way.

Later he came upon a young man sleeping under a tree, and asked him if he would kindly lend him a pair of arms, as he did not appear to be using them. The young man agreed, and the Head thanked him and went on his way.

Later still he reached a river-bank where fishermen sat singing and mending their cone-shaped net. The Head asked if any one of them would lend him a pair of legs, as they were all sitting and not walking. One of the fishermen agreed, and the Head thanked him and went on his way.

But now he had legs, arms, and a body, and so appeared like any other man.

In the evening he reached a town and saw maidens dancing while the onlookers threw coins to those they favoured. The Head threw all his coins to one of the dancers, and she so much admired his handsome form that she consented to marry him and go to live with him in his own country.

Next day they set out, but when they came to the river-bank, the stranger took off his legs and gave them back to the fisherman. Later they reached the young man, who still lay sleeping under the tree, and to him the Head gave back his arms. Finally they came to the cottage, where the old woman stood watching, and here the stranger gave up his body.

When the bride saw that her husband was merely a Head, she was filled with horror, and ran away as fast as she could go.

Now that the Head had neither body, arms, nor legs, he could not overtake her, and so lost her forever.

THE ELEPHANT'S TRUNK

Now it is a matter of common knowledge that Elephant has a long trunk, which he uses both as a nose and as a sort of hand—a very useful trunk indeed. But he was once without it, and had a very ordinary short snout like other animals.

Elephant was always inquisitive and went sniffing about the forest, prying into the secrets of the other animals. One day he came across a dark hole in the ground, and into this hole he poked his nose, to see what was there.

He at once regretted his curiosity, for a large snake, who lived in the hole, seized him by the nose and tried to swallow him. At this, Elephant made a great uproar, and his wife came rushing to his assistance. She seized his tail and pulled and pulled, and Elephant himself also pulled and pulled, but the snake would not leave go.

And as a result, Elephant's nose was drawn out into the long trunk which he still has.

At first he was ashamed to appear in the forest, on account of his trunk, but now the other animals envy him.

One day the monkey, which imitates everybody, looked down the same hole, thinking it would be good to have a long trunk so as to be able to swing from the trees by his nose. But the big snake who lived in the hole swallowed him, and since then nobody else has tried to imitate Elephant.

Key Terms

Dreamtime   In Australian indigenous religions, the mythical period in which, according to Aboriginal tradition, ancestral beings moved across the face of the earth forming its physical features. The Dreamtime is re-created in art, painting, chanting, dancing, and cult ceremonies.

shaman   (1) An ecstatic priest-magician among the Tungu people of Siberia. (2) By extension, a similar figure in other indigenous religions and ancient religions. Shamans induce a trance experience in which they are believed to leave the body and visit other worlds. The shaman's role is to convey sacrifices to the gods, to escort the dead to their destination and to return with divine prophecies.

taboo   Polynesian word applied to an object, place, or person prohibited because of its holy or dangerous character. It may include the sense of being "marked off" and therefore separate from everyday usage.

Annotated Bibliography

Bell, Diane. *Daughters of the Dreaming*. 2nd edition. Minneapolis: University of Minnesota Press, 1993.
In this anthropological study of Aboriginal women and their lives, the author includes excerpts from her many interviews and first-hand accounts of rituals and daily life in Aboriginal communities. She describes one woman's dance in this way: "When Nampiyinpa dances for Wakulpa [her land] . . . one of her favourite sequences is of food gathering west of Karlukarla. The images and the humour of her dancing draw on her experience of the country and family. Her ritual range extends from her mother's country in the south and west and, by following rain dreaming out of Wakulpa into Warumungu country, goes as far north as Tennant Creek; it is underwritten by her unbroken contact with the country celebrated in the ceremonies."

Fienup-Riordan, Ann. *Eskimo Essays: Yup'ik Lives and How We See Them*. New Brunswick, NJ: Rutgers University Press, 1990.
This book, written by an American anthropologist and including photographs, attempts to address stereotypes and "half-truths" about the Yup'ik people while specifically analyzing "the intersection between Yup'ik and Western thought and cultural representation."

Lugira, Aloysius M. *African Religion: World Religions*. Revised edition. New York: Facts on File, 2004.
This is a survey textbook on African religions. It discusses both general characteristics of religion indigenous to the continent and specific traditions and practices. Photographs of art, artifacts, people at worship, etc., enhance the text. Examples of practices and beliefs described in detail include a Zulu wedding, the concept of *Iwa* (character) in Yoruba tradition, and the deities in the pantheon of the Baganda (a Ugandan ethnic group).

Stories of Traditional Navajo Life and Culture by Twenty-two Navajo Men and Women. Edited by Broderick H. Johnson. Tsaile, AZ: Navajo Community College Press, 1997.
Twenty-two elderly Navajos, age fifty-six to ninety-six, recall their childhoods, describe their education and work lives, and discuss their concerns about modern life and the next generation. From one account that describes a "Beauty Way" ritual: "Everyone chanted many blessing songs all night, until dawn. . . . During the progress of a sing, every so often a pinch of [corn] pollen is handed to a person, starting from the doorway

clockwise. Each one takes a pinch of pollen and places it on the tip of his tongue; another bit is placed on the forehead and the last pinch is offered to Mother Earth, Sky and Sun."

"Who the Dongria Kondh Are, What Niyamgiri Is to Them." *Resources Research* (blog), August 26, 2010. http://makanaka.wordpress.com/2010/08/26/who-the-dongria-kondh-are-what-niyamgiri-is-to-them/.

This is an excerpt from an investigation committee's report about a bauxite mine proposed by the Orissa Mining Company for Kondh land; it discusses the Kondh's culture and belief system as well as the environmental impact of the proposed mine. It quotes one of the Kondh as saying, "We can never leave Niyamgiri. If the mountains are mined, the water will dry up. The crops won't ripen. The medicinal plants will disappear. The air will turn bad. Our gods will be angry. How will we live? We cannot leave Niyamgiri."

Questions for Study and Discussion

1. Using examples from two or three of the case studies, explain the relationship between taboos and rituals in some indigenous religions.
2. Compare indigenous South American shamanism to Norse shamanism, identifying two to three shared traits and two to three differences.
3. Explain the significance of the number four to many Native Americans, such as the Dakota.
4. In your own words, briefly describe three of the common characteristics of indigenous African religions.
5. Describe the role of the shades in Zulu religion.
6. James Cox describes an experience he had in Zimbabwe with a traditional healer and diviner (pp. 159–60). How would you characterize his retelling of the experience in terms of the theories and methodologies described in Part 1? Do you feel the author has maintained objectivity? How might the tone or perspective of his story change if he used a different method, such as phenomenology or psychology?

Questions for Reflection

Write your personal reflections to each of these questions in the space provided.

1. Why are terms like "primitive" and "primal" not appropriate for indigenous religions? (See pp. 130–31.)

2. What kinds of roles do shamans play in indigenous religions? (Think across the case studies.)

3. What are some of the various types of spirits and their roles or interactions with humans? (Think across the case studies.)

4. What types of myths are prevalent in indigenous religions that you find similar to one in your own tradition? (Hint: Water is a common element in creation stories; watch for it. Think across the case studies.)

5. Reflect on the similarities among the case studies and what they may tell us about being human.

6. What is the difference between ancestor worship and adoration of saints?

Selected Online Resources

▶ "Sacred Texts: Australia"—links to selected texts from the nineteenth and early twentieth centuries about aboriginal cultures of Australia
http://www.sacred-texts.com/aus/index.htm

▶ African Traditional Religion—extensive list of links to a wide range of topics related to indigenous African religions
http://www.afrikaworld.net/afrel/

▶ NativeWeb Resources: Religion & Spirituality—a list of sites related to the religions of indigenous people around the world, with an emphasis on North America
http://www.nativeweb.org/resources/religion_spirituality/

▶ "Shamanism in Siberia"—a 1914 essay explaining the author's observations from studying Siberian shamanism
http://www.sacred-texts.com/sha/sis/

Part 4: Hinduism

Chapter Summaries

31. A Historical Overview

Hinduism, unlike other world religions, has no single historical founder, no central revelation or creed, no single doctrine of salvation, and no centralized authority. Its origins can be traced to the Indus Valley around 2000 BCE. Scholars don't agree on the historical developments in that early period, but two theories are that the Aryans replaced the original communities and that Aryan culture developed indigenously. The Vedas, written in Sanskrit, provide important insight into the Aryans and are regarded by many Hindus as timeless revelation. They were mostly liturgical texts used in rituals of sacrifice.

Early Hinduism created elaborate systems of ritual and taught yoga and meditation as ways to liberation or salvation. Eventually sectarian worship developed and spread. Sanskrit narrative traditions also grew, including epics and devotional texts. Temple cities were established, with large complexes symbolizing the king's dharmic rule over his realm.

Hindu reform movements arose during British colonial rule. Today it is part of a resurgence of religious nationalism in India. On a global scale Hinduism continues to be inclusive and universal in orientation.

32. Philosophy

The orthodox or *astika* schools view the universe as having neither beginning nor end but issuing forth from Brahman, the divine ground of being. Life exists as a constant cycle with death and rebirth; the causal principle of karma connects each event in *samsara*. A Hindu tries to live in accordance with *dharma* as part of the effort to reach *moksha*, or ultimate liberation. Some of the Vedantic schools expounded a belief in a nondualistic view of existence; the philosopher Ramanuja proposed that the individual *atman* retains its particular qualities even though part of the Brahman. Another important figure, Madhva, wrote commentaries on sacred texts and established a new, dualistic interpretation of Vedanta.

33. Sacred Writings

Most Hindu scriptures are in Sanskrit, but some are in regional languages. Scriptures are in either of two categories: heard or revealed (*Sruti*), which were communicated directly by God to the sages, and remembered (*Smriti*), which include epics, law, and myths. The four types of Vedas include the earliest known Hindu religious literature; the *Upanishads* is an important set of commentaries discussing such themes as the *atman* or soul, Brahman, and internal sacrifice. To progress toward *moksha* Hindus are encouraged to read the epics *Ramayana* and *Mahabharata*, whose underlying theme is about salvation and the ongoing struggle between good and evil. The *Bhagavad Gita*, part of the *Mahabharata*, is highly influential within the tradition, seeking to unite theological strands while arguing for the way of devotion (*bhakti*) as the highest of all paths to enlightenment.

34. Beliefs

Hindus may be polytheistic, monotheistic, monistic (believing all reality is one), or even atheistic. Many believe there is one God, Brahman, who can be worshipped in many forms. The two preeminent gods are Shiva, the lord of yogis (ascetics), and Vishnu, who maintains the dharma and is typically worshipped via his *avatars*, Rama and Krishna. Goddesses can be distinct deities or forms of the (Maha) devi, or Great Goddess. Sita, the wife of Rama, has been upheld as a model for Hindu wives. Many Hindus believe the power (*shakti*) of a god is present in its image, so that they worship consecrated images. Dharma is a complex concept that includes social and cosmic order as well as individual religious and social duties. Central to the teaching about reincarnation is the idea of the endless cycle of *samsara* and a belief in karma—one's actions determine one's condition in this life and one's next rebirth.

The three paths to spiritual fulfillment are *jnana* (wisdom), karma (action), and *bhakti* (devotion). Many modern Hindu teachers and gurus teach that all three paths are linked and liberating knowledge can be gained through all. Hinduism recognizes four life goals for believers: *artha* (worldly success), *kama* (pleasure), dharma (virtue), and *moksha* (spiritual liberation).

Hindu complex beliefs about the afterlife tend to involve karma-driven rebirth and the possibility of some kind of *moksha*, which may mean the ultimate union with *Brahman* or experience of paradise.

35. Worship and Festivals

Early Hindu worship focused on sacrificial ritual, or *yajna*, addressed to nature gods. Today *puja* is a common ritual of devotional worship: the temple priest ritually purifies himself and the shrine and worships the image of the deity through ritual bathing and adorning, symbolic feeding, and circling it with a lamp. Some Hindus believe *puja* to be significant, while others prefer a more inward mode of spiritual practice. Other forms of worship include *bhajana* (hymn singing) and the recitation of the thousand names of the gods and goddesses. Hindu cosmology includes sacred rivers as well as animals such as the cow, the monkey, and the snake. Holy figures are believed to be capable of performing miracles and ensuring their followers' well-being. The Hindu lunar calendar features a series of festivals, usually marked by processions involving the deity's image.

36. Family and Society

Hindu society is organized into castes, which determine all social relationships in terms of superiority and inferiority and levels of purity. In traditional Indian society caste determined most aspects of a person's life. The joint family system determined each person's place within the household, with the men having the most power and the sole ability to inherit. Marriage is a central Hindu institution, typically arranged between similar-caste families. Today, women's roles are changing, and one's caste no longer wholly determines one's path in life. Families still tend to be closely connected through multiple generations, and parents often play a major role in their children's life choices.

37. Hinduism in the Modern World

Many contemporary Hindus consult astrologers and gurus, contributing to the rise of the cult phenomenon. Nationalism is also a strong force within and outside of India. Hindu political parties promote India as a Hindu, rather than multireligious, nation. Westernized Hindu ideas, a result of the diaspora, have increased awareness of mystical traditions and other forms of Hindu spirituality. The caste system has been strengthened, even while some people of lower castes have turned to Hindu worship over their traditional practices. Women first became involved in modern Indian politics through Gandhi's campaign for independence; women are now well represented in public life throughout India.

Key Personalities

Shankara (788–820 CE)

The best-known exponent of classical Hindu philosophy. Developing the thought of the Upanishads, he declared that only the eternal being is real; the diverse, phenomenal world is an illusion of *maya*. Even the notion of a personal God is part of *maya*. Liberation comes from realizing oneness with the absolute, which is defined as Being, Consciousness and Bliss.

"Shankara's underlying assumption is that the Veda is eternal truth, and on the basis of this he asks the classic questions: what is the nature of the self (atman) and of Brahman? The world seems to be multiple and to provide us with multiple experience, but what is its real ontological status? What is the nature of human experience and what is it to be enlightened? Like all Indian philosophers, he is not concerned to provide his own answers to these questions, but only with expanding Vedic teaching. . . .

"The teaching of the Veda, says Shankara, reveals that . . . there is only Brahman, eternal Being, Consciousness and Bliss: the multiple world which we seem to see and to experience has no more reality than the imagined snake which a person mistakenly

"superimposes" onto a piece of rope in the twilight, and a similar process of mistaken superimposition of qualities upon Brahman is responsible for our everyday interpretation of reality."

("Shankara," *Overview of World Religions*, http://www.philtar.ac.uk/encyclopedia/hindu/ascetic/shank.html)

ADDITIONAL RESOURCE

▶ "Shankara's Crest-Jewel of Wisdom, Vivekachudamani" (revision of a 1946 translation of Shankara's work) http://oaks.nvg.org/crest-jewel.html

Madhva (1197–1276 CE)

Indian philosopher who founded a dualist school in opposition to the monism of Shankara. He was a devotee of Vishnu, and believed that God was eternally distinct from the natural world. He may have been influenced by Christian teachings.

"Madhvacharya presented a very simple vision of the world. It was clear to him that there were differences and distinctions in the world. Matter was distinct from mind. One material thing was distinct from another, one person from another. Above all, there was a radical difference between God and the world. This in a nutshell is his doctrine of Panchabeda or five differences, which stated that there was an absolute distinction between God and the soul, God and matter, souls and matter, each individual soul and another, and each material thing and another. There is an unbridgeable gulf between God and all other beings because God is the only independent Reality."

(Roy Abraham Varghese, *The Wonder of the World: A Journey from Modern Science to the Mind of God* [Fountain Hills, AZ: Tyr, 2003], https://sites.google.com/site /harshalarajesh/wonders-of-the-world)

ADDITIONAL RESOURCE

▶ "Madhva" (biographical essay) http://www.dlshq.org/saints/madhva.htm

Vivekananda (about 1863–1902)

Follower of Ramakrishna, and founder of the Ramakrishna Mission in 1897. An apologist for Vedanta, he criticized the dogmatism of Christianity. Attending the World's Parliament of Religions in Chicago in 1893, he commended Vedanta as the highest form of religion.

"Of the different philosophies, the tendency of the Hindu is not to destroy, but to harmonise everything. If any new idea comes into India, we do not antagonise it, but simply try to take it in, to harmonise it, because this method was taught first by our prophet, God incarnate on earth, Shri Krishna. . . . We do not say that ours is the only way to salvation. Perfection can be had by everybody, and what is the proof? Because we see the holiest of men in all countries, good men and women everywhere, whether born in our faith or not."

(Swami Vivekananda, speaking to a gathering in Detroit, February 21, 1894, http://www.vivekananda.net/ByTopic /Vol8/Notes/11_HindusChristians.html)

ADDITIONAL RESOURCE

▶ Complete Works of Swami Vivekananda (online text representing nine volumes, plus additional material, including contemporary newspaper articles)

http://www.ramakrishnavivekananda.info /vivekananda/complete_works.htm

Ram Mohan Roy (1772–1833)

Hindu reformer who founded the Brahma Samaj, an ethical organization with monotheistic tendencies, in opposition to the idolatry of popular devotion. He believed the Vedas taught monotheism, though he also used Christian and Muslim ideas.

"Roy's efforts to abolish the practice of Sati were largely driven by his concern for the moral dimensions of religion. . . . He delved into the scriptures in great detail and proved that the practice of Sati could not gain *moksha* (salvation) for the husband as each man was responsible for his own destiny. He also realized that very often it was greedy relatives interested in the property of the dead husband who were behind promoting the practice. . . . Roy also succeeded in starting a revolution for women's education and women's right to property. By delving into Hindu scriptures, he showed that women enjoyed equal freedom with men."

(Melanie P. Kumar, "Raja Ram Mohan Roy: A Man for All Times," *Boloji*, May 11, 2003, http://www.boloji.com /people/04003.htm)

ADDITIONAL RESOURCE

▶ "Sati: Nonfiction, Rajah Rammohun Roy" (excerpt from a transcript of an 1818 debate over the practice of *sati*, with Roy arguing against it) http://chnm.gmu.edu/wwh/p/101.html

Mohandas Gandhi (1869–1948)

Leader of the Indian independence movement and the greatest spiritual and political figure of modern India. Disowning violence, he advocated political change through nonviolent resistance. After independence he tried to reconcile the Hindu and Muslim communities. He also campaigned against the social exclusion of untouchables. He was assassinated by a Hindu fanatic.

"Non-violence is a matchless weapon, which can help every one. I know we have not done much by way of non-violence and therefore, if such changes come about, I will take it that it is the result of our labors during the last twenty-two years and that God has helped us to achieve it. . . . My democracy means that every one is his own master. I have read sufficient history, and I have not seen such an experiment on such a large scale for the establishment of democracy by non-violence. Once you understand these things you will forget the differences between the Hindus and Moslems."

("Mohandas K. Gandhi's Speech [Excerpts] to the All-India Congress," *New York Times*, August 8, 1942, http://www.ibiblio.org/pha/policy/1942/420807a.html)

"According to Gandhi, God and *dharma* are inseparably linked, and both are combined with moksha. Religion and politics could not therefore be divided. Dharma and moksha were social not individual concepts. In the [*Bhagavad*] *Gita*, *Krishna* (God) is a friend (*bandhu*) who comes to Arjuna in his time of distress. This should be remembered when we read that for Gandhi, 'Truth is God.' Truth is no impersonal absolute nor a substitute for God. Truth clarifies what God meant when he used the term. It is also a source of power; hence his use of the word *satyagraha*, truth force."

(Vijay Mehta, "Why We Value Gandhi: A Hindu Perspective," speech given at the Annual Multi-Faith Service, London, 2005, http://arcwebsite.org/pages/why_we_value_gandhi.htm)

ADDITIONAL RESOURCES

- ▶ "Mohandas 'Mahatma' Gandhi" (biographic essay along with transcript of a 2004 BBC program about the conversations Gandhi had with the British wife of one of his assistants) http://www.bbc.co.uk/religion/religions/hinduism/people/gandhi_1.shtml
- ▶ *The Gandhi Reader: A Sourcebook of His Life and Writings* (selections available through Google Books) http://books.google.com/books?id=pjN3jZQ74AoC

Sarvepalli Radhakrishnan (1888–1975)

Indian philosopher who became vice president and then president of India. He taught that there is a basic unity of all religions and that Hinduism is a useful meeting ground because of its breadth and tolerance.

"As an Advaitin, Radhakrishnan embraced a metaphysical idealism. But Radhakrishnan's idealism was such that it recognized the reality and diversity of the world of experience (prakrti) while at the same time preserving the notion of a wholly transcendent Absolute (Brahman), an Absolute that is identical to the self (Atman). While the world of experience and of everyday things is certainly not ultimate reality, as it is subject to change and is characterized by finitude and multiplicity, it nonetheless has its origin and support in the Absolute (Brahman) which is free from all limits, diversity, and distinctions (nirguna). Brahman is the source of the world and its manifestations, but these modes do not affect the integrity of Brahman."

(Michael Hawley, "Radhakrishnan, Sarvepalli," *Internet Encyclopedia of Philosophy*, October 12, 2006, http://www.iep.utm.edu/radhakri/)

ADDITIONAL RESOURCE

- ▶ "Fellowship of the Spirit" (audio of a speech given by Radhakrishnan at the Center for the Study of World Religions, Harvard Divinity School, November 21, 1960) http://www.hds.harvard.edu/multimedia/audio/fellowship-of-the-spirit

Primary Source Readings

The following excerpted readings represent some of the important primary sources mentioned in the main text. Additional primary sources are available both in print and online, and students are encouraged to contact their instructors for further information.

IV.1 *The* Rig Veda

Source: *Rig Veda*, trans. Ralph T. H. Griffith (1896), Book 10, http://www.sacred-texts.com/hin/rigveda/rvi10.htm

HYMN XVI. AGNI

1. Burn him not up, nor quite consume him, Agni: let not his body or his skin be scattered.

O Jātavedas, when thou hast matured him, then send him on his way unto the Fathers.

2 When thou hast made him ready, Jātavedas, then do thou give him over to the Fathers.

When he attains unto the life that waits him, he shall become the Deities' controller.

3 The Sun receive thine eye, the Wind thy spirit; go, as thy merit is, to earth or heaven.

Go, if it be thy lot, unto the waters; go, make thine home in plants with all thy members.

4 Thy portion is the goat: with heat consume him: let thy fierce flame, thy glowing splendour, burn him

With thine auspicious forms, o Jātavedas, bear this man to the region of the pious.

5 Again, O Agni, to the Fathers send him who, offered in thee, goes with our oblations.

Wearing new life let him increase his offspring: let him rejoin a body, Jātavedas.

6 What wound soe'er the dark bird hath inflicted, the emmet, or the serpent, or the jackal,

May Agni who devoureth all things heal it and Soma who hath passed into the Brahmans.

7 Shield thee with flesh against the flames of Agni, encompass thee about with fat and marrow,

So will the Bold One, eager to attack thee with fierce glow fail to girdle and consume thee.

8 Forbear, O Agni, to upset this ladle: the Gods and they who merit Soma love it.

This ladle, this which serves the Gods to drink from, in this the Immortal Deities rejoice them.

9 I send afar flesh eating Agni, bearing off stains may he depart to Yama's subjects.

But let this other Jātavedas carry oblation to the Gods, for he is skilful.

10 I choose as God for Father-worship Agni, flesh-eater, who hath past within your dwelling,

While looking on this other Jātavedas. Let him light flames in the supreme assembly.

11 With offerings meet let Agni bring the Fathers who support the Law.

Let him announce oblations paid to Fathers and to Deities.

12 Right gladly would we set thee down, right gladly make thee burn and glow.

Gladly bring yearning Fathers nigh to cat the food of sacrifice.

13 Cool, Agni, and again refresh the spot which thou hast scorched and burnt.

Here let the water-lily grow, and tender grass and leafy herb.

14 O full of coolness, thou cool Plant, full of fresh moisture, freshening Herb,

Come hither with the female frog: fill with delight this Agni here.

HYMN LXXII. THE GODS

1. Let us with tuneful skill proclaim these generations of the Gods,

That one may see them when these hymns are chanted in a future age.

2 These Brahmanaspati produced with blast and smelting, like a Smith,

Existence, in an earlier age of Gods, from Non-existence sprang.

3 Existence, in the earliest age of Gods, from Non-existence sprang.

Thereafter were the regions born. This sprang from the Productive Power.

4 Earth sprang from the Productive Power the regions from the earth were born.

Daksa was born of Aditi, and Aditi was Daksa's Child.

5 For Aditi, O Daksa, she who is thy Daughter, was brought forth.

After her were the blessed Gods born sharers of immortal life.

6 When ye, O Gods, in yonder deep closeclasping one another stood,

Thence, as of dancers, from your feet a thickening cloud of dust arose.

7 When, O ye Gods, like Yatis, ye caused all existing things to grow,

Then ye brought Sūrya forward who was lying hidden in the sea.

8 Eight are the Sons of Adid who from her body sprang to life.

With seven she went to meet the Gods she cast Martanda far away.

9 So with her Seven Sons Aditi went forth to meet the earlier age.

She brought Martanda thitherward to spring to life and die again.

Hymn XC. Purusa.

1. A thousand heads hath Purusa, a thousand eyes, a thousand feet.

On every side pervading earth he fills a space ten fingers wide.

2 This Purusa is all that yet hath been and all that is to be;

The Lord of Immortality which waxes greater still by food.

3 So mighty is his greatness; yea, greater than this is Purusa.

All creatures are one-fourth of him, three-fourths eternal life in heaven.

4 With three-fourths Purusa went up: one-fourth of him again was here.

Thence he strode out to every side over what cats not and what cats.

5 From him Virāj was born; again Purusa from Virāj was born.

As soon as he was born he spread eastward and westward o'er the earth.

6 When Gods prepared the sacrifice with Purusa as their offering,

Its oil was spring, the holy gift was autumn; summer was the wood.

7 They balmed as victim on the grass Purusa born in earliest time.

With him the Deities and all Sādhyas and Rsis sacrificed.

8 From that great general sacrifice the dripping fat was gathered up.

He formed the creatures of the air, and animals both wild and tame.

9 From that great general sacrifice Rcas and Sāma-hymns were born:

Therefrom were spells and charms produced; the Yajus had its birth from it.

10 From it were horses born, from it all cattle with two rows of teeth:

From it were generated kine, from it the goats and sheep were born.

11 When they divided Purusa how many portions did they make?

What do they call his mouth, his arms? What do they call his thighs and feet?

12 The Brahman was his mouth, of both his arms was the Rājanya made.

His thighs became the Vaiśya, from his feet the Śūdra was produced.

13 The Moon was gendered from his mind, and from his eye the Sun had birth;

Indra and Agni from his mouth were born, and Vāyu from his breath.

14 Forth from his navel came mid-air the sky was fashioned from his head

Earth from his feet, and from his car the regions. Thus they formed the worlds.

15 Seven fencing-sticks had he, thrice seven layers of fuel were prepared,

When the Gods, offering sacrifice, bound, as their victim, Purusa.

16 Gods, sacrificing, sacrificed the victim these were the earliest holy ordinances.

The Mighty Ones attained the height of heaven, there where the Sādhyas, Gods of old, are dwelling.

Hymn CXXIX. Creation.

1. Then was not non-existent nor existent: there was no realm of air, no sky beyond it.

What covered in [sic], and where? and what gave shelter? Was water there, unfathomed depth of water?

2 Death was not then, nor was there aught immortal: no sign was there, the day's and night's divider.

That One Thing, breathless, breathed by its own nature: apart from it was nothing whatsoever.

3 Darkness there was: at first concealed in darkness this All was indiscriminated chaos.

All that existed then was void and form less: by the great power of Warmth was born that Unit.

4 Thereafter rose Desire in the beginning, Desire, the primal seed and germ of Spirit.

Sages who searched with their heart's thought discovered the existent's kinship in the non-existent.

5 Transversely was their severing line extended: what was above it then, and what below it?

There were begetters, there were mighty forces, free action here and energy up yonder

6 Who verily knows and who can here declare it, whence it was born and whence comes this creation?

The Gods are later than this world's production. Who knows then whence it first came into being?

7 He, the first origin of this creation, whether he formed it all or did not form it,

Whose eye controls this world in highest heaven, he verily knows it, or perhaps he knows not.

Hymn CXXX. Creation.

1. The sacrifice drawn out with threads on every side, stretched by a hundred sacred ministers and one,—

This do these Fathers weave who hitherward are come: they sit beside the warp and cry, Weave forth, weave back.

2 The Man extends it and the Man unbinds it: even to this vault of heaven hath he outspun it.

These pegs are fastened to the seat of worship: they made the Sāma-hymns their weaving shuttles.

3 What were the rule, the order and the model? What were the wooden fender and the butter?

What were the hymn, the chant, the recitation, when to the God all Deities paid worship?

4 Closely was Gāyatrī conjoined with Agni, and closely Savitar combined with Usnih.

Brilliant with Ukthas, Soma joined Anustup: Brhaspati's voice by Brhati was aided.

5 Virāj adhered to Varuna and Mitra: here Tristup day by day was Indra's portion.

Jagatī entered all the Gods together: so by this knowledge men were raised to Rsis.

6 So by this knowledge men were raised to Rsis, when ancient sacrifice sprang up, our Fathers.

With the mind's eye I think that I behold them who first performed this sacrificial worship.

7 They who were versed in ritual and metre, in hymns and rules, were the Seven Godlike Rsis.

Viewing the path of those of old, the sages have taken up the reins like chariot-drivers.

IV.2 The Yoga Sutras of Patanjali

Source: *The Yoga Sutras of Patanjali: The Threads of Union*, trans. BonGiovanni, http://www.sacred-texts.com/hin/yoga sutr.htm

Before beginning any spiritual text it is customary to clear the mind of all distracting thoughts, to calm the breath, and to purify the heart.

Part 1 on Contemplation

1.1 Now, instruction in Union.

1.2. Union is restraining the thought-streams natural to the mind.

1.3. Then the seer dwells in his own nature.

1.4. Otherwise he is of the same form as the thought-streams.

1.5. The thought-streams are five-fold, painful and not painful.

1.6. Right knowledge, wrong knowledge, fancy, sleep and memory.

1.7. Right knowledge is inference, tradition and genuine cognition.

1.8. Wrong knowledge is false, illusory, erroneous beliefs or notions.

1.9. Fancy is following after word-knowledge empty of substance.

1.10. Deep sleep is the modification of the mind which has for its substratum nothingness.

1.11. Memory is not allowing mental impressions to escape.

1.12. These thought-streams are controlled by practice and non-attachment.

1.13. Practice is the effort to secure steadiness.

1.14. This practice becomes well-grounded when continued with reverent devotion and without interruption over a long period of time.

1.15. Desirelessness towards the seen and the unseen gives the consciousness of mastery.

1.16. This is signified by an indifference to the three attributes, due to knowledge of the Indweller.

1.17. Cognitive meditation is accompanied by reasoning, discrimination, bliss and the sense of 'I am.'

1.18. There is another meditation which is attained by the practice of alert mental suspension until only subtle impressions remain.

1.19. For those beings who are formless and for those beings who are merged in unitive consciousness, the world is the cause.

1.20. For others, clarity is preceded by faith, energy, memory and equalminded contemplation.

1.21. Equalminded contemplation is nearest to those whose desire is most ardent.

1.22. There is further distinction on account of the mild, moderate or intense means employed.

1.23. Or by surrender to God.

1.24. God is a particular yet universal indweller, untouched by afflictions, actions, impressions and their results.

1.25. In God, the seed of omniscience is unsurpassed.

1.26. Not being conditioned by time, God is the teacher of even the ancients.

1.27. God's voice is Om.

1.28. The repetition of Om should be made with an understanding of its meaning.

1.29. From that is gained introspection and also the disappearance of obstacles.

1.30. Disease, inertia, doubt, lack of enthusiasm, laziness, sensuality, mind-wandering, missing the point, instability—these distractions of the mind are the obstacles.

1.31. Pain, despair, nervousness, and disordered inspiration and expiration are co-existent with these obstacles.

1.32. For the prevention of the obstacles, one truth should be practiced constantly.

1.33. By cultivating friendliness towards happiness and compassion towards misery, gladness towards virtue and indifference towards vice, the mind becomes pure.

1.34. Optionally, mental equanimity may be gained by the even expulsion and retention of energy.

1.35. Or activity of the higher senses causes mental steadiness.

1.36. Or the state of sorrowless Light.

1.37. Or the mind taking as an object of concentration those who are freed of compulsion.

1.38. Or depending on the knowledge of dreams and sleep.

1.39. Or by meditation as desired.

1.40. The mastery of one in Union extends from the finest atomic particle to the greatest infinity.

1.41. When the agitations of the mind are under control, the mind becomes like a transparent crystal and has the power of becoming whatever form is presented. knower, act of knowing, or what is known.

1.42. The argumentative condition is the confused mixing of the word, its right meaning, and knowledge.

1.43. When the memory is purified and the mind shines forth as the object alone, it is called non-argumentative.

1.44. In this way the meditative and the ultra-meditative having the subtle for their objects are also described.

1.45. The province of the subtle terminates with pure matter that has no pattern or distinguishing mark.

1.46. These constitute seeded contemplations.

1.47. On attaining the purity of the ultra-meditative state there is the pure flow of spiritual consciousness.

1.48. Therein is the faculty of supreme wisdom.

1.49. The wisdom obtained in the higher states of consciousness is different from that obtained by inference and testimony as it refers to particulars.

1.50. The habitual pattern of thought stands in the way of other impressions.

1.51. With the suppression of even that through the suspension of all modifications of the mind, contemplation without seed is attained.

Part 2 on Spiritual Disciplines

2.1 Austerity, the study of sacred texts, and the dedication of action to God constitute the discipline of Mystic Union.

2.2 This discipline is practised for the purpose of acquiring fixity of mind on the Lord, free from all impurities and agitations, or on One's Own Reality, and for attenuating the afflictions.

2.3 The five afflictions are ignorance, egoism, attachment, aversion, and the desire to cling to life.

2.4 Ignorance is the breeding place for all the others whether they are dormant or attenuated, partially overcome or fully operative.

2.5 Ignorance is taking the non-eternal for the eternal, the impure for the pure, evil for good and non-self as self.

2.6 Egoism is the identification of the power that knows with the instruments of knowing.

2.7 Attachment is that magnetic pattern which clusters in pleasure and pulls one towards such experience.

2.8 Aversion is the magnetic pattern which clusters in misery and pushes one from such experience.

2.9 Flowing by its own energy, established even in the wise and in the foolish, is the unending desire for life.

2.10 These patterns when subtle may be removed by developing their contraries.

2.11 Their active afflictions are to be destroyed by meditation.

2.12 The impressions of works have their roots in afflictions and arise as experience in the present and the future births.

2.13 When the root exists, its fruition is birth, life and experience.

2.14 They have pleasure or pain as their fruit, according as their cause be virtue or vice.

2.15 All is misery to the wise because of the pains of change, anxiety, and purificatory acts.

2.16 The grief which has not yet come may be avoided.

2.17 The cause of the avoidable is the superimposition of the external world onto the unseen world.

2.18 The experienced world consists of the elements and the senses in play. It is of the nature of cognition, activity and rest, and is for the purpose of experience and realization.

2.19 The stages of the attributes effecting the experienced world are the specialized and the unspecialized, the differentiated and the undifferentiated.

2.20 The indweller is pure consciousness only, which though pure, sees through the mind and is identified by ego as being only the mind.

2.21 The very existence of the seen is for the sake of the seer.

2.22 Although Creation is discerned as not real for the one who has achieved the goal, it is yet real in that Creation remains the common experience to others.

2.23 The association of the seer with Creation is for the distinct recognition of the objective world, as well as for the recognition of the distinct nature of the seer.

2.24 The cause of the association is ignorance.

2.25 Liberation of the seer is the result of the disassociation of the seer and the seen, with the disappearance of ignorance.

2.26 The continuous practice of discrimination is the means of attaining liberation.

2.27 Steady wisdom manifests in seven stages.

2.28 On the destruction of impurity by the sustained practice of the limbs of Union, the light of knowledge reveals the faculty of discrimination.

2.29 The eight limbs of Union are self-restraint in actions, fixed observance, posture, regulation of energy, mind-control in sense engagements, concentration, meditation, and realization.

2.30 Self-restraint in actions includes abstention from violence, from falsehoods, from stealing, from sexual engagements, and from acceptance of gifts.

2.31 These five willing abstentions are not limited by rank, place, time or circumstance and constitute the Great Vow.

2.32 The fixed observances are cleanliness, contentment, austerity, study and persevering devotion to God.

2.33 When improper thoughts disturb the mind, there should be constant pondering over the opposites.

2.34 Improper thoughts and emotions such as those of violence—whether done, caused to be done, or even approved of—indeed, any thought originating in desire, anger or delusion, whether mild medium or intense—do all result in endless pain and misery. Overcome such distractions by pondering on the opposites.

2.35 When one is confirmed in non-violence, hostility ceases in his presence.

2.36 When one is firmly established in speaking truth, the fruits of action become subservient to him.

2.37 All jewels approach him who is confirmed in honesty.

2.38 When one is confirmed in celibacy, spiritual vigor is gained.

2.39 When one is confirmed in non-possessiveness, the knowledge of the why and how of existence is attained.

2.40 From purity follows a withdrawal from enchantment over one's own body as well as a cessation of desire for physical contact with others.

2.41 As a result of contentment there is purity of mind, one-pointedness, control of the senses, and fitness for the vision of the self.

2.42 Supreme happiness is gained via contentment.

2.43 Through sanctification and the removal of impurities, there arise special powers in the body and senses.

2.44 By study comes communion with the Lord in the Form most admired.

2.45 Realization is experienced by making the Lord the motive of all actions.

2.46 The posture should be steady and comfortable.

2.47 In effortless relaxation, dwell mentally on the Endless with utter attention.

2.48 From that there is no disturbance from the dualities.

2.49 When that exists, control of incoming and outgoing energies is next.

2.50 It may be external, internal, or midway, regulated by time, place, or number, and of brief or long duration.

2.51 Energy-control which goes beyond the sphere of external and internal is the fourth level—the vital.

2.52 In this way, that which covers the light is destroyed.

2.53 Thus the mind becomes fit for concentration.

2.54 When the mind maintains awareness, yet does not mingle with the senses, nor the senses with sense impressions, then self-awareness blossoms.

2.55 In this way comes mastery over the senses.

PART 3 ON DIVINE POWERS

3.1 One-pointedness is steadfastness of the mind.

3.2 Unbroken continuation of that mental ability is meditation.

3.3 That same meditation when there is only consciousness of the object of meditation and not of the mind is realization.

3.4 The three appearing together are self-control.

3.5 By mastery comes wisdom.

3.6 The application of mastery is by stages.

3.7 The three are more efficacious than the restraints.

3.8 Even that is external to the seedless realization.

3.9 The significant aspect is the union of the mind with the moment of absorption, when the outgoing thought disappears and the absorptive experience appears.

3.10 From sublimation of this union comes the peaceful flow of unbroken unitive cognition.

3.11 The contemplative transformation of this is equalmindedness, witnessing the rise and destruction of distraction as well as one-pointedness itself.

3.12 The mind becomes one-pointed when the subsiding and rising thought-waves are exactly similar.

3.13 In this state, it passes beyond the changes of inherent characteristics, properties and the conditional modifications of object or sensory recognition.

3.14 The object is that which preserves the latent characteristic, the rising characteristic or the yet-to-be-named characteristic that establishes one entity as specific.

3.15 The succession of these changes in that entity is the cause of its modification.

3.16 By self-control over these three-fold changes (of property, character and condition), knowledge of the past and the future arises.

3.17 The sound of a word, the idea behind the word, and the object the idea signifies are often taken as being one thing and may be mistaken for one another. By self-control over their distinctions, understanding of all languages of all creatures arises.

3.18 By self-control on the perception of mental impressions, knowledge of previous lives arises.

3.19 By self-control on any mark of a body, the wisdom of the mind activating that body arises.

3.20 By self-control on the form of a body, by suspending perceptibility and separating effulgence therefrom, there arises invisibility and inaudibility.

3.21 Action is of two kinds, dormant and fruitful. By self-control on such action, one portends the time of death.

3.22 By performing self-control on friendliness, the strength to grant joy arises.

3.23 By self-control over any kind of strength, such as that of the elephant, that very strength arises.

3.24 By self-control on the primal activator comes knowledge of the hidden, the subtle, and the distant.

3.25 By self-control on the Sun comes knowledge of spatial specificities.

3.26 By self-control on the Moon comes knowledge of the heavens.

3.27 By self-control on the Polestar arises knowledge of orbits.

3.28 By self-control on the navel arises knowledge of the constitution of the body.

3.29 By self-control on the pit of the throat one subdues hunger and thirst.

3.30 By self-control on the tube within the chest one acquires absolute steadiness.

3.31 By self-control on the light in the head one envisions perfected beings.

3.32 There is knowledge of everything from intuition.

3.33 Self-control on the heart brings knowledge of the mental entity.

3.34 Experience arises due to the inability of discerning the attributes of vitality from the indweller, even though they are indeed distinct from one another. Self-control brings true knowledge of the indweller by itself.

3.35 This spontaneous enlightenment results in intuitional perception of hearing, touching, seeing and smelling.

3.36 To the outward turned mind, the sensory organs are perfections, but are obstacles to realization.

3.37 When the bonds of the mind caused by action have been loosened, one may enter the body of another by knowledge of how the nerve-currents function.

3.38 By self-control of the nerve-currents utilising the lifebreath, one may levitate, walk on water, swamps, thorns, or the like.

3.39 By self-control over the maintenance of breath, one may radiate light.

3.40 By self-control on the relation of the ear to the ether one gains distant hearing.

3.41 By self-control over the relation of the body to the ether, and maintaining at the same time the thought of the lightness of cotton, one is able to pass through space.

3.42 By self-control on the mind when it is separated from the body—the state known as the Great Transcorporeal—all coverings are removed from the Light.

3.43 Mastery over the elements arises when their gross and subtle forms, as well as their essential characteristics, and the inherent attributes and experiences they produce, is examined in self-control.

3.44 Thereby one may become as tiny as an atom as well as having many other abilities, such as perfection of the body, and non-resistance to duty.

3.45 Perfection of the body consists in beauty, grace, strength and adamantine hardness.

3.46 By self-conresistance changes that the sense-organs endure when contacting objects, and on the power of the sense of identity, and of the influence of the attributes, and the experience all these produce—one masters the senses.

3.47 From that come swiftness of mind, independence of perception, and mastery over primordial matter.

3.48 To one who recognizes the distinctive relation between vitality and indweller comes omnipotence and omniscience.

3.49 Even for the destruction of the seed of bondage by desirelessness there comes absolute independence.

3.50 When invited by invisible beings one should be neither flattered nor satisfied, for there is yet a possibility of ignorance rising up.

3.51 By self-control over single moments and their succession there is wisdom born of discrimination.

3.52 From that there is recognition of two similars when that difference cannot be distinguished by class, characteristic or position.

3.53 Intuition, which is the entire discriminative knowledge, relates to all objects at all times, and is without succession.

3.54 Liberation is attained when there is equal purity between vitality and the indweller.

Part 4 on Realizations

4.1 Psychic powers arise by birth, drugs, incantations, purificatory acts or concentrated insight.

4.2 Transformation into another state is by the directed flow of creative nature.

4.3 Creative nature is not moved into action by any incidental cause, but by the removal of obstacles,

as in the case of a farmer clearing his field of stones for irrigation.

4.4 Created minds arise from egoism alone.

4.5 There being difference of interest, one mind is the director of many minds.

4.6 Of these, the mind born of concentrated insight is free from the impressions.

4.7 The impressions of unitive cognition are neither good nor bad. In the case of the others, there are three kinds of impressions.

4.8 From them proceed the development of the tendencies which bring about the fruition of actions.

4.9 Because of the magnetic qualities of habitual mental patterns and memory, a relationship of cause and effect clings even though there may be a change of embodiment by class, space and time.

4.10 The desire to live is eternal, and the thought-clusters prompting a sense of identity are beginningless.

4.11 Being held together by cause and effect, substratum and object—the tendencies themselves disappear on the dissolution of these bases.

4.12 The past and the future exist in the object itself as form and expression, there being difference in the conditions of the properties.

4.13 Whether manifested or unmanifested they are of the nature of the attributes.

4.14 Things assume reality because of the unity maintained within that modification.

4.15 Even though the external object is the same, there is a difference of cognition in regard to the object because of the difference in mentality.

4.16 And if an object known only to a single mind were not cognized by that mind, would it then exist?

4.17 An object is known or not known by the mind, depending on whether or not the mind is colored by the object.

4.18 The mutations of awareness are always known on account of the changelessness of its Lord, the indweller.

4.19 Nor is the mind self-luminous, as it can be known.

4.20 It is not possible for the mind to be both the perceived and the perceiver simultaneously.

4.21 In the case of cognition of one mind by another, we would have to assume cognition of cognition, and there would be confusion of memories.

4.22 Consciousness appears to the mind itself as intellect when in that form in which it does not pass from place to place.

4.23 The mind is said to perceive when it reflects both the indweller (the knower) and the objects of perception (the known).

4.24 Though variegated by innumerable tendencies, the mind acts not for itself but for another, for the mind is of compound substance.

4.25 For one who sees the distinction, there is no further confusing of the mind with the self.

4.26 Then the awareness begins to discriminate, and gravitates towards liberation.

4.27 Distractions arise from habitual thought patterns when practice is intermittent.

4.28 The removal of the habitual thought patterns is similar to that of the afflictions already described.

4.29 To one who remains undistracted in even the highest intellection there comes the equal-minded realization known as The Cloud of Virtue. This is a result of discriminative discernment.

4.30 From this there follows freedom from cause and effect and afflictions.

4.31 The infinity of knowledge available to such a mind freed of all obscuration and property makes the universe of sensory perception seem small.

4.32 Then the sequence of change in the three attributes comes to an end, for they have fulfilled their function.

4.33 The sequence of mutation occurs in every second, yet is comprehensible only at the end of a series.

4.34 When the attributes cease mutative association with awareness, they resolve into dormancy in Nature, and the indweller shines forth as pure consciousness. This is absolute freedom.

IV.3 The Laws of Manu

Source: *Sacred Books of the East*, vol. 25, *The Laws of Manu*, trans. George Bühler, http://www.sacred-texts.com/hin/manu.htm

THE FOUR STAGES OF LIFE

6.87. The student, the householder, the hermit, and the ascetic, these (constitute) four separate orders, which all spring from (the order of) householders.

88. But all (or even (any of) these orders, assumed successively in accordance with the Institutes (of the sacred law), lead the Brahmana who acts by the preceding (rules) to the highest state.

89. And in accordance with the precepts of the Veda and of the Smriti, the housekeeper is declared to be superior to all of them; for he supports the other three.

7.352 Men who commit adultery with the wives of others, the king shall cause to be marked by punishments which cause terror, and afterwards banish

353. For by (adultery) is caused a mixture of the castes among men; from that (follows) sin, which cuts up even the roots and causes the destruction of everything.

2.36. In the eighth year after conception, one should perform the initiation (upanayana) of a Brahmana, in the eleventh after conception (that) of a Kshatriya, but in the twelfth that of a Vaisya.

69. Having performed the (rite of) initiation, the teacher must first instruct the (pupil) in (the rules of) personal purification, of conduct, of the fire-worship, and of the twilight devotions.

176. Every day, having bathed, and being purified, he must offer libations of water to the gods, sages and manes, worship (the images of) the gods, and place fuel on (the sacred fire).

177. Let him abstain from honey, meat, perfumes, garlands, substances (used for) flavouring (food), women, all substances turned acid, and from doing injury to living creatures.

178. From anointing (his body), applying collyrium to his eyes, from the use of shoes and of an

umbrella (or parasol), from (sensual) desire, anger, covetousness, dancing, singing, and playing (musical instruments),

179. From gambling, idle disputes, backbiting, and lying, from looking at and touching women, and from hurting others.

199. Let him not pronounce the mere name of his teacher (without adding an honorific title) behind his back even, and let him not mimic his gait, speech, and deportment.

200. Wherever (people) justly censure or falsely defame his teacher, there he must cover his ears or depart thence to another place.

201. By censuring (his teacher), though justly, he will become (in his next birth) an ass, by falsely defaming him, a dog; he who lives on his teacher's substance, will become a worm, and he who is envious (of his merit), a (larger) insect.

3.1. The vow (of studying) the three Vedas under a teacher must be kept for thirty-six years, or for half that time, or for a quarter, or until the (student) has perfectly learnt them.

2. (A student) who has studied in due order the three Vedas, or two, or even one only, without breaking the (rules of) studentship, shall enter the order of householders.

4. Having bathed, with the permission of his teacher, and performed according to the rule the Samavartana (the rite on returning home), a twice-born man shall marry a wife of equal caste who is endowed with auspicious (bodily) marks.

75. Let (every man) in this (second order, at least) daily apply himself to the private recitation of the Veda, and also to the performance of the offering to the gods; for he who is diligent in the performance of sacrifices, supports both the movable and the immovable creation.

76. An oblation duly thrown into the fire, reaches the sun; from the sun comes rain, from rain food, therefrom the living creatures (derive their subsistence).

77. As all living creatures subsist by receiving support from air, even so (the members of) all orders subsist by receiving support from the householder.

78. Because men of the three (other) orders are daily supported by the householder with (gifts of) sacred knowledge and food, therefore (the order of) householders is the most excellent order.

4.2. A Brahmana must seek a means of subsistence which either causes no, or at least little pain (to others), and live (by that) except in times of distress.

3. For the purpose of gaining bare subsistence, let him accumulate property by (following those) irreproachable occupations (which are prescribed for) his (caste), without (unduly) fatiguing his body.

11. Let him never, for the sake of subsistence, follow the ways of the world; let him live the pure, straightforward, honest life of a Brahmana.

THE DUTIES OF THE FOUR SOCIAL CLASSES

Brahmin

4.74. Let him never play with dice, nor himself take off his shoes; let him not eat, lying on a bed, nor what has been placed in his hand or on a seat.

75. Let him not eat after sunset any (food) containing sesamum grains; let him never sleep naked, nor go anywhere unpurified (after meals).

76. Let him eat while his feet are (yet) wet (from the ablution), but let him not go to bed with wet feet. He who eats while his feet are (still) wet, will attain long life.

77. Let him never enter a place, difficult of access, which is impervious to his eye; let him not look at urine or ordure, nor cross a river (swimming) with his arms.

78. Let him not step on hair, ashes, bones, potsherds, cotton-seed or chaff, if he desires long life.

79. Let him not stay together with outcasts, nor with Kandalas, nor with Pukkasas, nor with fools, nor with overbearing men, nor with low-caste men, nor with Antyavasayins.

80. Let him not give to a Sudra advice, nor the remnants (of his meal), nor food offered to the gods; nor let him explain the sacred law (to such a man), nor impose (upon him) a penance.

81. For he who explains the sacred law (to a Sudra) or dictates to him a penance, will sink

together with that (man) into the hell (called) Asamvrita.

82. Let him not scratch his head with both hands joined; let him not touch it while he is impure, nor bathe without (submerging) it.

83. Let him avoid (in anger) to lay hold of (his own or other men's) hair, or to strike (himself or others) on the head. When he has bathed (submerging) his head, he shall not touch any of his limbs with oil.

84. Let him not accept presents from a king who is not descended from the Kshatriya race, nor from butchers, oil-manufacturers, and publicans, nor from those who subsist by the gain of prostitutes.

85. One oil-press is as (bad) as ten slaughter-houses, one tavern as (bad as) ten oil-presses, one brothel as (bad as) ten taverns, one king as (bad as) ten brothels.

86. A king is declared to be equal (in wickedness) to a butcher who keeps a hundred thousand slaughter-houses; to accept presents from him is a terrible (crime).

87. He who accepts presents from an avaricious king who acts contrary to the Institutes (of the sacred law), will go in succession to the following twenty-one hells:

88. Tamisra, Andhatamisra, Maharaurava, Raurava, the Kalasutra hell, Mahanaraka,

89. Samgivana, Mahaviki, Tapana, Sampratapana, Samghata, Sakakola, Kudmala, Putimrittika,

90. Lohasanku, Rigisha, Pathin, the (flaming) river, Salmala, Asipatravana, and Lohakaraka.

91. Learned Brahmanas, who know that, who study the Veda and desire bliss after death, do not accept presents from a king.

92. Let him wake in the muhurta, sacred to Brahman, and think of (the acquisition of) spiritual merit and wealth, of the bodily fatigue arising therefrom, and of the true meaning of the Veda.

93. When he has risen, has relieved the necessities of nature and carefully purified himself, let him stand during the morning twilight, muttering for a long time (the Gayatri), and at the proper time (he must similarly perform) the evening (devotion).

94. By prolonging the twilight devotions, the sages obtained long life, wisdom, honour, fame, and excellence in Vedic knowledge.

95. Having performed the Upakarman according to the prescribed rule on (the full moon of the month) Sravana, or on that of Praushthapada (Bhadrapada), a Brahmana shall diligently study the Vedas during four months and a half.

96. When the Pushya-day (of the month Pausha), or the first day of the bright half of Magha has come, a Brahmana shall perform in the forenoon the Utsargana of the Vedas.

97. Having performed the Utsarga outside (the village), as the Institutes (of the sacred law) prescribe, he shall stop reading during two days and the intervening night, or during that day (of the Utsarga) and (the following) night.

98. Afterwards he shall diligently recite the Vedas during the bright (halves of the months), and duly study all the Angas of the Vedas during the dark fortnights.

99. Let him not recite (the texts) indistinctly, nor in the presence of Sudras; nor let him, if in the latter part of the night he is tired with reciting the Veda, go again to sleep.

100. According to the rule declared above, let him recite the daily (portion of the) Mantras, and a zealous Brahmana, (who is) not in distress, (shall study) the Brahmana and the Mantrasamhita.

101. Let him who studies always avoid (reading) on the following occasions when the Veda-study is forbidden, and (let) him who teaches pupils according to the prescribed rule (do it likewise).

102. Those who know the (rules of) recitation declare that in the rainy season the Veda-study must be stopped on these two (occasions), when the wind is audible at night, and when it whirls up the dust in the day-time.

Kshatriya

7.18. Punishment alone governs all created beings, punishment alone protects them, punishment watches over them while they sleep; the wise declare punishment (to be identical with) the law.

19. If (punishment) is properly inflicted after (due) consideration, it makes all people happy; but inflicted without consideration, it destroys everything.

20. If the king did not, without tiring, inflict punishment on those worthy to be punished, the stronger would roast the weaker, like fish on a spit;

21. The crow would eat the sacrificial cake and the dog would lick the sacrificial viands, and ownership would not remain with any one, the lower ones would (usurp the place of) the higher ones.

22. The whole world is kept in order by punishment, for a guiltless man is hard to find; through fear of punishment the whole world yields the enjoyments (which it owes).

88. Not to turn back in battle, to protect the people, to honour the Brahmanas, is the best means for a king to secure happiness.

89. Those kings who, seeking to slay each other in battle, fight with the utmost exertion and do not turn back, go to heaven.

144. The highest duty of a Kshatriya is to protect his subjects, for the king who enjoys the rewards, just mentioned, is bound to (discharge that) duty.

198. He should (however) try to conquer his foes by conciliation, by (well-applied) gifts, and by creating dissension, used either separately or conjointly, never by fighting, (if it can be avoided.)

199. For when two (princes) fight, victory and defeat in the battle are, as experience teaches, uncertain; let him therefore avoid an engagement.

Vaishya

9.326. After a Vaisya has received the sacraments and has taken a wife, he shall be always attentive to the business whereby he may subsist and to (that of) tending cattle.

327. For when the Lord of creatures (Pragapati) created cattle, he made them over to the Vaisya; to the Brahmana, and to the king he entrusted all created beings.

328. A Vaisya must never (conceive this) wish, I will not keep cattle; and if a Vaisya is willing (to keep them), they must never be kept by (men of) other (castes).

329. (A Vaisya) must know the respective value of gems, of pearls, of coral, of metals, of (cloth) made of thread, of perfumes, and of condiments.

330. He must be acquainted with the (manner of) sowing of seeds, and of the good and bad qualities of fields, and he must perfectly know all measures and weights.

331. Moreover, the excellence and defects of commodities, the advantages and disadvantages of (different) countries, the (probable) profit and loss on merchandise, and the means of properly rearing cattle.

332. He must be acquainted with the (proper), wages of servants, with the various languages of men, with the manner of keeping goods, and (the rules of) purchase and sale.

333. Let him exert himself to the utmost in order to increase his property in a righteous manner, and let him zealously give food to all created beings.

Shudra

8.334. With whatever limb a thief in any way commits (an offence) against men, even of that (the king) shall deprive him in order to prevent (a repetition of the crime).

335. Neither a father, nor a teacher, nor a friend, nor a mother, nor a wife, nor a son, nor a domestic priest must be left unpunished by a king, if they do not keep within their duty.

413. But a Sudra, whether bought or unbought, he may compel to do servile work; for he was created by the Self-existent (Svayambhu) to be the slave of a Brahmana.

414. A Sudra, though emancipated by his master, is not released from servitude; since that is innate in him, who can set him free from it?

10.128. The more a (Sudra), keeping himself free from envy, imitates the behaviour of the virtuous, the more he gains, without being censured, (exaltation in) this world and the next.

Key Terms

avatars   Term meaning "one who descends." In popular Hinduism, Lord Vishnu appears on earth at intervals to assert ancient values and destroy illusion. The main tradition refers to ten descents, nine of which have already happened. Krishna is the most famous avatar. Some modern cults claim to worship a living avatar.

Bhagavad Gita   ("Song of the Lord") A section of the Mahabharata in the form of a battlefield dialogue between the warrior prince Arjuna and Krishna, disguised as his charioteer. Arjuna is unwilling to fight his kinsmen, but Krishna encourages him, teaching him that wisdom requires him to fulfill his proper role while at the same time renouncing the consequences of his actions.

bhakti   Love of, or devotion to, God. It is one of the Hindu paths to union with God. It is expressed in popular religion in which the worshipper develops a sense of personal relationship to God, responding to him as though to a father, mother, friend, lover or child, and looking to him for grace.

caste system   The division of a society into groups reflecting and defining the division of labor. In Hinduism, caste is traditionally seen as the creation of Brahma, each caste emerging symbolically from different parts of his body. There are four chief groups: Brahmans, priests, come from Brahma's mouth; Kshatriyas, warriors, come from Brahma's arms; Vaishyas, commoners, come from Brahma's thighs; Sudras, servants, come from Brahma's feet. Groups of no definite caste were regarded as untouchables and were banished from society.

dharma   In Hinduism, cosmic order, the law of existence, right conduct.

dukkha   Buddhist term for unsatisfactoriness or suffering. Birth, illness, decay, death, and rebirth are symptoms of a restless and continuous "coming-to-be," which marks all existence as *dukkha*.

guru   ("Teacher") Specifically a spiritual teacher or guide who, in Indian religion, awakens a disciple to a realization of his or her own divine nature. In Sikh religion it refers to the ten teachers, from Guru Nanak to Guru Gobindh Singh, who ruled the community.

karma   Sanskrit word for work or action. In Indian belief every action has inevitable consequences which attach themselves to the doer requiring reward or punishment. Karma is thus the moral law of cause and effect. It explains the inequalities of life as the consequences of actions in previous lives. The notion of karma probably developed among the Dravidian people of India. In Mahayana Buddhism the concept is transformed by the idea of the Bodhisattva. Merit can be transferred by grace or faith, thus changing the person's karma.

maya   Illusion or deception in Hindu thought. Maya is concerned with the diverse phenomenal world perceived by the senses. It is the trick of maya to convince people that this is all that exists and thus blind them to the reality of Brahman and the oneness of existence.

moksha   Sanskrit word meaning liberation from the cycle of birth, death, and rebirth. Permanent spiritual perfection experienced by an enlightened soul after the physical body has died. No further incarnations will be endured.

puja   ("Reverence") Refers particularly to temple worship in Hinduism and to the keeping of rites and ceremonies prescribed by the Brahmans.

Puranas A vast corpus of sacred writings (c. 350–950 CE), which include mythologies of Hindu deities and avatars of Vishnu, the origins of the cosmos and of humanity, pilgrimage, ritual, law codes, caste obligations, and so on. There are eighteen principal Puranas, each exalting a member of the *Trimurti* (Brahma, Vishnu, Shiva). They are very important in popular Hinduism, the most popular being the *Bhagavata Purana*, which deals with Krishna's early life and encourages devotion to him (bhakti).

samsara Sanskrit word meaning "stream of existence," which refers to the cycle of birth and death followed by rebirth as applied both to individuals and to the universe itself.

Sanskrit The language of the Aryan peoples and of the Hindu scriptures. It is an Indo-European language related to Latin, Greek and Persian.

untouchables Indians who belong to no caste and are therefore banished from normal social life. Mahatma Gandhi called them "children of God" and worked for their acceptance in Indian society.

Upanishads The last books of the Indian Vedas, which were written in Sanskrit between 800 and 400 BCE. They develop the concept of *brahman* as the holy power released in sacrifice to the point where it becomes the underlying reality of the universe. The soul, *atman*, is identified with the holy power, *brahman*. They include speculation on how the soul can realize its oneness with *brahman* through contemplative techniques.

Vedas Scriptures that express the religion of the Aryan people of India. They comprise hymns, instructions for ritual, and cosmological speculations. There are four divisions: *Rig Veda*, hymns to the Aryan gods, who are personifications of natural forces; *Sama Veda*, verses selected for chanting; *Yajur Veda*, prose instructions on matters of ritual; *Atharva Veda*, rites and spells in verse, especially concerned with curing illness.

yoga A way to union with God in Hindu philosophy. It also forms one of the six classical systems of Indian thought. Traditionally there are eight stages of yoga: restraint; discipline; posture; breathing; detachment; concentration; meditation, and trance. In the *Bhagavad Gita* the three paths to spiritual fulfillment are: *jnanayoga* (the path of knowledge/wisdom), *karmayoga* (the path of work/action) and *bhaktiyoga* (the path of devotion).

Questions for Study and Discussion

1. What is the *karma-samsara-moksha* doctrine?
2. What are the three central presuppositions of Hindu thought?
3. Explain the view of salvation as expressed in the *Bhagavad Gita* and its significance for Hinduism.
4. Explain how Naren Patel's description of his daily life and beliefs (see "I am a Hindu," pp. 194–95) correspond to one or more of the three paths of spiritual fulfillment and to one or more of the four goals of Hinduism.
5. What is appealing about Hinduism to contemporary non-Hindu Westerners? How has Western culture "imported" into India affected Hindu practice there today?
6. Select two of the photographs or illustrations in the chapter and explain how they demonstrate major philosophical assumptions, beliefs, or practices of Hinduism.
7. "It is more accurate to discuss Hinduism*s* than Hinduism." Argue for or against this statement using evidence from the text.

Questions for Reflection

Write your personal reflections to each of these questions in the space provided.

1. How does Hindu belief emerge from ancient India, given there is no founder? (See pp. 168–70.)

2. Describe how religion was integrated into social life in India. Does it appear to be an integration *all* would be satisfied with? (See p. 170.)

3. Discuss how religion and politics have come together in India. (See pp. 172–74.)

4. What is the relationship of the worshiper to the statue? (See pp. 187–88.)

5. List the aspects found in both Hindu worship and indigenous religions and what they tell us about the relationship of indigenous religions and world religions.

Selected Online Resources

▶ "India Temples"—essays and photographs of temples organized by region, deity, etc. (part of a tour agency website)
http://www.pilgrimage-india.com/india-temples.html
▶ Sacred Texts: Hinduism—English translations of the Vedas, Upanishads, Bhagavad Gita, etc.
http://www.sacred-texts.com/hin/index.htm
▶ Hinduism in Kashmir—one example of a particular ethnic group's Hindu beliefs and practices; includes explanations of traditions as well as descriptions of deities and photographs
http://www.koausa.org/religion.html

Part 5: Buddhism

Chapter Summaries

38. A Historical Overview

Siddhartha Gautama, the founder of Buddhism, lived sometime around 400 BCE. His teachings about truth and the path to enlightenment are at the core of the religion. He was probably a high-born man who left his family to wander the world and to seek the ultimate truth. He became the Buddha when he became enlightened. He taught that to overcome *dukkha*, or suffering one has to see things the way they really are. One must understand one's own ignorance and attachment to impermanent things contribute to *dukkha*. After death, the flow of consciousness continues in the cycle of rebirth, determined by karma. Only through meditation and a complete letting go can one escape this cycle.

The Buddhist monastic tradition of Sangha developed gradually. The Buddha himself said the Dharma, his teachings, were his only successor. So different monastic groups evolved; the best known and one of the earliest is Theravada.

Within Buddhism is the Mahayana tradition, which encompasses many doctrinal schools. It distinguishes between being free from suffering and being a Buddha, who is both spiritually free and also compassionate. Those who aspire to become Buddhas are known as bodhisattvas.

Buddhism spread from India to Sri Lanka to Southeast Asia and East Asia over the centuries. Mahayana scriptures tended to hold authority in early East Asian Buddhist society. Zen Buddhism stresses direct insight to awaken the Buddha nature that is present in everyone. Tantras are ritual texts that often claim to have special knowledge of how to attain enlightenment or certain powers. While controversial, Tantric traditions were also incorporated into Mahayana Buddhism, becoming part of the Buddhism of Tibet.

39. Sacred Writings

Oral tradition kept the earliest Buddhist teachings alive. Eventually the texts recited at the First Buddhist Council were written down to form the canon; they are divided into *sutras* (discourses and teachings) and *vinaya* (monastic rules). Later writings on higher teachings, *abhidharma*, were added. Other, later scriptures were written in or translated into other languages. They all were preserved by the *Sangha*; the Pali Canon was held by the Theravada. Mahayana *sutras* are apocryphal: they may have originated in meditative visions of the Buddha. Tantras are texts associated with ritual magic, while *shastras* are scholarly treatises.

40. Beliefs

Buddhism is a path leading from suffering to the end of suffering, from ignorance to compassion and wisdom. The heart of Buddhism is the Three Jewels, where Buddhists take refuge: the Buddha, the Dharma (teaching), and the Sangha (Buddhist community). Once one fully understands that life is defined by impermanence, unsatisfactoriness, and not-self, one can begin to take steps to living a holy life. One must also accept the Four Noble Truths, which acknowledges *Dukkha* and the Eightfold Path to ending *Dukkha*. Moral discipline defines the Buddhist path; it involves abstention from harm and cultivating loving-kindness. Meditation is a tool that helps the Buddhist along the path: mindfulness of the present moment helps the person let go of distractions and attachments. Rebirth is the fate of all beings except those who attain nirvana, the ultimate goal of the Buddhist path.

41. Family and Society

While monks and nuns might be seen as on the easier path to attaining nirvana, householders could still attain a higher level of purity. The Fourfold Society concept recognizes monks, nuns, laymen, and laywomen as interdependent. Marriage is an entirely secular matter, but children are valued. Family relationships are regulated by specific duties assigned to each member. In Buddhist tradition the state is influenced by the Dharma and advised by the Sangha; even today the Sangha may play a role in government. Buddhism itself promotes loving-kindness as a societal practice.

42. Buddhism in the Modern World

Imperialism had a significant impact on Buddhism's historical development. Western interpretation emphasized the tradition's written texts, and Asian Buddhism went through revival as part of its resistance against Christian missionary work. In China Buddhists were attacked, and the Chinese takeover of Tibet caused the Dalai Lama to flee and prompted the looting of monasteries and the imprisonment, torture, and execution of some monks. Cambodia is now attempting to rebuild the Buddhist communities destroyed under the Khmer Rouge. Buddhism has spread throughout the West, with new Buddhist strands emerging. Buddhism's nonviolence stance has generally led its followers to oppose war. Women, both lay and religious, have become active in Buddhist projects and the promotion of Buddhist teachings around the world. Thich Nhat Hanh founded Engaged Buddhism to raise awareness of poverty and oppression and promote Buddhist engagement in social justice work.

Key Personalities

Siddhartha Gautama (around fifth century BCE)

The historical person known as the Buddha. Born in India to a wealthy family, he ultimately sought enlightenment in the life of a wandering seeker and ascetic. His teaching, called the *Dharma*, is what Buddhists strive to follow.

"If he recites many teachings, but—heedless man—doesn't do what they say, like a cowherd counting the cattle of others, he has no share in the contemplative life. If he recites next to nothing but follows the Dhamma in line with the Dhamma; abandoning passion, aversion, delusion; alert, his mind well-released, not clinging either here or hereafter: he has his share in the contemplative life."

("Yamakavagga: Pairs," verses 19–20, *Dhammapada: The Path of Dhamma*, translated by Thanissaro Bhikku, 1997–2011, http://www.accesstoinsight.org/tipitaka/kn/dhp/dhp .01.than.html)

"At that time the World-Honored One calmly arose from his samadhi and addressed Shariputra, saying: 'The wisdom of the Buddhas is infinitely profound and immeasurable. The door to this wisdom is difficult to understand and difficult to enter. Not one of the voice-hearers or pratyekabuddhas is able to comprehend it.

'What is the reason for this? A Buddha has personally attended a hundred, a thousand, ten thousand, a million, a countless number of Buddhas and has fully carried out an immeasurable number of religious practices. He has exerted himself bravely and vigorously, and his name is universally known. He has realized the Law that is profound and never known before, and preaches it in accordance with what is appropriate, yet his intention is difficult to understand.

'Shariputra, ever since I attained Buddhahood I have through various causes and various similes widely expounded my teachings and have used countless expedient means to guide living beings and cause them to renounce attachments. Why is this? Because the Thus Come One is fully possessed by both expedient means and the paramita [perfection] of wisdom.

'Shariputra, the wisdom of the Thus Come One is expansive and profound. He has immeasurable [mercy], unlimited [eloquence], power, fearlessness, concentration, emancipation, and samadhis, and has deeply entered the boundless and awakened to the Law never before attained.

'Shariputra, the Thus Come One knows how to make various kinds of distinctions and to expound the teachings skillfully. His words are soft and gentle and delight the hearts of the assembly.

'Shariputra, to sum it up: the Buddha has fully realized the Law that is limitless, boundless, never attained before.

'But stop, Shariputra, I will say no more. Why? Because what the Buddha has achieved is the rarest and most difficult-to-understand Law. The true entity of all phenomena can only be understood and shared between Buddhas. This reality consists of the appearance, nature, entity, power, influence, inherent cause, relation, latent effect, manifest effect, and their consistency from beginning to end.'"

(Chapter 2, "Expedient Means," *The Lotus Sutra*, translated by Burton Watson, n.d., http://nichiren.info/buddhism /lotussutra/text/chap02.html)

Ngo Van Chieu (1878–1926)

The founder of the Vietnamese sect Cao Dai and governor under the French colonial authority in Cochin China. He had a vision in 1919 in which the Supreme Being told him that all the religions of the world should return to the their one common origin, and he was instructed to deliver this message to the world.

Hyunh Phu So (1919–1947)

The founder of the Hoa Hao, a neo-Buddhist sect. His survival of a nervous illness led to his preaching and teaching a new religion, which focused on

Buddhist rituals without recourse to an intermediary or sacred center of worship.

Thich Nhat Hanh (born 1926)

A Vietnamese Zen Buddhist monk who has lived in exile in France since 1966 as a result of his leading a nonviolent movement against the Diem regime. As the co-founder of Engaged Buddhism, he has inspired people worldwide to apply Buddhist insight and practice to improve social conditions for the poor and to work for international peace.

"Hope is important, because it can make the present moment less difficult to bear. If we believe that tomorrow will be better, we can bear a hardship today. But that is the most that hope can do for us—to make some hardship lighter. When I think deeply about the nature of hope, I see something tragic. Since we cling to our hope in the future, we do not focus our energies and capabilities on the present moment. . . . Enlightenment, peace, and joy will not be granted by someone else. The well is within us, and if we dig deeply in the present moment, the water will spring forth. We must go back to the present moment in order to be really alive. When we practice conscious breathing, we practice going back to the present moment where everything is happening."

(Thich Nhat Hanh, *Peace Is Every Step: The Path of Mindfulness in Everyday Life*, ed. Arnold Kotler [New York: Bantam, 1991], 41)

Primary Source Readings

The following excerpted readings represent some of the important primary sources mentioned in the main text. Additional primary sources are available both in print and online, and students are encouraged to contact their instructors for further information.

V.1 The Birth of Gotama (Gautama)

Source: E. J. Thomas, *Buddhist Scriptures*, 1913, http://www.sacred-texts.com/bud/busc/busc05.htm

The personal name of Buddha was Siddhattha, "one who has accomplished his aim." Whether it was actually the name given to him as a child we do not know. His family name was Gotama, and it is as "sir, Gotama" or "the ascetic Gotama," that members of other sects are represented as addressing him. By the Buddhists he is called up to the time of his enlightenment the Bodhisatta, "being of enlightenment," a term applied to any one who is destined to become a Buddha. After his enlightenment he is called the Buddha "the enlightened one," and addressed as Bhagavan, "the Lord." Buddha, when speaking of himself, calls himself the Tathāgata, literally "one who has gone thus." The exact significance is disputed, but it probably means, "one who has gone in the way of previous Buddhas."

The queen Mahāmāyā, bearing the Bodhisatta like oil in a vessel for ten months, desired, when her time was come, to go to her relatives' home, and addressed king Suddhodana, "Your Majesty, I wish to go to Devadaha, the city of my people." "Good," said the king, and he caused the road from Kapilavatthu to the city of Devadaha to be made smooth, adorned it with plantains in pots, flags and banners, seated the queen in a golden palanquin borne by a thousand courtiers, and sent her forth with a great retinue. Between the two cities, and belonging to the inhabitants of both, is a pleasure-grove of sal-trees, called the Lumbini grove. At that time from the roots to the ends of the branches the whole grove was in full flower, and among the branches and flowers were numberless bees of the five colours, and flocks of various kinds of birds, singing with sweet sounds. The whole Lumbini grove seemed like the heavenly Cittalatā grove or like an adorned banqueting pavilion for a mighty king.

When the queen saw it, the desire arose in her heart of sporting therein. The courtiers with the queen entered the sal-grove. She went to the foot of a royal sal-tree, and desired to take hold of a branch. The sal-tree branch, like the tip of a supple reed, bowed down, and came within reach of the queen's hand. She put out her hand and seized the branch. Then she was shaken by the pangs of birth. The multitude put round her a curtain and retired. Taking hold of the sal-branch and standing up she was delivered. And even at that moment the four pure-minded Mahābrahmas [of the different Brahma-heavens] came and brought a golden net, and with the golden net they received the Bodhisatta and set him before his mother, "Rejoice, O queen, a mighty son is born to thee," they said. And as other beings at their birth are born with disagreeable impurity and stain, so was not the Bodhisatta. But the Bodhisatta, like a preacher of the doctrine descending from his seat of doctrine, like a man descending stairs, stretched forth his two hands and feet, and standing unsoiled, unstained by any impurity from the sojourn of his birth, like a jewel placed in Benares cloth, thus brilliant did he descend from his mother. And yet in honour of the Bodhisatta and the Bodhisatta's mother two showers of water descended from the sky on the body of the Bodhisatta and his mother.

V.2 The Buddha's First Sermon at Sarnath

Source: *Dhammacakkappavattana Sutta: Setting the Wheel of Dhamma in Motion*, trans. Thanissaro Bhikkhu, 1993, http://www.accesstoinsight.org/tipitaka/sn/sn56/sn56.011.than.html

I have heard that on one occasion the Blessed One was staying at Varanasi in the Game Refuge at Isipatana. There he addressed the group of five monks:

"There are these two extremes that are not to be indulged in by one who has gone forth. Which two? That which is devoted to sensual pleasure with reference to sensual objects: base, vulgar, common, ignoble, unprofitable; and that which is devoted to self-affliction: painful, ignoble, unprofitable. Avoiding both of these extremes, the middle way realized by the Tathagata—producing vision, producing knowledge—leads to calm, to direct knowledge, to self-awakening, to Unbinding.

"And what is the middle way realized by the Tathagata that—producing vision, producing knowledge—leads to calm, to direct knowledge, to self-awakening, to Unbinding? Precisely this Noble Eightfold Path: right view, right resolve, right speech, right action, right livelihood, right effort, right mindfulness, right concentration. This is the middle way realized by the Tathagata that—producing vision, producing knowledge—leads to calm, to direct knowledge, to self-awakening, to Unbinding.

"Now this, monks, is the noble truth of stress: Birth is stressful, aging is stressful, death is stressful; sorrow, lamentation, pain, distress, & despair are stressful; association with the unbeloved is stressful, separation from the loved is stressful, not getting what is wanted is stressful. In short, the five clinging-aggregates are stressful.

"And this, monks, is the noble truth of the origination of stress: the craving that makes for further becoming—accompanied by passion & delight, relishing now here & now there—i.e., craving for sensual pleasure, craving for becoming, craving for non-becoming.

"And this, monks, is the noble truth of the cessation of stress: the remainderless fading & cessation, renunciation, relinquishment, release, & letting go of that very craving.

"And this, monks, is the noble truth of the way of practice leading to the cessation of stress: precisely this Noble Eightfold Path—right view, right resolve, right speech, right action, right livelihood, right effort, right mindfulness, right concentration.

"Vision arose, insight arose, discernment arose, knowledge arose, illumination arose within me with regard to things never heard before: 'This is the noble truth of stress.' Vision arose, insight arose, discernment arose, knowledge arose, illumination arose within me with regard to things never heard before: 'This noble truth of stress is to be comprehended.' Vision arose, insight arose, discernment arose, knowledge arose, illumination arose within me with regard to things never heard before:' This noble truth of stress has been comprehended.'

"Vision arose, insight arose, discernment arose, knowledge arose, illumination arose within me with regard to things never heard before: 'This is the noble truth of the origination of stress'. . . 'This noble truth of the origination of stress is to be abandoned'. . . 'This noble truth of the origination of stress has been abandoned.'

"Vision arose, insight arose, discernment arose, knowledge arose, illumination arose within me with regard to things never heard before: 'This is the noble truth of the cessation of stress'. . . 'This noble truth of the cessation of stress is to be directly experienced'. . . 'This noble truth of the cessation of stress has been directly experienced.'

"Vision arose, insight arose, discernment arose, knowledge arose, illumination arose within me with regard to things never heard before: 'This is the noble truth of the way of practice leading to the cessation of stress'. . . 'This noble truth of the way of practice leading to the cessation of stress is to be developed'. . . 'This noble truth of the way of practice leading to the cessation of stress has been developed.'

"And, monks, as long as this—my three-round, twelve-permutation knowledge & vision concerning these four noble truths as they have come to be—was not pure, I did not claim to have directly awakened to the right self-awakening unexcelled in the cosmos with its deities, Maras, & Brahmas, with its contemplatives & priests, its royalty & commonfolk. But as soon as this—my three-round, twelve-permutation knowledge & vision concerning these four noble truths as they have come to be—was truly pure, then I did claim to have directly awakened to the right self-awakening unexcelled in the cosmos with its deities, Maras & Brahmas, with its contemplatives & priests, its royalty & commonfolk. Knowledge & vision arose in me: 'Unprovoked is my release. This is the last birth. There is now no further becoming.'"

V.3 Âkankheyya-Sutta: If He Should Desire

Source: *The Sacred Books of the East*, vol. 11, *Buddhist Suttas*, trans. T. W. Rhys Davids (Oxford: Clarendon, 1881), http://www.sacred-texts.com/bud/sbe11/sbe1106.htm

1. Thus have I heard. The Blessed One was once staying at Sâvatthi in Anâtha Pindika's park.

There the Blessed One addressed the Brethren, and said, 'Bhikkhus.' 'Yea, Lord!' said the Brethren, in assent, to the Blessed One.

Then spake the Blessed One:

2. 'Continue, Brethren, in the practice of Right Conduct, adhering to the Rules of the Order; continue enclosed by the restraint of the Rules of the Order, devoted to uprightness in life; train yourselves according to the Precepts, taking them upon you in the sense of the danger in the least offence.

3. 'If a Bhikkhu should desire, Brethren, to become beloved, popular, respected among his fellow-disciples, let him then fulfil all righteousness, let him be devoted to that quietude of heart which springs from within, let him not drive back the ecstasy of contemplation, let him look through things, let him be much alone!'

4. 'If a Bhikkhu should desire, Brethren, to receive the requisites—clothing, food, lodging, and medicine, and other necessaries for the sick—let him then fulfil all righteousness, let him be devoted to that quietude of heart which springs from within, let him not drive back the ecstasy of contemplation, let him look through things, let him be much alone!'

5. 'If a Bhikkhu should desire, Brethren, that to those people among whom he receives the requisites—clothing, food, lodging, and medicine, and other necessaries for the sick—that charity of theirs should redound to great fruit and great advantage, let him then fulfil all righteousness, let him be devoted to that quietude of heart which springs from within, let him not drive back the ecstasy of contemplation, let him look through things, let him be much alone!'

6. 'If a Bhikkhu should desire, Brethren, that those relatives of his, of one blood with him, dead and gone, who think of him with believing heart should find therein great fruit and great advantage, let him then fulfil all righteousness, let him be devoted to that quietude of heart which springs from within, let

him not drive back the ecstasy of contemplation, let him look through things, let him be much alone!'

7. 'If a Bhikkhu should desire, Brethren, that he should be victorious over discontent and lust, that discontent should never overpower him, that he should master and subdue any discontent that had sprung up within him, let him then fulfil all righteousness, let him be devoted to that quietude of heart which springs from within, let him not drive back the ecstasy of contemplation, let him look through things, let him be much alone!'

8. 'If a Bhikkhu should desire, Brethren, that he should be victorious over (spiritual) danger and dismay, that neither danger nor dismay should ever overcome him, that he should master and subdue every danger and dismay, let him then fulfil all righteousness, let him be devoted to that quietude of heart which springs from within, let him not drive back the ecstasy of contemplation, let him look through things, let him be much alone!'

9. 'If a Bhikkhu should desire, Brethren, to realise the hopes of those spiritual men who live in the bliss which comes, even in this present world, from the four *Ghânas*, should he desire not to fall into the pains and difficulties (which they avoid), let him then fulfil all righteousness, let him be devoted to that quietude of heart which springs from within, let him not drive back the ecstasy of contemplation, let him look through things, let him be much alone!'

10. 'If a Bhikkhu should desire, Brethren, to reach with his body and remain in those stages of deliverance which are incorporeal, and pass beyond phenomena, let him then fulfil all righteousness, let him be devoted to that quietude of heart which springs from within, let him not drive back the ecstasy of contemplation, let him look through things, let him be much alone!'

11. 'If a Bhikkhu should desire, Brethren, by the complete destruction of the three Bonds to become converted, to be no longer liable to be reborn in a state of suffering, and to be assured of final salvation, let him then fulfil all righteousness, let him

be devoted to that quietude of heart which springs from within, let him not drive back the ecstasy of contemplation, let him look through things, let him be much alone!'

12. 'If a Bhikkhu should desire, Brethren, by the complete destruction of the three Bonds, and by the reduction to a minimum of lust, hatred, and delusion, to become a Sakadâgâmin, and (thus) on his first return to this world to make an end of sorrow, let him then fulfil all righteousness, let him be devoted to that quietude of heart which springs from within, let him not drive back the ecstasy of contemplation, let him look through things, let him be much alone!'

13. 'If a Bhikkhu should desire, Brethren, by the complete destruction of the five Bonds which bind people to this earth, to become an inheritor of the highest heavens, there to pass entirely away, thence

14. 'If a Bhikkhu should desire, Brethren, to exercise one by one each of the different Iddhis, being one to become multiform, being multiform to become one; to become visible, or to become invisible; to go without being stopped to the further side of a wall, or a fence, or a mountain, as if through air; to penetrate up and down through solid ground, as if through water; to walk on the water without dividing it, as if on solid ground; to travel cross-legged through the sky, like the birds on wing; to touch and feel with the hand even the sun and the moon, mighty and powerful though they be; and to reach in the body even up to the heaven of Brahmâ; let him then fulfil all righteousness, let him be devoted to that quietude of heart which springs from within, let him not drive back the ecstasy of contemplation, let him look through things, let him be much alone!'

15. 'If a Bhikkhu should desire, Brethren, to hear with clear and heavenly ear, surpassing that of men, sounds both human and celestial, whether far or near, let him then fulfil all righteousness, let him be devoted to that quietude of heart which springs from within, let him not drive back the ecstasy of contemplation, let him look through things, let him be much alone!'

16. 'If a Bhikkhu should desire, Brethren, to comprehend by his own heart the hearts of other beings and of other men; to discern the passionate mind to be passionate, and the calm mind calm; the angry mind to be angry, and the peaceable peaceable; the deluded mind to be deluded, and the wise mind wise; the concentrated thoughts to be concentrated, and the scattered to be scattered; the lofty mind to be lofty, and the narrow mind narrow; the sublime thoughts to be sublime, and the mean to be mean; the steadfast mind to be steadfast, and the wavering to be wavering; the free mind to be free, and the enslaved mind to be enslaved; let him then fulfil all righteousness, let him be devoted to that quietude of heart which springs from within, let him not drive back the ecstasy of contemplation, let him look through things, let him be much alone!'

17. 'If a Bhikkhu should desire, Brethren, to be able to call to mind his various temporary states in days gone by; such as one birth, two births, three, four, five, ten, twenty, thirty, forty, fifty, a hundred or a thousand, or a hundred thousand births; his births in many an aeon of destruction, in many an aeon of renovation, in many an aeon of both destruction and renovation; (so as to be able to say), "In that place such was my name, such my family, such my caste, such my subsistence, such my experience of comfort or of pain, and such the limit of my life; and when I passed from thence, I took form again in that other place where my name was so and so, such my family, such my caste, such my subsistence, such my experience of comfort or of joy, and such my term

of life; and when I fell from thence, I took form in such and such a place;"—should he desire thus to call to mind his temporary states in days gone by in all their modes and all their details let him then fulfil all righteousness, let him be devoted to that quietude of heart which springs from within, let him not drive back the ecstasy of contemplation, let him look through things, let him be much alone!'

18. 'If a Bhikkhu should desire, Brethren, to see with pure and heavenly vision, surpassing that of

19. 'If a Bhikkhu should desire, Brethren, by the destruction of the great evils, by himself, and even in this very world, to know and realise and attain to Arahatship, to emancipation of heart, and emancipation of mind, let him then fulfil all righteousness, let him be devoted to that quietude of heart which springs from within, let him not drive back the ecstasy of contemplation, let him look through things, let him be much alone!'

20. 'Continue therefore, Brethren, in the practice of Right Conduct, adhering to the Rules of the Order; continue enclosed by the restraint of the Rules of the Order, devoted to uprightness in life; train yourselves according to the Precepts, taking them upon you in the sense of the danger in the least offence. For to this end alone has all, that has been said, been said!'

21. Thus spake the Blessed One. And those Brethren, delighted in heart, exalted the word of the Blessed One.

Key Terms

atman/atta   Sanskrit word meaning soul or self. The Upanishads teach that *atman* is identical to Brahman— that is, the soul is one with the divine.

bodhisattva   In Mahayana Buddhism a saint or semi-divine being who has voluntarily renounced *nirvana* in order to help others to salvation. In popular devotion *bodhisattvas* are worshipped as symbols of compassion.

Cao Dai   Religious and political movement which started in southern Vietnam around 1920. It is sometimes called the "Third Amnesty." Firmly nationalistic, its teachings are a mixture of Buddhism and Taoism.

Dharma/Dhamma   In Buddhism, the teaching of the Buddha.

dukkha   Buddhist term for unsatisfactoriness or suffering. Birth, illness, decay, death and rebirth are symptoms of a restless and continuous "coming-to-be" which marks all existence as *dukkha*.

Hoa Hao   Offshoot of the Vietnamese Cao Dai movement. It is Buddhist-based and has been strongly nationalistic.

karma   The belief every action has inevitable consequences which attach themselves to the doer requiring reward or punishment. Karma is thus the moral law of cause and effect. It explains the inequalities of life as the consequences of actions in previous lives. The notion of karma probably developed among the Dravidian people of India. In Mahayana Buddhism the concept is transformed by the idea of the bodhisattva. Merit can be transferred by grace or faith, thus changing the person's karma.

Lotus Sutra   Mahayana Buddhist scripture in the form of a sermon preached by the Buddha (1) to a vast throng of gods, demons, rulers and cosmic powers. It contains the essence of Mahayana teachings on the eternity of the Buddha, the universal capacity for Buddhahood and the compassion and power of the bodhisattvas. It is especially revered in Japan and is the basic scripture of the Nichiren Buddhist new religions.

Mahayana   ("Large vehicle") The form of Buddhism practiced in Nepal, China, Tibet, Korea and Japan. Mahayana accepts more scriptures than Theravada and has developed various forms of popular devotion based on the doctrine of the bodhisattvas.

mandala   A visual aid in the form of a series of colored concentric circles used in Tibetan Buddhism. Segments of the circles portray different aspects of the Buddha's compassion. Concentration on the mandala enables the disciple to see himself in relation to the Buddha's compassion and thus to achieve enlightenment.

mantra   A symbolic sound causing an internal vibration which helps to concentrate the mind and aids self-realization, e.g., the repeated syllable "om," and in Tibetan Buddhism the phrase "*om mani padme hum.*" In Hinduism the term originally referred to a few sacred verses from the Vedas. It came to be thought that they possessed spiritual power, and that repetition of them was a help to liberation. A mantra is sometimes given by a spiritual teacher to a disciple as an initiation.

nirvana/nibbana   ("Going out, becoming cool") In Buddhism, the state when dukkha ceases because the flames of desire are no longer fuelled. It is a state of unconditioned-ness and uncompounded-ness beyond any form of known or imagined existence.

sangha   Community of Buddhist monks which started with the Buddha's first disciples. The functions of the *sangha* are to promote through its own lifestyle the best conditions for attaining individual salvation and to teach the *dhamma* to all people.

Theravada   ("The doctrine of the elders") The form of Buddhism practiced in Sri Lanka, Myanmar (Burma), Thailand, Cambodia, and Laos; it sticks firmly to the teachings of the Vinaya Pitaka and rejects the doctrine of the bodhisattvas.

Vajrayana   ("Diamond vehicle") An expression sometimes used for Tibetan Buddhism, a form of Mahayana Buddhism which has distinctive doctrines and practices.

Zen   Japanese Buddhist movement that developed from the Chinese Ch'an school in the thirteenth century CE. It is characterized by the teaching that enlightenment is a spontaneous event, totally independent of concepts, techniques or rituals. Zen aims at harmony in living and uses secular arts such as tea-making and calligraphy to develop effortless skills.

Questions for Study and Discussion

1. According to Buddhism, what is the cause of *dukkha* (suffering)?
2. Briefly define Theravada Buddhism and Mahayana Buddhism. Why does the author say they are "not comparable phenomena"?
3. Give definitions in your own words for the following concepts: *dharma* (*dhamma*), *sangha*, and *nirvana* (*nibbana*).
4. Why are Mahayana *sutras* called "apocryphal"? What is their significance to Buddhism?
5. Briefly describe the basic precepts of the Cao Dai and Hoa Hao sects of Buddhism. What roles have they played in modern Vietnam?
6. Describe the relationship of "nonattachment" to the Buddhist concepts of morality and *karma* and practice of meditation.
7. Choose a quotation from among the sidebars of this chapter and explain how it demonstrates a core Buddhist belief or important aspect of Buddhist practice.

Questions for Reflection

Write your personal reflections to each of these questions in the space provided.

1. How might the Siddhartha Gautama's caste have influenced his beliefs? (See pp. 202.)

2. What does it mean to "see things the way they really are," a key teaching of the Buddha? (See p. 203.)

3. Discuss the importance of meditation to Buddhism. (See pp. 218–19.)

4. Buddhists have *rebirth* rather than *reincarnation*; explain. (See p. 220.)

5. Describe the similarities between Hinduism and Buddhism, and explain what they tell us about the historical relationship of religions.

Selected Online Resources

▶ Sacred Texts: Buddhism—both traditional texts and more modern ones are included here
   http://www.sacred-texts.com/bud/index.htm
▶ Buddhist Studies Virtual Library—frequently updated catalog of websites on all aspects and sects of Buddhism
   http://www.ciolek.com/WWWVL-Buddhism.html
▶ Karmapa the Black Hat Lama of Tibet—one example of a contemporary Buddhist organization with worldwide presence
   http://www.karmapa.org

Part 6: Jainism

Chapter Summaries

43. A Historical Overview

Jainism originated in India about the fifth century BCE and now has several different branches, associated with either the Digambara or the Shvetambara sects. Jains follow the teachings of the *jinas*, religious teachers who have attained enlightenment by conquering *samsara*. Twenty-four *jinas* are born and preach during the third and fourth phases of each half of the cosmic cycle. Jain tradition holds that after the death of Mahavira, the twenty-fourth *jina*, the cosmos entered a 21,000-year phase. Mahavira was a contemporary of the Buddha who lived and preached near Patna, India. His life story and teachings are recorded in Jain scriptures. Different Jain traditions tell different versions of his life, but according to most he renounced his privileged life, went wandering, practiced nonviolence and meditation, and eventually attained enlightenment.

Mahavira's original eleven disciples had hundreds of disciples of their own, who went on to found ascetic communities. Jainism spread through parts of western and southern India in the first few centuries CE and benefited from periods of royal support. The ascetic tradition ultimate divided between wandering and temple-dwelling ascetics. An institution of clerics developed later, the *bhattarakas*, who promoted Jainism through education and publications.

44. Sacred Writings

The collection of writings by Mahavira's disciples is called the *Twelve-Limbed Basket*. But the two main sects of Jainism refer to different canons: Shvetambara believe their scripture descends directly from the disciples, while the Digambara believe it was lost long ago. Digambara Jainism recognizes the *Scripture of Six Parts* and the *Treatise on the Passions* as well as certain texts written by revered ascetics. The Shvetambara canon is organized into three groups: the *Purva*, the *Twelve Limbs* (missing the twelfth text), and a group of texts written by later ascetics. Both sects accept the *Tattvarthasutra*, written by an early ascetic in Sanskrit and the first attempt to organize the Jain doctrine.

45. Beliefs

Jain doctrine is primarily concerned with the nature of the soul and its liberation from *samsara*. Karma is a physical substance that permeates the universe and obscures the soul's knowledge of its own pure nature, trapping the soul in a cycle of action and reaction. Jains believe in personal responsibility for liberation, which involves fourteen stages of purity. While Jains do not believe in a creator god, they venerate liberated souls as divine being. They believe all living creatures have souls, which are eternal, and have the capacity for suffering. Causing harm to another soul generates karma that attaches to one's own soul. The Jainist view of the cosmos includes seven realms of hell as well as seven heavenly realms. Liberation isn't currently possible during the cycle the world exists in now, but Jains believe rebirth in the *mahavideha*, in which *moksha* is attainable, is possible through religious effort.

46. Family and Society

Jain religious society is fourfold, consisting of female ascetics, male ascetics, laywomen, and laymen. Ascetic communities are hierarchical and headed by an *acharya*. Laypeople can become ascetics after progressing through eleven stages of renunciation and taking five vows. Ascetics have no permanent home and must depend on donations of food from laypeople. They renounce all worldly attachments and live as public figures who deliver sermons and advise laypeople on spiritual matters. Jain lay society is divided by sect and caste; intermarriage between Jains and Hindus of the same caste is not uncommon in India. Jains are prohibited from entering professions that cause harm to other living beings and practice vegetarianism and nonviolence in their daily lives.

47. Worship and Festivals

Jain worship is directed toward ascetics, who venerate their superiors as lay people venerate ascetics. The rite of veneration performed by a lay person is the *guru-vandan*. During the ritual *puja* Jains worship the *jinas* and express veneration through song. Images of *jinas* in marble or metal are common features of worship. Typical ritual worship is individual, not congregational. During festivals lay and ascetic Jains often come together to celebrate things like aspects of the lives of the *jinas*. During the Shvetambara festival of *Paryushan*, the closing of the year, some laypeople observe fasts, and ascetics deliver sermons. Ascetics relinquish worldly possessions and commit to complete nonviolence, which includes compassion toward others.

48. Jainism in the Modern World

Some Jains embrace modernization, while others uphold traditions. Some Jains point to scientific discoveries to justify certain traditional beliefs and practices. Advances in publishing technology have made Jain publications widely accessible. Jains in the diaspora must live without the spiritual guidance of ascetics, who cannot travel outside of India. Some modern Jain movements have addressed the problem of ascetic absence.

Key Personalities

Mahavira (died around 425 BCE)

Great Jain teacher who abolished the distinctions of the caste system and tried to spread his teaching among the Brahmans. He starved himself to death at the age of seventy-two, having spent his last years totally naked. Jains celebrate five auspicious moments in his life: his conception, birth, renunciation, enlightenment, and final spiritual liberation, or *moksha*.

"He said that, 'A living body is not merely an integration of limbs and flesh but it is the abode of the soul which potentially has perfect perception (Anant-darshana), perfect knowledge (Anant-jnana), perfect power (Anant-virya), and perfect bliss (Anant-sukha)'. . . . Lord Mahavir also preached the gospel of universal love, emphasizing that all living beings, irrespective of their size, shape, and form, how spiritually developed or under-developed, are equal and we should love and respect them."

(Pravin K. Shah, "Lord Mahavir and Jain Religion," Jain History, n.d., http://www.cs.colostate.edu/~malaiya /mahavira.html)

ADDITIONAL RESOURCE
- ▶ "Lord Mahavira and His Philosophy" (essay includes illustrations and brief biography) http://www.exoticindiaart.com/article /mahavira/

Trishala (fifth century BCE)

The mother of Mahavira and the wife of King Siddhartha.

"According to the Jain scriptures, Trishala had 16 dreams [according to the Digambara sect] and [according to the] Shvetabar sect . . . fourteen dreams after the conception of her son [Mahavira]. After having these dreams she woke her husband King Siddharth and told him about the dreams. The next day Siddharth summoned the scholars of the court and asked them to explain the meaning of the dreams. According to the scholars, these dreams

meant that the child would be born very strong, courageous, and full of virtue."

("Dreams of Lord Mahavira's Mother Trishala," Digambara Jain Online, 2003, http://www.digambarjainonline .com/dharma/trisala.htm)

Indrabhuti Gautama (fifth century BCE)

One of Mahavira's closest disciples, and one of the two who survived him.

"Indrabhuti became a very learned *pandita* and grew extremely vain of his learning. One day, however, an old man appeared and asked him to explain a certain verse. . . . The verse contained references . . . not one of which could Gautama understand. . . . He sought out Mahavira to ask for an explanation. The moment he was in the presence of the great ascetic, all his pride in his fancied learning fell from him, and he besought Mahavira to teach him. He not only became a convert himself, but took over with him his five hundred pupils and his three brothers."

(Kailash Chand Jain, *Lord Mahavira and His Times*, revised ed., Lal S. L. Jain Research Series [Delhi: Motilal Banarsidass Publishers, 1991], 59)

Sudharman (fifth century BCE)

One of Mahavira's closest disciples, and one of the two who survived him.

"It is not [Indrabhuti] Gautama . . . but his colleague Sudharman who is regarded as the source of the authoritative texts, for it was Sudharman who, when questioned by his own disciple Jambusvamin, provided the introduction to the exposition of the doctrine which then followed."

(A. N. Dwivedi, *Essentials of Hinduism, Jainism, and Buddhism* [New Delhi: Books Today, 1979], 78)

Shrimad Rajachandra (1867–1901)

A Jain layperson from Gujarat who urged his followers to devote themselves to authoritative gurus in order to achieve spiritual liberation. Because his movement's members follow lay gurus, who can travel, it has spread throughout the Jain diaspora.

"In my short life I have entertained all the thought-forms which were thought over by all the powerful saints and philosophers and by the formidable skeptics. I have thought of the universe of desires and aspirations which were discussed by the great rulers. I have also thought of the disinterestedness par excellence, an attitude of serene indifference. I have much meditated on the acquisition of immortality and of minute temporariness or transitoriness. Many similar great thoughts I have traversed in very few years of my life.

"I look at all of them as a seer, and I realize the unfathomable gap between my present state of knowledge and experience and the state of my being when I cherished or entertained these great and multifarious thought-systems."

(Shrimad Rajchandra quoted in "Life of Shrimad Rajchandra," n.d., http://www.cs.colostate.edu/~malaiya/rajchandra.html)

Primary Source Readings

The following excerpted readings represent some of the important primary sources mentioned in the main text. Additional primary sources are available both in print and online, and students are encouraged to contact their instructors for further information.

VI.1 The Kalpa Sutra

Source: *Jaina Sutras, Part 2*, trans. Hermann Jacobi, 1884, http://www.sacred-texts.com/jai/sbe22/sbe2281.htm

Note on italicized letters: "Italics are used to indicate distinctions between consonants in transliterated Sanskrit and Prakrit. Most notably in this system, 'j' (roughly, the initial sound of the English word 'jam') is written *g*, hence the spelling *G*ain throughout, which is pronounced 'Jain.'"

LIFE OF MAHÂVÎRA

Obeisance to the Arhats!

Obeisance to the Liberated Ones!

Obeisance to the Religious Guides!

Obeisance to the Religious Instructors! Obeisance to all Saints in the World!

This fivefold obeisance, destroying all sins, is of all benedictions the principal benediction.

In that period, in that age lived the Venerable Ascetic Mahâvîra, the five (most important moments of whose life happened) when the moon was in conjunction with the asterism Uttaraphalgunî; to wit, in Uttaraphalgunî he descended (from heaven), and having descended (thence), he entered the womb (of Devânandâ); in Uttaraphalgunî he was removed from the womb (of Devânandâ) to the womb (of Trisalâ); in Uttaraphalgunî he was born; in Uttaraphalgunî, tearing out his hair, he left the house and entered the state of houselessness; in Uttaraphalgunî he obtained the highest knowledge and intuition, called Kevala, which is infinite, supreme, unobstructed, unimpeded, complete, and perfect. But in Svâti the Venerable One obtained final liberation. . . .

In that night in which the Venerable Ascetic Mahâvîra took the form of an embryo in the womb of the Brâhma*n*î Devânandâ of the *G*âlandharâya*n*a gotra, the Brâhma*n*î Devânandâ was on her couch, taking fits of sleep, in a state between sleeping and waking, and having seen the following fourteen illustrious, beautiful, lucky, blest, auspicious, fortunate great dreams, she woke up. To wit:

An elephant, a bull, a lion, the anointing (of the goddess Srî), a garland, the moon, the sun, a flag, a vase, a lotus lake, the ocean, a celestial abode, a heap of jewels, and a flame.

When the Brâhma*n*î Devânandâ, having seen these dreams, woke up, she—glad, pleased, and joyful in her mind, delighted, extremely enraptured, with a heart widening under the influence of happiness, with the hair of her body all erect in their pores like the flowers of the Kadamba touched by rain-drops—firmly fixed the dreams (in her mind), and rose from her couch. Neither hasty nor trembling, with a quick and even gait, like that of the royal swan, she went to the Brâhma*n*a *R*ishabhadatta, and gave him the greeting of victory. Then she comfortably sat down in an excellent chair of state; calm and composed, joining the palms of her hands so as to bring the ten nails together, she laid the folded hands on her head, and spoke thus:

"O beloved of the gods, I was just now on my couch taking fits of sleep, in a state between sleeping and waking, when I saw the following fourteen illustrious, &c., great dreams; to wit, an elephant, &c.

"O beloved of the gods, what, to be sure, will be the happy result portended by these fourteen illustrious, &c., great dreams?"

When the Brâhma*n*a *Ri*shabhadatta had heard and perceived this news from the Brâhma*nî* Devânandâ, he, glad, pleased, and joyful rain-drops, firmly fixed the dreams (in his mind), and entered upon considering them. He grasped the meaning of those dreams with his own innate intellect and intuition, which were preceded by reflection, and thus spoke to the Brâhma*nî* Devânandâ:

"O beloved of the gods, you have seen illustrious dreams; O beloved of the gods, you have seen beautiful, lucky, blest, auspicious, fortunate dreams, which will bring health, joy, long life, bliss, and fortune! We shall have success, O beloved of the gods, we shall have pleasure; we shall have happiness, O beloved of the gods, we shall have a son! Indeed, O beloved of the gods, after the lapse of nine complete months and seven and a half days you will give birth to a lovely and handsome boy with tender hands and feet, with a body containing the entire and complete five organs of sense, with the lucky signs, marks, and good qualities; a boy on whose body all limbs will be well formed, and of full volume, weight, and length, of a lovely figure like that of the moon! And this boy, after having passed his childhood, and, with just ripened intellect, having reached the state of youth, will repeat, fully understand, and well retain (in his mind) the four Vedas: the *Ri*g-veda, Yagur-veda, Sâma-veda, Atharva-veda—to which the Itihâsa is added as a fifth, and the Nigghan*t*u as a sixth (Veda)—together with their Angas and Upângas, and the Rahasya; he will know the six Angas, he will

be versed in the philosophy of the sixty categories, and well grounded in arithmetic, in phonetics, ceremonial, grammar, metre, etymology, and astronomy, and in many other brahmanical [and monastic] sciences besides. Therefore, O beloved of the gods, you have seen illustrious dreams, &c."

In this way he repeatedly expressed his extreme satisfaction.

When the Brâhma*nî* Devânandâ had heard and perceived this news from the Brâhma*n*a *Ri*shabhadatta, she—glad, pleased, and joyful, &c.—joining the palms of her hands, &c. and spoke thus:

"That is so, O beloved of the gods; that is exactly so, O beloved of the gods; that is true, O beloved of the gods; that is beyond doubt, O beloved of the gods; that is what I desire, O beloved of the gods; that is what I accept, O beloved of the gods; that is what I desire and accept, O beloved of the gods; that matter is really such as you have pronounced it."

Thus saying, she accepted the true meaning of the dreams, and enjoyed together with *Ri*shabhadatta the noble permitted pleasures of human nature.

In that period, in that age, *Sakra*,—the chief and king of the gods, the wielder of the thunderbolt, the destroyer of towns, the performer of a hundred sacrifices, the thousand-eyed one, Maghavan, the punisher of the Daitya Pâka, the lord of the southern half of the earth, the lord of the thirty-two thousand celestial abodes, the bestrider of the elephant Airavata, the chief of the Suras . . . was in the Saudharma Kalpa, in the celestial abode Saudharma Avatamsaka, in the council-hall Sudharman, on his throne *Sakra*; he who exercises and maintains the supreme command, government, management, guidance, direction, and sovereign power and generalship over the thirty-two thousand gods of the celestial abodes, the eighty-four thousand gods of a rank equal with that of himself, the thirty-two chief gods, the four guardians of the world, the eight principal queens with their trains, the three courts, the seven armies, and the seven commanders of these armies. He was then enjoying the permitted pleasures of divine nature under the great din of uninterrupted story-telling, dramatical plays, singing, and music, as beating of time, performance on the Vînâ, the Tûrya, the great drum, and the Paṭupaṭaha.

And he viewed this whole continent Gambûd-vîpa with his extensive (knowledge called) Avadhi. There he saw in the continent Gambûdvîpa, in Bhâratavarsha, in the southern half of Bharata, in the brahmanical part of the town Kuṇḍagrâma, the Venerable Ascetic Mahâvira taking the form of an embryo in the womb of the Brâhmaṇî Devânandâ of the Gâlandharâyaṇa gotra, wife of the Brâhmaṇa Rishabhadatta of the gotra of Koḍâla. . . . The chief of the gods rose with confusion, hasty and trembling from his throne, descended from the footstool, took off his shoes which were by a clever artist set with Vaidûrya and excellent Rishṭa and Añgana, and ornamented with glittering jewels and precious stones, threw his seamless robe over his left shoulder, and, arranging the fingers of his hands in the shape of a bud, he advanced seven or eight steps towards the Tîrthakara. Bending his left knee and reposing on the right one, he three times placed his head on the ground and lifted it a little; then he raised his bracelet-encumbered arms, and joining the palms of his hands so as to bring the ten nails together, laid the hands on his head and spoke thus:

"Reverence to the Arhats and Bhagavats; to the Âdikaras, the Tîrthakaras, the perfectly-enlightened ones; to the highest of men, the lions among men, the flowers among mankind, the Gandhahastins among men; to the highest in the world, the guides of the world, the benefactors of the world, the lights of the world, the enlighteners of the world . . . reverence to the Ginas who have conquered fear. Reverence to the Venerable Ascetic Mahâvira, the Âdikara, the last of the Tîrthakaras who was predicted by the former Tîrthakaras, &c. I here adore the Revered One yonder, may the Revered One yonder see me here!" With these words he adored, he worshipped the Venerable Ascetic Mahâvira, and sat down on his excellent throne facing the east. Then the following internal, reflectional, desirable idea occurred to the mind of Sakra, the chief of kings and gods:

"It never has happened, nor does it happen, nor will it happen, that Arhats, Kakravartins, Baladevas, or Vasudevas, in the past, present, or future, should be born in low families, mean families, degraded families, poor families, indigent families, beggars' families, or brahmanical families. For indeed Arhats, Kakravartins, Baladevas, and Vasudevas, in the past, present, and future, are born in high families, noble families, royal families, noblemen's families, in families belonging to the race of Ikshvâku, or of Hari, or in other suchlike families of pure descent on both sides. . . . Hence it is the established custom of all past, present, and future Sakras, chiefs and kings of the gods, to cause the Arhats and Bhagavats to be removed from such-like low, mean, &c., families, to such-like high, noble, &c., families. It is, therefore, better that I should cause the Venerable Ascetic Mahâvîra, the last of the Tîrthakaras who was predicted by the former Tîrthakaras, to be removed from the brahmanical part of the town Kuṇḍagrâma, from the womb of the Brâhmaṇî Devânandâ of the Gâlandharâyaṇa gotra, wife of the Brâhmaṇa Rishabhadatta of the gotra of Koḍâla, to the Kshatriya part of the town Kuṇḍagrâma, and to be placed as an embryo in the womb of the Kshatriyâṇî Trisalâ of the Vâsishṭha gotra, wife of the Kshatriya Siddhârtha of the Kâsyapa gotra, belonging to the clan of the Gñâtri Kshatriya,; and to cause the embryo of the Kshatriyâṇî Trisalâ of the Vâsishṭha gotra to be placed in the womb of the Brâhmaṇî Devânandâ of the Gâlandharâyaṇa gotra." . . .

In that night in which the embryo of the Venerable Ascetic Mahâvira was removed from the womb of the Brâhmaṇî Devânandâ of the Gâlandharâyaṇa gotra to that of the Kshatriyâṇî Trisalâ of the Vâsishṭha gotra, the former was on her couch taking fits of sleep in a state between sleeping and waking; and seeing that these fourteen illustrious, beautiful, lucky, blest, auspicious, fortunate, great dreams were taken from her by the Kshatriyâṇî Trisalâ, she awoke. . . .

1. Then Trisalâ saw in her first dream a fine, enormous elephant, possessing all lucky marks, with strong thighs and four mighty tusks; who was whiter

than an empty great cloud, or a heap of pearls, or the ocean of milk, or the moon-beams, or spray of water, or the silver mountain (Vaitâdhya); whose temples were perfumed with fragrant musk-fluid, which attracted the bees; equalling in dimension the best elephant of the king of the gods (Airâvata); uttering a fine deep sound like the thunder of a big and large rain-cloud.

2. Then she saw a tame, lucky bull, of a whiter hue than that of the mass of petals of the white lotus, illumining all around by the diffusion of a glory of light; (a bull) whose lovely, resplendent, beautiful hump was delightful through the collection of its charms, whose glossy skin (was covered with) thin, fine, soft hairs; whose body was firm, well made, muscular, compact, lovely, well proportioned, and beautiful; whose horns were large, round, excellently beautiful, greased at their tops, and pointed; whose teeth were all equal, shining, and pure. He foreboded innumerable good qualities.

3. Then she saw a handsome, handsomely shaped, playful lion, jumping from the sky towards her face; a delightful and beautiful lion whiter than a heap of pearls, &c., who had strong and lovely fore-arms, and a mouth adorned with round, large, and well-set teeth; whose lovely lips, splendent through their proportions, and soft like a noble lotus, looked as if they were artificially ornamented; whose palate was soft and tender like the petals of the red lotus, and the top of whose tongue was protruding; whose eyes were like pure lightning, and revolved like red-hot excellent gold just poured out from the crucible; (a lion) with broad and large thighs, and with full and excellent shoulders, who was adorned with a mane of soft, white, thin, long hair of the finest quality; whose erect, well-shaped, and well-grown tail was flapping; the tops of whose nails were deeply set and sharp; whose beautiful tongue came out of his mouth like a shoot of beauty.

4. Then she, with the face of the full moon, saw the goddess of famous beauty, Srî, on the top of Mount Himavat, reposing on a lotus in the lotus lake, anointed with the water from the strong and large trunks of the guardian elephants. She sat on a lofty throne. Her firmly placed feet resembled golden tortoises, and her dyed, fleshy, convex, thin, red, smooth nails were set in swelling muscles. Her hands and feet were like the leaves of the lotus, and her fingers and toes soft and excellent; her round and well-formed legs were adorned with the Kuruvindâvarta, and her knees with dimples. Her fleshy thighs resembled the proboscis of an excellent elephant, and her lovely broad hips were encircled by a golden zone. Her large and beautiful belly was adorned by a circular navel, and contained a lovely row of hairs (black as) collyrium, bees, or clouds, straight, even, continuous, thin, admirable, handsome, soft, and downy. Her waist, which contained the three folds, could be encompassed with one hand. On all parts of her body shone ornaments and trinkets, composed of many jewels and precious stones, yellow and red gold. The pure cup-like pair of her breasts sparkled, encircled by a garland of Kunda flowers, in which glittered a string of pearls. She wore strings of pearls made by diligent and clever artists, shining with wonderful strings, a necklace of jewels with a string of Dînârâs, and a trembling pair of earrings, touching her shoulders, diffused a brilliancy; but the united beauties and charms of these ornaments were only subservient to the loveliness of her face. Her lovely eyes were large and pure like the water lily. She sprinkled about the sap from two lotus flowers which she held in her splendid hands, and gracefully fanned herself. Her glossy, black, thick, smooth hair hung down in a braid.

5. Then she saw, coming down from the firmament, a garland charmingly interwoven with fresh Mandâra flowers. It spread the delicious smell of Kampaka, Asoka, Nâga Punnâga, Priyangu, Sirîsha, Mudgara, Mallikâ, Gâti, Yûthika, Ankolla, Korantakapatra, Damanaka, Navamâlikâ, Bakula, Tilaka, Vâsantika, Nuphar, Nymphaea, Pâtala, Kunda, Atimukta, and Mango; and perfumed the ten divisions of the universe with its incomparably delightful fragrance. It was white through wreaths of fragrant flowers of all seasons, and brilliant through splendid, beautiful embellishments of many colours.

Towards it came humming swarms of different kinds of bees, and filled with their sweet noise the whole neighbourhood.

6. And the moon: white as cow-milk, foam, spray of water, or a silver cup, glorious, delighting heart and eyes, full, dispelling the compact darkness of the thickest wilderness, whose crescent shines at the end of the two halves of the month, opening the blossoms of the groups of Nymphaeas, adorning the night, resembling the surface of a well-polished mirror. She was of a white hue, like a flamingo, the stars' head-ornament, the quiver of Cupid's arrows, raising the waters of the ocean, burning as it were disconsolate people when absent from their sweethearts, the large, glorious, wandering headmark of the celestial sphere—beloved in heart and soul by Rohinî. Such was the glorious, beautiful, resplendent full moon which the queen saw.

7. Then she saw the large sun, the dispeller of the mass of darkness, him of radiant form, red like the Asoka, the open Kimsuka, the bill of a parrot, or the Guñgârdha, the adorner of the lotus groups, the marker of the starry host, the lamp of the firmament, throttling as it were the mass of cold, the illustrious leader of the troop of planets, the destroyer of night, who only at his rising and setting may be well viewed, but (at all other times) is difficult to be regarded, who disperses evil-doers that stroll about at night, who stops the influence of cold, who always circles round Mount Meru, whose thousand rays obscure the lustre of other lights.

8. Then she saw an extremely beautiful and very large flag, a sight for all people, of a form attractive to the beholders. It was fastened to a golden staff with a tuft of many soft and waving peacock's feathers of blue, red, yellow, and white colours, and seemed as if it would pierce the brilliant, celestial sphere, with the brilliant lion on its top, who was white like crystal, pearlmother, Anka-stone, Kunda-flowers, spray of water, or a silver cup.

9. Then she saw a full vase of costly metal, splendent with fine gold, filled with pure water, excellent, of brilliant beauty, and shining with a bouquet of water lilies. It united many excellencies and all-auspicious marks, and stood on a lotus-(shaped foot), shining with excellent jewels. It delighted the eyes, glittered and illumined all about; it was the abode of happy Fortune, free from all faults, fine, splendid, exquisitely beautiful, entwined with a wreath of fragrant flowers of all seasons.

10. Then she saw a lake, called Lotus Lake, adorned with water lilies. Its yellow water was perfumed by lotuses opening in the rays of the morning sun; it abounded with swarms of aquatic animals, and fed fishes. It was large, and seemed to burn through the wide-spreading, glorious beauty of all kinds of lotuses. Its shape and beauty were pleasing. The lotuses in it were licked by whole swarms of gay bees and mad drones. Pairs of swans, cranes, *Kakravâkas*, ducks, Indian cranes, and many other lusty birds resorted to its waters, and on the leaves of its lotuses sparkled water-drops like pearls. It was a sight, pleasing to the heart and the eye.

11. Then she whose face was splendid like the moon in autumn, saw the milk-ocean, equalling in beauty the breast of Lakshmî, which is white like the mass of moon-beams. Its waters increased in all four directions, and raged with ever-changing and moving, excessively high waves. It presented a splendid and pleasant spectacle as it rushed to and from the shore with its wind-raised, changeable, and moving billows, its tossing waves, and its rolling, splendid, transparent breakers. From it issued camphor-white foam under the lashing (tails) of great porpoises, fishes, whales, and other monsters of the deep. Its agitated waters were in great uproar, occasioned by the vortex Gangâvarta, which the vehemence and force of the great rivers produced; they rose, rushed onwards and backwards, and eddied.

12. Then she saw a celestial abode excelling among the best of its kind, like the lotus (among flowers). It shone like the morning sun's disk, and was of a dazzling beauty. Its thousand and eight excellent columns (inlaid with) the best gold and heaps of jewels diffused a brilliant light like a heavenly lamp, and the pearls fastened to its curtains glittered. It was

hung with brilliant divine garlands, and decorated with pictures of wolves, bulls, horses, men, dolphins, birds, snakes, Kinnaras, deer, Sarabhas, Yaks, Samsaktas, elephants, shrubs, and plants. There the Gandharvas performed their concerts, and the din of the drums of the gods, imitating the sound of big and large rain-clouds, penetrated the whole inhabited world. It was highly delightful through curling, scented fumes of black aloe, the finest Kundurukka and Turushka, burning frankincense and other perfumes. It (shed) continuous light, was white, of excellent lustre, delighting the best of gods, and affording joy and pleasure.

13. Then she saw an enormous heap of jewels containing Pulaka, Vagra, Indranîla, Sasyaka, Karketana, Lohitâksha, Marakata, Prabâla, Saugandhika, Sphatika, Hamsagarbha, Añgana, and Kandrakânta. Its base was on the level of the earth, and it illumined with its jewels even the sphere of the sky. It was high and resembled Mount Meru.

14. And a fire. She saw a fire in vehement motion, fed with much-shining and honey-coloured ghee, smokeless, crackling, and extremely beautiful with its burning flames. The mass of its flames, which rose one above the other, seemed to interpenetrate each other, and the blaze of its flames appeared to bake the firmament in some places.

After having seen these fine, beautiful, lovely, handsome dreams, the lotus-eyed queen awoke on her bed while the hair of her body bristled for joy.

Every mother of a Tîrthakara sees these fourteen dreams in that night in which the famous Arhat enters her womb. . . .

Then the Kshatriya Siddhârtha placed his wife Trisalâ behind the curtain, and taking flowers and fruits in his hands, addressed with utmost courtesy the interpreters of dreams:

"O beloved of the gods, the Kshatriyânî Trisalâ was just on her couch, &c. What to be sure, O beloved of the gods, will be the result portended by these fourteen illustrious great dreams?"

When the interpreters of dreams had heard and perceived this news from the Kshatriya Siddhârtha, they—glad, pleased, and joyful, &c.—fixed the dreams in their minds, entered upon considering them, and conversed together.

Having found, grasped, discussed, decided upon, and clearly understood the meaning of these dreams, they recited before king Siddhârtha the dream-books and spoke thus:

"O beloved of the gods, in our dream-books are enumerated forty-two (common) dreams and thirty great dreams. Now, O beloved of the gods, the mothers of universal monarchs or of Arhats wake up after seeing these fourteen great dreams out of the thirty great dreams, when the embryo of a universal monarch or an Arhat enters their womb; viz. an elephant, a bull, &c. The mothers of Vâsudevas wake up after seeing any seven great dreams out of these fourteen great dreams, when the embryo of a Vâsudeva enters their womb. The mothers of Baladevas wake up after seeing any four great dreams out of these fourteen great dreams, when the embryo of a Baladeva enters their womb. The mother of Mândalikas wake up after seeing a single great dream out of these fourteen great dreams, when the embryo of a Mândalika enters their womb. Now, O beloved of the gods, the Kshatriyânî Trisalâ has seen these fourteen great dreams, &c. And this boy, &c. the lord of a realm with a large and extensive army and train of wagons, a universal emperor or a Gina, the lord of the three worlds, the universal emperor of the law. Therefore, O beloved of the gods, the Kshatriyânî Trisalâ has seen illustrious dreams," &c.

When king Siddhârtha had heard and perceived this news from the interpreter of dreams, he—glad, pleased, and joyful, &c.—spoke to them thus:

"That is so, O beloved of the gods, &c. as you have pronounced it." . . .

In that night in which the Venerable Ascetic Mahâvîra was born, there was a divine lustre originated by many descending and ascending gods and goddesses, and in the universe, resplendent with one light, the conflux of gods occasioned great confusion and noise.

In that night in which the Venerable Ascetic Mahâvîra was born, many demons in Vaisramana's service belonging to the animal world, rained down on the palace of king Siddhârtha one great shower of silver, gold, diamonds, clothes, ornaments, leaves, flowers, fruits, seeds, garlands, perfumes, sandal, powder, and riches.

After the Bhavanapati, Vyantara, Gyotishka, and Vaimânika gods had celebrated the feast of the inauguration of the Tîrthakara's birthday, the Kshatriya Siddhârtha called, at the break of the morning, together the town policemen and addressed them thus:

"O beloved of the gods, quickly set free all prisoners in the town of Ku*nd*apura, increase measures and weights, give order that the whole town of Ku*nd*apura with its suburbs be sprinkled with water, swept, and smeared (with cowdung, &c.) that in triangular places, in places where three or four roads meet, in courtyards, in squares, and in thoroughfares, the middle of the road and the path along the shops be sprinkled, cleaned, and swept; that platforms be erected one above the other; that the town be decorated with variously coloured flags and banners, and adorned with painted pavilions; that the walls bear impressions in Gosîrsha, fresh red sandal, and Dardara of the hand with outstretched fingers; that luck-foreboding vases be put on the floor, and pots of the same kind be disposed round every door and arch; that big, round, and long garlands, wreaths, and festoons be hung low and high; that the town be furnished with offerings, &c. smelling box; that players, dancers, rope-dancers, wrestlers, boxers, jesters, story-tellers, ballad-singers, actors, messengers, pole-dancers, fruit-mongers, bag-pipers, lute-players, and many Tâlâkaras be present. Erect and order to erect thousands of pillars and poles, and report on the execution of my orders." . . .

The parents of the Venerable Ascetic Mahâvîra celebrated the birth of their heir on the first day, on the third day they showed him the sun and the moon,

on the sixth day they observed the religious vigil; after the eleventh day, when the impure operations and ceremonies connected with the birth of a child had been performed, and the twelfth day had come, they prepared plenty of food, drink, spices, and sweetmeats, invited their friends, relations, kinsmen, agnates, cognates, and followers, together with I the *Gñâtrika* Kshatriyas. Then they bathed, made offerings (to the house-gods), and performed auspicious rites and expiatory acts, put on excellent, lucky, pure court-dress, and adorned their persons with small but costly ornaments. At dinner-time they sat down on excellent, comfortable chairs in the dining-hall, and together with their friends, relations, kinsmen, agnates, cognates and followers, and with the *Gñâtrika* Kshatriyas they partook, ate, tasted, and interchanged (bits) of a large collation of food, drink, spices, and sweetmeats. . . .

The Venerable Ascetic Mahâvîra belonged to the Kâsyapa gotra. His three names have thus been recorded: by his parents he was called Vardhamâna; because he is devoid of love and hate, he is called Sra-ma*n*a (i.e. Ascetic); because he stands fast in midst of dangers and fears, patiently bears hardships and calamities, adheres to the chosen rules of penance, is wise, indifferent to pleasure and pain, rich in control, and gifted with fortitude, the name Venerable Ascetic Mahâvîra has been given him by the gods.

The Venerable Ascetic Mahâvîra's father belonged to the Kâsyapa gotra; he had three names: Siddhârtha, Sreyâm*s*a, and Gasam*s*a, &c. Seshavatî and Yasovatî.

The Venerable Ascetic Mahâvîra—clever, with the aspirations of a clever man, of great beauty, controlling (his senses), lucky, and modest; a *Gñâtri* Kshatriya, the son of a *Gñâtri* Kshatriya; the moon of the clan of the *Gñâtris*; a Videha, the son of Videhadattâ, a native of Videha, a prince of Videha—had lived thirty years in Videha when his parents went to the world of the gods (i.e. died), and he with the permission of his elder brother and the authorities of the kingdom fulfilled his promise. At that moment the Laukântika gods, following the established custom, praised and hymned him with these kind, pleasing, &c. sweet, and soft words:

"Victory, victory to thee, gladdener of the world! Victory, victory to thee, lucky one! Luck to thee, bull of the best Kshatriyas! Awake, reverend lord of the world! Establish the religion of the law which benefits all living beings in the whole universe! It will bring supreme benefit to all living beings in all the world!"

Thus they raised the shout of victory.

Before the Venerable Ascetic Mahâvîra had adopted the life of a householder (i.e. before his marriage) he possessed supreme, unlimited, unimpeded knowledge and intuition. The Venerable Ascetic Mahâvîra perceived with this his supreme unlimited knowledge and intuition that the time for his Renunciation had come. He left his silver, he left his gold, he left his riches, corn, majesty, and kingdom; his army, grain, treasure, storehouse, town, seraglio, and subjects; he quitted and rejected his real, valuable property, such as riches, gold, precious stones, jewels, pearls, conches, stones, corals, rubies, &c.; he distributed presents through proper persons, he distributed presents among indigent persons. . . .

Then the Venerable Ascetic Mahâvîra—gazed on by a circle of thousands of eyes, praised by a circle of thousands of mouths, extolled by a circle of thousands of hearts, being the object of many thousands of wishes, desired because of his splendour, beauty, and virtues, pointed out by a circle of thousands of forefingers, answering with (a salam) of his right hand a circle of thousands of joined hands of thousands of men and women, passing along a row of thousands of palaces, greeted by sweet and delightful music, as beating of time, performance on the Vînâ, Tûrya, and the great drum, in which joined shouts of victory, and the low and pleasing murmur of the people; accompanied by all his pomp, all his splendour, all his army, all his train, by all his retinue, by all his magnificence, by all his grandeur, by all his ornaments, by all the tumult, by all the throng, by all subjects, by all actors, by all time-beaters, by the whole seraglio; adorned with flowers, scented robes, garlands, and ornaments, &c. which were accompanied at the same time by trumpets—went right through Kundapura to a park called the Shandavana of the Gñâtris and proceeded to the excellent tree Asoka. There under the excellent tree Asoka he caused his palankin to stop, descended from his palankin, took off his ornaments, garlands, and finery with his own hands, and with his own hands plucked out his hair in five handfuls. When the moon was in conjunction with the asterism Uttaraphalgunî, he, after fasting two and a half days without drinking water, put on a divine robe, and quite alone, nobody else being present, he tore out his hair and leaving the house entered the state of houselessness.

The Venerable Ascetic Mahâvîra for a year and a month wore clothes; after that time he walked about naked, and accepted the alms in the hollow of his hand. For more than twelve years the Venerable Ascetic Mahâvira neglected his body and abandoned the care of it; he with equanimity bore, underwent, and suffered all pleasant or unpleasant occurrences arising from divine powers, men, or animals. . . .

When the Venerable Ascetic Mahâvîra had become a Gina and Arhat, he was a Kevalin, omniscient and comprehending all objects; he knew and saw all conditions of the world, of gods, men, and demons: whence they come, whither they go, whether they are born as men or animals (kyavana) or become gods or hell-beings (upapâda), the ideas, the thoughts of their minds, the food, doings, desires, the open and secret deeds of all the living beings in the whole world; he the Arhat, for whom there is no secret, knew and saw all conditions of all living beings in the world, what they thought, spoke, or did at any moment. . . .

In that night in which the Venerable Ascetic Mahâvîra died, &c. freed from all pains, a great confusion and noise was originated by many descending and ascending gods.

In that night in which the Venerable Ascetic Mahâvîra died, &c. freed from all pains, his oldest disciple, the monk Indrabhûti of the Gautama gotra, cut asunder the tie of friendship which he had for his master, and obtained the highest knowledge and intuition, called Kevala, which is infinite, supreme, &c., complete, and full. . . .

The Venerable Ascetic Mahâvîra instituted two epochs in his capacity of a Maker of an end: the epoch relating to generations, and the epoch relating to psychical condition; in the third generation ended the former epoch, and in the fourth year of his Kevaliship the latter.

In that period, in that age the Venerable Ascetic Mahâvîra lived thirty years as a householder, more than full twelve years in a state inferior to perfection, something less than thirty years as a Kevalin, forty-two years as a monk, and seventy-two years on the whole. When his Karman which produces Vedanîya (or what one has to experience in this world), Âyus (length of life), name, and family, had been exhausted, when in this Avasarpinî era the greater part of the Duhshamasushamâ period had elapsed and only three years and eight and a half months were left, when the moon was in conjunction with the asterism Svâti, at the time of early morning, in the town of Pâpâ, and in king Hastipâla's office of the writers, (Mahâvîra) single and alone, sitting in the Samparyanka posture, reciting the fifty-five lectures which detail the results of Karman, and the thirty-six unasked questions, when he just explained the chief lecture (that of Marudeva) he died, &c. freed from all pains.

VI.2 Rules for Yatis

Source: *Jaina Sutras, Part 2*, trans. Hermann Jacobi, 1884, http://www.sacred-texts.com/jai/sbe22/sbe2291.htm

1. In that period, in that age the Venerable Ascetic Mahâvîra commenced the Paggusan when a month and twenty nights of the rainy season had elapsed.

"Why has it been said that the Venerable Ascetic Mahâvîra commenced the Paggusan when a month and twenty nights of the rainy season had elapsed?"

"Because at that time the lay people have usually matted their houses, whitewashed them, strewn

them (with straw), smeared them (with cowdung), levelled, smoothed, or perfumed them (or the floor of them), have dug gutters and drains, have furnished their houses, have rendered them comfortable, and have cleaned them. Hence it has been said that the Venerable Ascetic Mahâvîra commenced the Paggusan when a month and twenty nights of the rainy season had elapsed."

As the Venerable Ascetic Mahâvîra commenced the Paggusan when a month and twenty nights of the rainy season had elapsed, so the Ganadharas commenced the Paggusan when a month and twenty nights of the rainy season had elapsed. As the Ganadharas have done, so the disciples of the Ganadharas have done. As they have done, so the Sthaviras have done. As they have done, so do the Nirgrantha Sramanas of the present time.

As they do, so our masters, teachers, &c. do. As they do, so do we commence the Paggusan after a month and twenty nights of the rainy season have elapsed. It is allowed to commence the Paggusan earlier, but not after that time.

2. Monks or nuns during the Paggusan are allowed to regard their residence as extending a Yogana and a Krosa all around, and to live there for a moderate time.

3. During the Paggusan monks or nuns are allowed to go and return, for the sake of collecting alms, not farther than a Yogana and a Krosa (from their lodgings). If there is (in their way) an always flowing river which always contains water, they are not allowed to travel for a Yogana and a Krosa. But if the river is like the Erâvatî near Kunâlâ, such that it can be crossed by putting one foot in the water and keeping the other in the air, there it is allowed to travel for a Yogana and a Krosa. But where that is impossible, it is not allowed to travel for a Yogana and a Krosa.

4. During the Paggusan the Âkârya will say, "Give, Sir!" Then he is allowed to give (food to a sick brother), but not to accept himself. If the Âkârya says, "Accept, Sir!" then he is allowed to accept (food), but not to give. If the Âkârya says, "Give, Sir!

accept, Sir!" then the patient is allowed to give and to accept (food).

5. Monks or nuns who are hale and healthy, and of a strong body, are not allowed during the Paggusan frequently to take the following nine drinks: milk, thick sour milk, fresh butter, clarified butter, oil, sugar, honey, liquor, and meat.

6. During the Paggusan a collector of alms might ask (the Âkârya), "Sir, is (anything of the just-mentioned articles) required for the sick man?" he (the Âkârya) says, "Yes, it is." Then (the sick man) should be asked, "How much do you require?" The Âkârya says, "So much is required for the sick man: you must take so much as he told you." And he (the collector of alms) should beg, and begging he should accept (the required food). Having obtained the quantity ordered, he should say, "No more!" Perchance (the giver of food) might ask, "Why do you say so, Sir?" (Then he should answer), "Thus much is required for the sick man." Perchance, after that answer the other may say, "Take it, Sir! You may after (the sick man has got his share) eat it or drink it." Thus he is allowed to accept it, but he is not allowed to accept it by pretending that it is for the sick man.

7. In householders' families which are converted, devoted, staunch adherers (to the law), and honour, praise, and permit (the visits of monks), Sthaviras, during the Paggusan, are not allowed to ask, "Sir, have you got such or such a thing?" if they do not see it.

"Why, Sir, has this been said?" "Because a devout householder might buy it or steal it."

8. During the Paggusan a monk eats only one meal a day, and should at one fixed time frequent the abodes of householders for the sake of collecting alms, except when he does services for the Âkârya, the teacher, an ascetic, or a sick man, likewise if he or she be a novice who has not yet the marks of ripe age. To a monk who during the Paggusan eats only one meal on every second day, the following special rule applies. Having gone out in the morning, he should eat and drink his pure dinner, then

he should clean and rub his alms-bowl. If his dinner was sufficient, he should rest content with it for that day; if not, he is allowed for a second time to frequent the abodes of householders for the sake of collecting alms. A monk who during the Paggusan eats on every third day, is allowed twice to frequent the abodes of householders for the sake of collecting alms. A monk who during the Paggusan eats one meal on every fourth day, is allowed three times to frequent the abodes of householders for the sake of collecting alms. A monk who keeps still more protracted fasts, is allowed at all (four) times to frequent the abodes of householders for the sake of collecting alms. . . .

20. During the Paggusan monks or nuns are not allowed to be without their proper bed or bench. This is the reason: A mendicant whose bed and bench are not reserved for his own use, are low and rickety, not sufficiently fastened, without a fixed place, and never exposed to the sun, and who is not circumspect in what he does, nor accustomed to inspect and clean the things of his use, will find it difficult to exercise control; but on the contrary, control will be easy to him.

21. During the Paggusan monks or nuns must always inspect three spots where to ease nature; not so in the summer and winter, as in the rainy season. 'Why has this been said, Sir?' 'For in the rainy season living beings, grass, seeds, mildew, and sprouts frequently come forth.'

22. During the Paggusan monks or nuns must have three pots, one for ordure, one for urine, and a spitting-box. Monks and nuns, who wear after the Paggusan their hair as short as that of a cow, are not allowed to do so during the Paggusan after that night (of the fifth Bhâdrapada); but a monk should shave his head or pluck out his hair. Shaving with a razor every month, cutting with scissors every half-month, plucking out every six months. This is the conduct chiefly of Sthaviras during the rainy season.

23. During the Paggusan monks or nuns should not use harsh words after the commencement of the Paggusan; if they do, they should be warned, "Reverend

brother (or sister), you speak unmannerly." One who (nevertheless) uses harsh words after the commencement of the Paggusan, should be excluded from the community. . . .

Of those Nirgrantha monks who follow, &c. . . . these (rules regulating) the conduct of Sthaviras in the rainy season, some will reach perfection, &c. be freed from all pains in that same life, some in the next life, some in the third birth; none will have to undergo more than seven or eight births.

In that period, in that age the Venerable Ascetic Mahâvîra, in the town of Râgagríha, in the *Kaitya Gunasilaka*, surrounded by many monks and nuns, by many men and women of the laity, by many gods and goddesses, said thus, spoke thus, declared thus, explained thus; he proclaimed again and again the Lecture called Paryushanâkalpa with its application, with its argumentation, with its information, with its text, with its meaning, with both text and meaning, with the examination of the meaning.

Thus I say.

Key Terms

Digambara   ("Sky-clad") Members of a major sect of Jains who followed Mahavira in believing in the virtue of total nudity. Numerous in the warm south of India, they tend to wear robes in public.

Diwali   Festival of light celebrated by Hindus, Jains, and Sikhs. For Jains it is the beginning of a new ritual and commercial year and celebrates Mahavira's transcendence to *moksha* and the enlightenment of his disciple Gautama.

Jina   Also called "Tirthankaras" ("ford-makers"), Jinas ("conquerors") are Jain religious teachers who have attained enlightenment and omniscience by conquering samsara (the continuous cycle of birth, death, and rebirth to which those with karma are bound).

karma   The belief every action has inevitable consequences which attach themselves to the doer requiring reward or punishment. Karma is thus the moral law of cause and effect. It explains the inequalities of life as the consequences of actions in previous lives. The notion of karma probably developed among the Dravidian people of India. In Mahayana Buddhism the concept is transformed by the idea of the bodhisattva. Merit can be transferred by grace or faith, thus changing the person's karma.

moksha   Sanskrit word meaning liberation from the cycle of birth, death and rebirth. Permanent spiritual perfection experienced by an enlightened soul after the physical body has died. No further incarnations will be endured.

puja   ("Reverence") Refers particularly to temple worship in Hinduism, and to the keeping of rites and ceremonies prescribed by the Brahmans.

samsara   ("Stream of existence") Sanskrit word that refers to the cycle of birth and death followed by rebirth as applied both to individuals and to the universe itself.

Shvetambara   ("White-clad") Members of a major Jain sect who rejected the Digambaras' stress on the virtues of nudity. They are numerous in the north of India.

Questions for Study and Discussion

1. Name three significant differences between Digambara and Shvetambara Jainism.
2. What are the important characteristics of the *Tattvarthasutra*?
3. Name and describe two of the fourteen *gunasthanas*.
4. What specific aspects of the *puja* of eight substances demonstrate core spiritual and philosophical beliefs of Jainism?
5. Briefly explain the importance of ascetic communities to Jainism. How does this affect Jains living in the diaspora today?
6. Compare the Jain concept of karma to the Hindu concept of karma. Why is the idea of "good karma," which is part of Hindu belief, impossible from the Jain point of view?
7. In Samani Charitra Prajna's story ("I am a Jain," pp. 256–57), what elements of her religious beliefs and lifestyle seem to be closest to traditional Jainism? What evidence is there of the influence of the modern world on her beliefs or practices?

Questions for Reflection

Write your personal reflections on each of these questions in the space provided.

1. Describe how Jainism emerges from or is related to Hinduism. (See pp. 236–37.)

2. What do Jainism and Buddhism share as a religious ideal? (See p. 237.)

3. How is karma described or visualized? (See pp. 245–46.)

4. What concept or definition of god is absent in Jainism? (See pp. 246–47.)

5. Describe the similarities between Hinduism and Jainism and what they tell us about the historical relationship of religions.

Selected Online Resources

▶ Life of Lord Mahavir—virtual illustrated book with the story of Mahavira (also spelled "Mahavir"), created by the Jain Society of Ottawa-Carleton
http://jainoc.tripod.com/mahavir/mahavir.html

▶ Jainism Potpourri—featuring history, a glossary, and photographs
http://www.kamat.com/kalranga/jain/index.htm

▶ Jainism Global Resource Center—educational materials, e-books, discussion forum, and other resources in English from a Jain organization based in the United States
http://www.jainworld.com/

Part 7: Chinese Religions

Chapter Summaries

49. Chinese Religions: Sages and Immortals

Chinese religions developed in isolation, contributing to their unique features. During the Shang dynasty people used oracle bones to divine knowledge from the spirit world. The concept of the yin and yang probably evolved from the concern for the balance of nature, as did the Will of Heaven, or *t'ien-ming*.

Confucianism and Taoism can be seen as both philosophies and religions, since they include intellectual traditions as well as teachings and devotions. Confucianism, or *Ju*, is known for its moral philosophy, developed by great thinkers like Confucius and Mencius. The *Chung-yung*, a Confucian book, states that the sage becomes one with Heaven and Earth through realizing true integrity. Confucianism emphasizes ethical meaning in human relationships. Mencius proclaimed an inner doctrine revolving around human nature and the Way of Heaven.

Later developments in Confucianism led to pantheism and mystical ideas. Neo-Confucianism focused on achieving sagehood. Chu Hsi believed in a careful examination of ethical and spiritual states of the mind in order to perfect one's nature. Wang Yang-ming believed only the absolute unity of the person's mind with the mind of Tao would achieve sagehood.

The Taoist seeks fulfillment in contemplation of nature and transcendence of human limitations. Taoist religion, as opposed to the classical philosophy, developed a mystical tradition involving wonder-working immortals and esoteric teachings. The quest for freedom—from political constraints or from mortality itself—marks all Taoist sects. The Tao is all-embracing and includes all that changes as well as all that is unchanging.

Buddhism's entry into China influenced both Taoism and Confucianism. During the Ming dynasty many thinkers sought to harmonize the three great religions of China in one syncretic faith.

50. Christianity in Contemporary China

Chinese Christianity has undergone a process of indigenization (sinicization) that has embedded it within Chinese cultures and traditions. Under Communist rule Christian communities continued their worship practices even in isolation. In the post-Mao era Christianity remains strong, though somewhat influenced by globalization. State control has liberalized, and the official Three Self Church has flourished in both rural and urban areas.

Christianity came to China as early as 635 in the form of a Nestorian Christian community. The Jesuits brought scientific knowledge with them in the sixteenth century. In the nineteenth century missionaries were supported by imperial powers, while in the twentieth missionaries tended to be educators and medical care providers.

Today's Chinese churches are generally sanctioned by the government. Bibles are rare, as are trained clergy. Indigenous churches have sprung up and even spread beyond the country's boundaries.

Key Personalities

Confucius (551–479 BCE)

Chinese civil servant and administrator who became known as a teacher, opening his classes to everyone regardless of wealth or class. His teachings, especially the idea of Li, became the basis of a system of social ethics which greatly influenced Chinese society after his death.

"Confucius' social philosophy largely revolves around the concept of ren, 'compassion' or 'loving others.' Cultivating or practicing such concern for others involved deprecating oneself. . . . For Confucius, such concern for others is demonstrated through the practice of forms of the Golden Rule: "What you do not wish for yourself, do not do to others;" "Since you yourself desire standing then help others achieve it, since you yourself desire success then help others attain it." (Lunyu 12.2, 6.30). He regards devotion to parents and older siblings as the most basic form of promoting the interests of others before one's own and teaches that such altruism can be accomplished only by those who have learned self-discipline."

(Jeffrey Riegel, "Confucius," *Stanford Encyclopedia of Philosophy*, 2006, http://plato.stanford.edu/entries/confucius)

Mencius (370–286 BCE)

Confucian teacher who expanded and developed Confucius's teachings. He believed that the universe followed a moral order and that knowledge of this order could be attained by meditation.

"Mencius said, 'That whereby the superior man is distinguished from other men is what he preserves in his heart; namely, benevolence and propriety. The benevolent man loves others. The man of propriety shows respect to others. He who loves others is constantly loved by them. He who respects others is constantly respected by them. Here is a man, who treats me in a perverse and unreasonable manner. The superior man in such a case will turn and say to himself—"I must have been wanting in benevolence; I must have been wanting in propriety: how should this have happened to me?" He examines himself, and is specially benevolent. He turns to consider himself, and is specially observant of propriety. The perversity and unreasonableness of the other, however, are still the same. The superior man will again rebuke himself—"I must have been failing to do my utmost."'"

("Mencius," adapted from *The Chinese Classics*, vol. 2: *The Works of Mencius*, trans. James Legge [Oxford: Clarendon, 1895], http://www.humanistictexts.org/mencius.htm)

Hsün-tzu (third century BCE)

Chinese Confucian scholar who blended the philosophies of Confucianism and Taoism. He believed in the correct observance of ceremonial which helped to improve evil human nature. He was critical of superstition and reinterpreted popular religious practices in rationalistic terms.

Chu His (1130–1200)

Chinese philosopher who expounded a system rather similar to that of Plato. He believed that by quiet daily meditation one could see through diversity to the supreme reality behind all phenomena.

Lao-tzu

Traditionally the author of the *Tao Te Ching* and a contemporary of Confucius. His name means "old master," which could have applied to any wandering teacher.

The enlightened possess understanding
So profound they can not be understood.
Because they cannot be understood
I can only describe their appearance:
Cautious as one crossing thin ice,

Undecided as one surrounded by danger,
Modest as one who is a guest.
Unbounded as melting ice,
Genuine as unshaped wood,
Broad as a valley,
Seamless as muddy water.

Who stills the water that the mud may settle,
Who seeks to stop that he may travel on,
Who desires less than what may transpire,
Decays, but will not renew.

(*Tao Te Ching*, http://www.taoteching.org/chapters/15.htm)

Chuang-tzu (fourth and third centuries BCE)

Chinese Taoist teacher who commended a way of life according to nature which disregarded the conventions of Confucianism. His writings stress spiritual discipline that should lead to meditation on the formless Tao.

Primary Source Reading

Additional primary sources are available both in print and online, and students are encouraged to contact their instructors for further information.

VII.1 Book of Mencius (Confucianism)

Source: *Chinese Classics*, vol. 2, *The Works of Mencius*, trans. James Legge, 1895, http://www.sacred-texts.com/cfu/menc/index.htm

CHAPTER 6

1. Mencius said, 'He who, using force, makes a pretence to benevolence is the leader of the princes. A leader of the princes requires a large kingdom. He who, using virtue, practises benevolence is the sovereign of the kingdom. To become the sovereign of the kingdom, a prince need not wait for a large kingdom. T'ang did it with only seventy lî, and king Wan with only a hundred.

2. 'When one by force subdues men, they do not submit to him in heart. They submit, because their strength is not adequate to resist. When one subdues men by virtue, in their hearts' core they are pleased, and sincerely submit, as was the case with the seventy disciples in their submission to Confucius. What is said in the Book of Poetry,

"From the west, from the east,

From the south, from the north,

There was not one who thought of refusing submission,"

is an illustration of this.'

1. Mencius said, 'Benevolence brings glory to a prince, and the opposite of it brings disgrace. For the princes of the present day to hate disgrace and yet to live complacently doing what is not benevolent, is like hating moisture and yet living in a low situation.

2. 'If a prince hates disgrace, the best course for him to pursue, is to esteem virtue and honour virtuous scholars, giving the worthiest among them places of

dignity, and the able offices of trust. When throughout his kingdom there is leisure and rest from external troubles, let him, taking advantage of such a season, clearly digest the principles of his government with its legal sanctions, and then even great kingdoms will be constrained to stand in awe of him.

3. 'It is said in the Book of Poetry,

"Before the heavens were dark with rain,

I gathered the bark from the roots of the mulberry trees,

And wove it closely to form the window and door of my nest;

Now, I thought, ye people below,

Perhaps ye will not dare to insult me."

Confucius said, "Did not he who made this ode understand the way of governing?" If a prince is able rightly to govern his kingdom, who will dare to insult him?

4. 'But now the princes take advantage of the time when throughout their kingdoms there is leisure and rest from external troubles, to abandon themselves to pleasure and indolent indifference;—they in fact seek for calamities for themselves.

5. 'Calamity and happiness in all cases are men's own seeking.

6. 'This is illustrated by what is said in the Book of Poetry,—

Be always studious to be in harmony with the ordinances of God,

So you will certainly get for yourself much happiness;"

and by the passage of the Tâi Chiah,—"When Heaven sends down calamities, it is still possible to escape from them; when we occasion the calamities ourselves, it is not possible any longer to live."'

1. Mencius said, 'If a ruler give honour to men of talents and virtue and employ the able, so that offices shall all be filled by individuals of distinction and

mark;—then all the scholars of the kingdom will be pleased, and wish to stand in his court.

2. 'If, in the market-place of his capital, he levy a ground-rent on the shops but do not tax the goods, or enforce the proper regulations without levying a ground-rent;—then all the traders of the kingdom will be pleased, and wish to store their goods in his market-place.

3. 'If, at his frontier-passes, there be an inspection of persons, but no taxes charged on goods or other articles, then all the travellers of the kingdom will be pleased, and wish to make their tours on his roads.

4. 'If he require that the husbandmen give their mutual aid to cultivate the public field, and exact no other taxes from them;—then all the husbandmen of the kingdom will be pleased, and wish to plough in his fields.

5. 'If from the occupiers of the shops in his market-place he do not exact the fine of the individual idler, or of the hamlet's quota of cloth, then all the people of the kingdom will be pleased, and wish to come and be his people.

6. 'If a ruler can truly practise these five things, then the people in the neighbouring kingdoms will look up to him as a parent. From the first birth of mankind till now, never has any one led children to attack their parent, and succeeded in his design. Thus, such a ruler will not have an enemy in all the kingdom, and he who has no enemy in the kingdom is the minister of Heaven. Never has there been a ruler in such a case who did not attain to the royal dignity.'

1. Mencius said, 'All men have a mind which cannot bear to see the sufferings of others.

2. 'The ancient kings had this commiserating mind, and they, as a matter of course, had likewise a commiserating government. When with a commiserating mind was practised a commiserating government, to rule the kingdom was as easy a matter as to make anything go round in the palm.

3. 'When I say that all men have a mind which cannot bear to see the sufferings of others, my meaning

may be illustrated thus:—even now-a-days, if men suddenly see a child about to fall into a well, they will without exception experience a feeling of alarm and distress. They will feel so, not as a ground on which they may gain the favour of the child's parents, nor as a ground on which they may seek the praise of their neighbours and friends, nor from a dislike to the reputation of having been unmoved by such a thing.

4. 'From this case we may perceive that the feeling of commiseration is essential to man, that the feeling of shame and dislike is essential to man, that the feeling of modesty and complaisance is essential to man, and that the feeling of approving and disapproving is essential to man.

5. 'The feeling of commiseration is the principle of benevolence. The feeling of shame and dislike is the principle of righteousness. The feeling of modesty and complaisance is the principle of propriety. The feeling of approving and disapproving is the principle of knowledge.

6. 'Men have these four principles just as they have their four limbs. When men, having these four principles, yet say of themselves that they cannot develop them, they play the thief with themselves, and he who says of his prince that he cannot develop them plays the thief with his prince.

7. 'Since all men have these four principles in themselves, let them know to give them all their development and completion, and the issue will be like that of fire which has begun to burn, or that of a spring which has begun to find vent. Let them have their complete development, and they will suffice to love and protect all within the four seas. Let them be denied that development, and they will not suffice for a man to serve his parents with.'

1. Mencius said, 'Is the arrow-maker less benevolent than the maker of armour of defence? And yet, the arrow-maker's only fear is lest men should not be hurt, and the armour-maker's only fear is lest men should be hurt. So it is with the priest and the coffin-maker. The choice of a profession, therefore, is a thing in which great caution is required.

2. 'Confucius said, "It is virtuous manners which constitute the excellence of a neighbourhood. If a man, in selecting a residence, do not fix on one where such prevail, how can he be wise?" Now, benevolence is the most honourable dignity conferred by Heaven, and the quiet home in which man should dwell. Since no one can hinder us from being so, if yet we are not benevolent;—this is being not wise.

3. 'From the want of benevolence and the want of wisdom will ensue the entire absence of propriety and righteousness;—he who is in such a case must be the servant of other men. To be the servant of men and yet ashamed of such servitude, is like a bowmaker's being ashamed to make bows, or an arrow-maker's being ashamed to make arrows.

4. 'If he be ashamed of his case, his best course is to practise benevolence.

5. 'The man who would be benevolent is like the archer. The archer adjusts himself and then shoots. If he misses, he does not murmur against those who surpass himself. He simply turns round and seeks the cause of his failure in himself.'

1. Mencius said, 'When any one told Tsze-lû that he had a fault, he rejoiced.

2. 'When Yü heard good words, he bowed to the speaker.

3. 'The great Shun had a still greater delight in what was good. He regarded virtue as the common property of himself and others, giving up his own way to follow that of others, and delighting to learn from others to practise what was good.

4. 'From the time when he ploughed and sowed, exercised the potter's art, and was a fisherman, to the time when he became emperor, he was continually learning from others.

5. 'To take example from others to practise virtue, is to help them in the same practice. Therefore, there is no attribute of the superior man greater than his helping men to practise virtue.'

1. Mencius said, 'Po-î would not serve a prince whom he did not approve, nor associate with a friend whom he did not esteem. He would not stand in a bad prince's court, nor speak with a bad man. To stand in a bad prince's court, or to speak with a bad man, would have been to him the same as to sit with his court robes and court cap amid mire and ashes. Pursuing the examination of his dislike to what was evil, we find that he thought it necessary, if he happened to be standing with a villager whose cap was not rightly adjusted, to leave him with a high air, as if he were going to be defiled. Therefore, although some of the princes made application to him with very proper messages, he would not receive their gifts.—He would not receive their gifts, counting it inconsistent with his purity to go to them.

2. 'Hûi of Liû-hsiâ was not ashamed to serve an impure prince, nor did he think it low to be an inferior officer. When advanced to employment, he did not conceal his virtue, but made it a point to carry out his principles. When neglected and left without office, he did not murmur. When straitened by poverty, he did not grieve. Accordingly, he had a saying, "You are you, and I am I. Although you stand by my side with breast and aims bare, or with your body naked, how can you defile me?" Therefore, self-possessed, he companied with men indifferently, at the same time not losing himself. When he wished to leave, if pressed to remain in office, he would remain.—He would remain in office, when pressed to do so, not counting it required by his purity to go away.'

3. Mencius said, 'Po-î was narrow-minded, and Hûi of Liû-hsiâ was wanting in self-respect. The superior man will not manifest either narrow-mindedness, or the want of self-respect.'

Chapter 13

1. Mencius said, 'The power of vision of Lî Lâu, and skill of hand of Kung-shû, without the compass and square, could not form squares and circles. The acute ear of the music-master K'wang, without the pitch-tubes, could not determine correctly the five notes. The principles of Yâo and Shun, without a benevolent government, could not secure the tranquil order of the kingdom.

2. 'There are now princes who have benevolent hearts and a reputation for benevolence, while yet the people do not receive any benefits from them, nor will they leave any example to future ages;—all because they do not put into practice the ways of the ancient kings.

3. 'Hence we have the saying:—"Virtue alone is not sufficient for the exercise of government; laws alone cannot carry themselves into practice."

4. It is said in the Book of Poetry,

"Without transgression, without forgetfulness,

Following the ancient statutes."

Never has any one fallen into error, who followed the laws of the ancient kings.

5. 'When the sages had used the vigour of their eyes, they called in to their aid the compass, the square, the level, and the line, to make things square, round, level, and straight:—the use of the instruments is inexhaustible. When they had used their power of hearing to the utmost, they called in the pitch-tubes to their aid to determine the five notes:—the use of those tubes is inexhaustible. When they had exerted to the utmost the thoughts of their hearts, they called in to their aid a government that could not endure to witness the sufferings of men:—and their benevolence overspread the kingdom.

6. 'Hence we have the saying:—"To raise a thing high, we must begin from the top of a mound or a hill; to dig to a great depth, we must commence in the low ground of a stream or a marsh." Can he be pronounced wise, who, in the exercise of government, does not proceed according to the ways of the former kings?

7. 'Therefore only the benevolent ought to be in high stations. When a man destitute of benevolence is in a high station, he thereby disseminates his wickedness among all below him.

8. 'When the prince has no principles by which he examines his administration, and his ministers have no laws by which they keep themselves in the discharge of their duties, then in the court obedience is not paid to principle, and in the office obedience is not paid to rule. Superiors violate the laws of righteousness, and inferiors violate the penal laws. It is only by a fortunate chance that a State in such a case is preserved.

9. 'Therefore it is said, "It is not the exterior and interior walls being incomplete, and the supply of weapons offensive and defensive not being large, which constitutes the calamity of a kingdom. It is not the cultivable area not being extended, and stores and wealth not being accumulated, which occasions the ruin of a State." When superiors do not observe the rules of propriety, and inferiors do not learn, then seditious people spring up, and that State will perish in no time.

10. 'It is said in the Book of Poetry,

"When such an overthrow of Châu is being produced by Heaven,

Be not ye so much at your ease!"

11. '"At your ease;"—that is, dilatory.

12. 'And so dilatory may those officers be deemed, who serve their prince without righteousness, who take office and retire from it without regard to propriety, and who in their words disown the ways of the ancient kings.

13. 'Therefore it is said, "To urge one's sovereign to difficult achievements may be called showing respect for him. To set before him what is good and repress his perversities may be called showing reverence for him. He who does not do these things, saying to himself,—My sovereign is incompetent to this, may be said to play the thief with him."'

1. Mencius said, 'The compass and square produce perfect circles and squares. By the sages, the human relations are perfectly exhibited.

2. 'He who as a sovereign would perfectly discharge the duties of a sovereign, and he who as a minister would perfectly discharge the duties of a minister, have only to imitate—the one Yâo, and the other Shun. He who does not serve his sovereign as Shun served Yâo, does not respect his sovereign; and he who does not rule his people as Yâo ruled his, injures his people.

3. 'Confucius said, "There are but two courses, which can be pursued, that of virtue and its opposite."

4. 'A ruler who carries the oppression of his people to the highest pitch, will himself be slain, and his kingdom will perish. If one stop short of the highest pitch, his life will notwithstanding be in danger, and his kingdom will be weakened. He will be styled "The Dark," or "The Cruel," and though he may have filial sons and affectionate grandsons, they will not be able in a hundred generations to change the designation.

5. 'This is what is intended in the words of the Book of Poetry,

"The beacon of Yin is not remote,

It is in the time of the (last) sovereign of Hsiâ."'

1. Mencius said, 'It was by benevolence that the three dynasties gained the throne, and by not being benevolent that they lost it.

2. 'It is by the same means that the decaying and flourishing, the preservation and perishing, of States are determined.

3. 'If the sovereign be not benevolent, be cannot preserve the throne from passing from him. If the Head of a State be not benevolent, he cannot preserve his rule. If a high noble or great officer be not benevolent, he cannot preserve his ancestral temple. If a scholar or common man be not benevolent, be cannot preserve his four limbs.

4. 'Now they hate death and ruin, and yet delight in being not benevolent;—this is like hating to be drunk, and yet being strong to drink wine!

1. Mencius said, 'If a man love others, and no responsive attachment is shown to him, let him turn inwards and examine his own benevolence. If he is trying to rule others, and his government is unsuccessful, let him turn inwards and examine his wisdom. If he treats others politely, and they do not return his politeness, let him turn inwards and examine his own feeling of respect.

2. 'When we do not, by what we do, realise what we desire, we must turn inwards, and examine ourselves in every point. When a man's person is correct, the whole kingdom will turn to him with recognition and submission.

3. 'It is said in the Book of Poetry,

"Be always studious to be in harmony with the ordinances of God,

And you will obtain much happiness." '

Mencius said, 'People have this common saying,— "The kingdom, the State, the family." The root of the kingdom is in the State. The root of the State is in the family. The root of the family is in the person of its Head.'

Mencius said, 'The administration of government is not difficult;—it lies in not offending the great families. He whom the great families affect, will be affected by the whole State; and he whom any one State affects, will be affected by the whole kingdom. When this is the case, such an one's virtue and teachings will spread over all within the four seas like the rush of water.'

1. Mencius said, 'When right government prevails in the kingdom, princes of little virtue are submissive to those of great, and those of little worth to those of great. When bad government prevails in the kingdom, princes of small power are submissive to those of great, and the weak to the strong. Both these cases are the rule of Heaven. They who accord with Heaven are preserved, and they who rebel against Heaven perish.

2. 'The duke Ching of Ch'î said, "Not to be able to command others, and at the same time to refuse to

receive their commands, is to cut one's self off from all intercourse with others." His tears flowed forth while he gave his daughter to be married to the prince of Wû.

3. 'Now the small States imitate the large, and yet are ashamed to receive their commands. This is like a scholar's being ashamed to receive the commands of his master.

4. 'For a prince who is ashamed of this, the best plan is to imitate king Wan. Let one imitate king Wan, and in five years, if his State be large, or in seven years, if it be small, he will be sure to give laws to the kingdom.

5. 'It is said in the Book of Poetry,

"The descendants of the sovereigns of the Shang dynasty,

Are in number more than hundreds of thousands,

But, God having passed His decree,

They are all submissive to Châu.

They are submissive to Châu,

Because the decree of Heaven is not unchanging.

The officers of Yin, admirable and alert,

Pour out the libations, and assist in the capital of Châu."

Confucius said, "As against so benevolent a sovereign, they could not be deemed a multitude." Thus, if the prince of a state love benevolence, he will have no opponent in all the kingdom.

6. 'Now they wish to have no opponent in all the kingdom, but they do not seek to attain this by being benevolent. This is like a man laying hold of a heated substance, and not having first dipped it in water. It is said in the Book of Poetry,

"Who can take up a heated substance,

Without first dipping it (in water)?" '

1. Mencius said, 'How is it possible to speak with those princes who are not benevolent ? Their perils

they count safety, their calamities they count profitable, and they have pleasure in the things by which they perish. If it were possible to talk with them who so violate benevolence, how could we have such destruction of States and ruin of Families?

2. 'There was a boy singing,

"When the water of the Ts'ang-lang is clear,

It does to wash the strings of my cap;

When the water of the Ts'ang-lang is muddy,

It does to wash my feet."

3. 'Confucius said, "Hear what he sings, my children. When clear, then he will wash his cap-strings; and when muddy, he will wash his feet with it. This different application is brought by the water on itself."

4. 'A man must first despise himself, and then others will despise him. A family must first destroy itself, and then others will destroy it. A State must first smite itself, and then others will smite it.

5. 'This is illustrated in the passage of the T'âi Chiâ, "When Heaven sends down calamities, it is still possible to escape them. When we occasion the calamities ourselves, it is not possible any longer to live."'

1. Mencius said, 'Chieh and Châu's losing the throne, arose from their losing the people, and to lose the people means to lose their hearts. There is a way to get the kingdom:—get the people, and the kingdom is got. There is a way to get the people:—get their hearts, and the people are got. There is a way to get their hearts:—it is simply to collect for them what they like, and not to lay on them what they dislike.

2. 'The people turn to a benevolent rule as water flows downwards, and as wild beasts fly to the wilderness.

3. 'Accordingly, as the otter aids the deep waters, driving the fish into them, and the hawk aids the thickets, driving the little birds to them, so Chieh and Châu aided T'ang and Wû, driving the people to them.

4. 'If among the present rulers of the kingdom, there were one who loved benevolence, all the other princes would aid him, by driving the people to him. Although he wished not to become sovereign, he could not avoid becoming so.

5. 'The case of one of the present princes wishing to become sovereign is like the having to seek for mugwort three years old, to cure a seven years' sickness. If it have not been kept in store, the patient may all his life not get it. If the princes do not set their wills on benevolence, all their days will be in sorrow and disgrace, and they will be involved in death and ruin.

6. 'This is illustrated by what is said in the Book of Poetry,

"How otherwise can you improve the kingdom?

You will only with it go to ruin."'

1. Mencius said, 'With those who do violence to themselves, it is impossible to speak. With those who throw themselves away, it is impossible to do anything. To disown in his conversation propriety and righteousness, is what we mean by doing violence to one's self. To say—"I am not able to dwell in benevolence or pursue the path of righteousness," is what we mean by throwing one's self away.

2. 'Benevolence is the tranquil habitation of man, and righteousness is his straight path.

3. 'Alas for them, who leave the tranquil dwelling empty and do not reside in it, and who abandon the right path and do not pursue it?'

CHAPTER 21

1. The philosopher Kâo said, 'Man's nature is like the ch'î-willow, and righteousness is like a cup or a bowl. The fashioning benevolence and righteousness out of man's nature is like the making cups and bowls from the ch'î-willow.'

2. Mencius replied, 'Can you, leaving untouched the nature of the willow, make with it cups and bowls? You must do violence and injury to the willow, before you can make cups and bowls with it. If you must do violence and injury to the willow in order to make cups and bowls with it, on your principles you must

in the same way do violence and injury to humanity in order to fashion from it benevolence and righteousness! Your words, alas! would certainly lead all men on to reckon benevolence and righteousness to be calamities.'

1. The philosopher Kâo said, 'Man's nature is like water whirling round in a corner. Open a passage for it to the east, and it will flow to the east; open a passage for it to the west, and it will flow to the west. Man's nature is indifferent to good and evil, just as the water is indifferent to the east and west.'

2. Mencius replied, 'Water indeed will flow indifferently to the east or west, but will it flow indifferently up or down? The tendency of man's nature to good is like the tendency of water to flow downwards. There are none but have this tendency to good, just as all water flows downwards.

3. 'Now by striking water and causing it to leap up, you may make it go over your forehead, and, by damming and leading it you may force it up a hill;—but are such movements according to the nature of water? It is the force applied which causes them. When men are made to do what is not good, their nature is dealt with in this way.'

1. The philosopher Kâo said, 'Life is what we call nature!'

2. Mencius asked him, 'Do you say that by nature you mean life, just as you say that white is white?' 'Yes, I do,' was the reply. Mencius added, 'Is the whiteness of a white feather like that of white snow, and the whiteness of white snow like that of white jade?' Kâo again said 'Yes.'

3. 'Very well,' pursued Mencius. 'Is the nature of a dog like the nature of an ox, and the nature of an ox like the nature of a man?'

1. The philosopher Kâo said, 'To enjoy food and delight in colours is nature. Benevolence is internal and not external; righteousness is external and not internal.'

2. Mencius asked him, 'What is the ground of your saying that benevolence is internal and righteousness

external?' He replied, 'There is a man older than I, and I give honour to his age. It is not that there is first in me a principle of such reverence to age. It is just as when there is a white man, and I consider him white; according as he is so externally to me. On this account, I pronounce of righteousness that it is external.'

3. Mencius said, 'There is no difference between our pronouncing a white horse to be white and our pronouncing a white man to be white. But is there no difference between the regard with which we acknowledge the age of an old horse and that with which we acknowledge the age of an old man? And what is it which is called righteousness?—the fact of a man's being old? or the fact of our giving honour to his age?'

4. Kâo said, 'There is my younger brother;—I love him. But the younger brother of a man of Ch'in I do not love: that is, the feeling is determined by myself, and therefore I say that benevolence is internal. On the other hand, I give honour to an old man of Ch'û, and I also give honour to an old man of my own people: that is, the feeling is determined by the age, and therefore I say that righteousness is external.'

5. Mencius answered him, 'Our enjoyment of meat roasted by a man of Ch'in does not differ from our enjoyment of meat roasted by ourselves. Thus, what you insist on takes place also in the case of such things, and will you say likewise that our enjoyment of a roast is external?'

1. The disciple Mang Chî asked Kung-tû, saying, 'On what ground is it said that righteousness is internal?'

2. Kung-tû replied, 'We therein act out our feeling of respect, and therefore it is said to be internal.'

3. The other objected, 'Suppose the case of a villager older than your elder brother by one year, to which of them would you show the greater respect?' 'To my brother,' was the reply. 'But for which of them would you first pour out wine at a feast?' 'For the villager.' Mang Chî argued, 'Now your feeling of reverence rests on the one, and now the honour due to age is rendered to the other;—this is certainly determined

by what is without, and does not proceed from within.'

4. Kung-tû was unable to reply, and told the conversation to Mencius. Mencius said, 'You should ask him, "Which do you respect most,—your uncle, or your younger brother?" He will answer, "My uncle." Ask him again, "If your younger brother be personating a dead ancestor, to which do you show the greater respect,—to him or to your uncle?" He will say, "To my younger brother." You can go on, "But where is the respect due, as you said, to your uncle?" He will reply to this, "I show the respect to my younger brother, because of the position which he occupies," and you can likewise say, "So my respect to the villager is because of the position which he occupies. Ordinarily, my respect is rendered to my elder brother; for a brief season, on occasion, it is rendered to the villager." '

5. Mang Chî heard this and observed, 'When respect is due to my uncle, I respect him, and when respect is due to my younger brother, I respect him;—the thing is certainly determined by what is without, and does not proceed from within.' Kung-tû replied, 'In winter we drink things hot, in summer we drink things cold; and so, on your principle, eating and drinking also depend on what is external!'

1. The disciple Kung-tû said, 'The philosopher Kâo says, "Man's nature is neither good nor bad."

2. 'Some say, "Man's nature may be made to practise good, and it may be made to practise evil, and accordingly, under Wan and Wû, the people loved what was good, while under Yû and Lî, they loved what was cruel."

3. 'Some say, "The nature of some is good, and the nature of others is bad. Hence it was that under such a sovereign as Yâo there yet appeared Hsiang; that with such a father as Kû-sâu there yet appeared Shun; and that with Châu for their sovereign, and the son of their elder brother besides, there were found Ch'î, the viscount of Wei, and the prince Pî-Kan.

4. 'And now you say, "The nature is good." Then are all those wrong?'

5. Mencius said, 'From the feelings proper to it, it is constituted for the practice of what is good. This is what I mean in saying that the nature is good.

6. 'If men do what is not good, the blame cannot be imputed to their natural powers.

7. 'The feeling of commiseration belongs to all men; so does that of shame and dislike; and that of reverence and respect; and that of approving and disapproving. The feeling of commiseration implies the principle of benevolence; that of shame and dislike, the principle of righteousness; that of reverence and respect, the principle of propriety; and that of approving and disapproving, the principle of knowledge. Benevolence, righteousness, propriety, and knowledge are not infused into us from without. We are certainly furnished with them. And a different view is simply owing to want of reflection. Hence it is said, "Seek and you will find them. Neglect and you will lose them." Men differ from one another in regard to them;—some as much again as others, some five times as much, and some to an incalculable amount:—it is because they cannot carry out fully their natural powers.

8. 'It is said in the Book of Poetry,

"Heaven in producing mankind,

Gave them their various faculties and relations with their specific laws.

These are the invariable rules of nature for all to hold,

And all love this admirable virtue."

Confucius said, "The maker of this ode knew indeed the principle of our nature!" We may thus see that every faculty and relation must have its law, and since there are invariable rules for all to hold, they consequently love this admirable virtue.'

1. Mencius said, 'In good years the children of the people are most of them good, while in bad years the most of them abandon themselves to evil. It is not owing to any difference of their natural powers conferred by Heaven that they are thus different. The

abandonment is owing to the circumstances through which they allow their minds to be ensnared and drowned in evil.

2. 'There now is barley.—Let it be sown and covered up; the ground being the same, and the time of sowing likewise the same, it grows rapidly up, and, when the full time is come, it is all found to be ripe. Although there may be inequalities of produce, that is owing to the difference of the soil, as rich or poor, to the unequal nourishment afforded by the rains and dews, and to the different ways in which man has performed his business in reference to it.

3. 'Thus all things which are the same in kind are like to one another;—why should we doubt in regard to man, as if he were a solitary exception to this? The sage and we are the same in kind.

4. 'In accordance with this the scholar Lung said, "If a man make hempen sandals without knowing the size of people's feet, yet I know that he will not make them like baskets." Sandals are all like one another, because all men's feet are like one another.

5. 'So with the mouth and flavours;—all mouths have the same relishes. Yî-yâ only apprehended before me what my mouth relishes. Suppose that his mouth in its relish for flavours differed from that of other men, as is the case with dogs or horses which are not the same in kind with us, why should all men be found following Yî-yâ in their relishes? In the matter of tastes all the people model themselves after Yî-yâ; that is, the mouths of all men are like one another.

6. 'And so also it is with the ear. In the matter of sounds, the whole people model themselves after the music-master K'wang; that is, the ears of all men are like one another.

7. 'And so also it is with the eye. In the case of Tsze-tû, there is no man but would recognise that he was beautiful. Any one who would not recognise the beauty of Tsze-tû must have no eyes.

8. 'Therefore I say,—Men's mouths agree in having the same relishes; their ears agree in enjoying the same sounds; their eyes agree in recognising the same beauty:—shall their minds alone be without that which the similarly approve? What is it then of which they similarly approve? It is, I say, the principles of our nature, and the determinations of righteousness. The sages only apprehended before me that of which my mind approves along with other men. Therefore the principles of our nature and the determinations of righteousness are agreeable to my mind, just as the flesh of grass and grain-fed animals is agreeable to my mouth.'

1. Mencius said, 'The trees of the Niû mountain were once beautiful. Being situated, however, in the borders of a large State, they were hewn down with axes and bills;—and could they retain their beauty? Still through the activity of the vegetative life day and night, and the nourishing influence of the rain and dew, they were not without buds and sprouts springing forth, but then came the cattle and goats and browsed upon them. To these things is owing the bare and stripped appearance of the mountain, and when people now see it, they think it was never finely wooded. But is this the nature of the mountain?

2. 'And so also of what properly belongs to man;—shall it be said that the mind of any man was without benevolence and righteousness? The way in which a man loses his proper goodness of mind is like the way in which the trees are denuded by axes and bills. Hewn down day after day, can it—the mind—retain its beauty? But there is a development of its life day and night, and in the calm air of the morning, just between night and day, the mind feels in a degree those desires and aversions which are proper to humanity, but the feeling is not strong, and it is fettered and destroyed by what takes place during the day. This fettering taking place again and again, the restorative influence of the night is not sufficient to preserve the proper goodness of the mind; and when this proves insufficient for that purpose, the nature becomes not much different from that of the irrational animals, and when people now see it, they think that it never had those powers which I assert. But does this condition represent the feelings proper to humanity?

3. 'Therefore, if it receive its proper nourishment, there is nothing which will not grow. If it lose its proper nourishment, there is nothing which will not decay away.

4. 'Confucius said, "Hold it fast, and it remains with you. Let it go, and you lose it. Its outgoing and incoming cannot be defined as to time or place." It is the mind of which this is said!'

CHAPTER 25

1. Mencius said, 'He who has exhausted all his mental constitution knows his nature. Knowing his nature, he knows Heaven.

2. 'To preserve one's mental constitution, and nourish one's nature, is the way to serve Heaven.

3. 'When neither a premature death nor long life causes a man any double-mindedness, but he waits in the cultivation of his personal character for whatever issue;—this is the way in which he establishes his Heaven-ordained being.'

1. Mencius said, 'There is an appointment for everything. A man should receive submissively what may be correctly ascribed thereto.

2. 'Therefore, he who has the true idea of what is Heaven's appointment will not stand beneath a precipitous wall.

3. 'Death sustained in the discharge of one's duties may correctly be ascribed to the appointment of Heaven.

4. 'Death under handcuffs and fetters cannot correctly be so ascribed.'

1. Mencius said, 'When we get by our seeking and lose by our neglecting;—in that case seeking is of use to getting, and the things sought for are those which are in ourselves.

2. 'When the seeking is according to the proper course, and the getting is only as appointed;—in that case the seeking is of no use to getting, and the things sought are without ourselves.'

1. Mencius said, 'All things are already complete in us.

2. 'There is no greater delight than to be conscious of sincerity on self-examination.

3. 'If one acts with a vigorous effort at the law of reciprocity, when he seeks for the realization of perfect virtue, nothing can be closer than his approximation to it.'

2. 'Those who form contrivances and versatile schemes distinguished for their artfulness, do not allow their sense of shame to come into action.

3. 'When one differs from other men in not having this sense of shame, what will he have in common with them?'

Mencius said, 'The able and virtuous monarchs of antiquity loved virtue and forgot their power. And shall an exception be made of the able and virtuous scholars of antiquity, that they did not do the same? They delighted in their own principles, and were oblivious of the power of princes. Therefore, if kings and dukes did not show the utmost respect, and observe all forms of ceremony, they were not permitted to come frequently and visit them. If they thus found it not in their power to pay them frequent visits, how much less could they get to employ them as ministers?'

1. Mencius said to Sung Kâu-ch'ien, 'Are you fond, Sir, of travelling to the different courts? I will tell you about such travelling.

2. 'If a prince acknowledge you and follow your counsels, be perfectly satisfied. If no one do so, be the same.'

3. Kâu-ch'ien said, 'What is to be done to secure this perfect satisfaction?' Mencius replied, 'Honour virtue and delight in righteousness, and so you may always be perfectly satisfied.

4. 'Therefore, a scholar, though poor, does not let go his righteousness; though prosperous, he does not leave his own path.

5. 'Poor and not letting righteousness go;—it is thus that the scholar holds possession of himself. Prosperous and not leaving the proper path;—it is thus that the expectations of the people from him are not disappointed.

6. 'When the men of antiquity realized their wishes, benefits were conferred by them on the people. If they did not realize their wishes, they cultivated their personal character, and became illustrious in the world. If poor, they attended to their own virtue in solitude; if advanced to dignity, they made the whole kingdom virtuous as well.'

Mencius said, 'The mass of men wait for a king Wan, and then they will receive a rousing impulse. Scholars distinguished from the mass, without a king Wan, rouse themselves.'

Mencius said, 'Add to a man the families of Han and Wei. If he then look upon himself without being elated, he is far beyond the mass of men.'

Mencius said, 'Let the people be employed in the way which is intended to secure their ease, and though they be toiled, they will not murmur. Let them be put to death in the way which is intended to preserve their lives, and though they die, they will not murmur at him who puts them to death.'

1. Mencius said, 'Under a chief, leading all the princes, the people look brisk and cheerful. Under a true sovereign, they have an air of deep contentment.

2. 'Though he slay them, they do not murmur. When he benefits them, they do not think of his merit. From day to day they make progress towards what is good, without knowing who makes them do so.

3. 'Wherever the superior man passes through, transformation follows; wherever he abides, his influence is of a spiritual nature. It flows abroad, above and beneath, like that of Heaven and Earth. How can it be said that he mends society but in a small way!'

1. Mencius said, 'Kindly words do not enter so deeply into men as a reputation for kindness.

2. 'Good government does not lay hold of the people so much as good instructions.

3. 'Good government is feared by the people, while good instructions are loved by them. Good government gets the people's wealth, while good instructions get their hearts.'

1. Mencius said, 'The ability possessed by men without having been acquired by learning is intuitive ability, and the knowledge possessed by them without the exercise of thought is their intuitive knowledge.

2. 'Children carried in the arms all know to love their parents, and when they are grown a little, they all know to love their elder brothers.

3. 'Filial affection for parents is the working of benevolence. Respect for elders is the working of righteousness. There is no other reason for those feelings;—they belong to all under heaven.'

Mencius said, 'When Shun was living amid the deep retired mountains, dwelling with the trees and rocks, and wandering among the deer and swine, the difference between him and the rude inhabitants of those remote hills appeared very small. But when he heard a single good word, or saw a single good action, he was like a stream or a river bursting its banks, and flowing out in an irresistible flood.'

2. 'They are the friendless minister and concubine's son, who keep their hearts under a sense of peril, and use deep precautions against calamity. On this account they become distinguished for their intelligence.'

2. 'There are ministers who seek the tranquility of the State, and find their pleasure in securing that tranquility.

3. 'There are those who are the people of Heaven. They, judging that, if they were in office, they could carry out their principles, throughout the kingdom, proceed so to carry them out.

4. 'There are those who are great men. They rectify themselves and others are rectified.'

2. 'That his father and mother are both alive, and that the condition of his brothers affords no cause for anxiety;—this is one delight.

3. 'That, when looking up, he has no occasion for shame before Heaven, and, below, he has no occasion to blush before men;—this is a second delight.

4. 'That he can get from the whole kingdom the most talented individuals, and teach and nourish them;—this is the third delight.

5. 'The superior man has three things in which he delights, and to be ruler over the kingdom is not one of them.'

1. Mencius said, 'Wide territory and a numerous people are desired by the superior man, but what he delights in is not here.

2. 'To stand in the centre of the kingdom, and tranquillize the people within the four seas;—the superior man delights in this, but the highest enjoyment of his nature is not here.

3. What belongs by his nature to the superior man cannot be increased by the largeness of his sphere of action, nor diminished by his dwelling in poverty and retirement;—for this reason that it is determinately apportioned to him by Heaven.

4. 'What belongs by his nature to the superior man are benevolence, righteousness, propriety, and knowledge. These are rooted in his heart; their growth and manifestation are a mild harmony appearing in the countenance, a rich fullness in the back, and the character imparted to the four limbs. Those limbs understand to arrange themselves, without being told.'

1. Mencius said, 'Po-î, that he might avoid Châu, was dwelling on the coast of the northern sea when he heard of the rise of king Wan. He roused himself and said, "Why should I not go and follow him? I have heard that the chief of the West knows well how to nourish the old." T'âi-kung, to avoid Châu, was dwelling on the coast of the eastern sea. When he heard of the rise of king Wan, he said, "Why should I not go and follow him? I have heard that the chief of the West knows well how to nourish the old." If there were a prince in the kingdom, who knew well how to nourish the old, all men of virtue would feel that he was the proper object for them to gather to.

2. 'Around the homestead with its five mâu, the space beneath the walls was planted with mulberry trees, with which the women nourished silkworms, and thus the old were able to have silk to wear. Each family had five brood hens and two brood sows, which were kept to their breeding seasons, and thus the old were able to have flesh to eat. The husbandmen cultivated their farms of 100 mâu, and thus their families of eight mouths were secured against want.

3. 'The expression, "The chief of the West knows well how to nourish the old," refers to his regulation of the fields and dwellings, his teaching them to plant the mulberry and nourish those animals, and his instructing the wives and children, so as to make them nourish their aged. At fifty, warmth cannot be maintained without silks, and at seventy flesh is necessary to satisfy the appetite. Persons not kept warm nor supplied with food are said to be starved and famished, but among the people of king Wan, there were no aged who were starved or famished. This is the meaning of the expression in question.'

1. Mencius said, 'Let it be seen to that their fields of grain and hemp are well cultivated, and make the taxes on them light;—so the people may be made rich.

2. 'Let it be seen to that the people use their resources of food seasonably, and expend their wealth only on the prescribed ceremonies:—so their wealth will be more than can be consumed.

3. 'The people cannot live without water and fire, yet if you knock at a man's door in the dusk of the evening, and ask for water and fire, there is no man who will not give them, such is the abundance of these things. A sage governs the kingdom so as to cause pulse and grain to be as abundant as water and fire. When pulse and grain are as abundant as water and fire, how shall the people be other than virtuous?'

Key Terms

Confucianism   The system of social ethics taught by Confucius and given imperial recognition in China in the second century CE. Opinion is divided on whether or not Confucianism should be regarded as a religion.

Taoism   Chinese philosophy outlined in the Tao Te Ching. Its aim is to achieve harmony with all that is by pursuing inaction and effortlessness. Taoism gradually evolved an elaborate mythological system and incorporated notions of spirit possession, alchemy and divination.

Yin and Yang   The polarity of energies in Chinese philosophy. Yang is masculine, dynamic, bright and good; yin is feminine, passive, dark and bad. Their production and interplay is represented in a circular diagram. *Yin* and *yang* produce the elements and the cycle of the seasons. They also provided the theoretical basis for the Taoist practice of alchemy

Nestorianism   Christian movement that claimed that two separate persons, human and divine, existed in the incarnate Christ (as opposed to the orthodox view that God assumed human nature as one person in Christ). Although condemned in 431 CE it continued to flourish in Persia. A few groups of Nestorians survive in the present day.

Questions for Study and Discussion

1. Briefly describe Mencius's and Hsün-tzu's contributions to Confucianism.
2. Compare one of the quotations from a Confucian (such as Chu Hsi, p. 267) with a Taoist quotation (such as one on p. 270). What marks each as coming from its particular tradition? Are there any common assumptions or values that are demonstrated by both texts?
3. Define "sincization," and explain its significance.
4. What is the Three Self Policy? How does it affect Christianity's presence in China?

Questions for Reflection

Write your personal reflections to each of these questions in the space provided.

1. How was divination expressed in ancient China? (See p. 262.)

2. Explain *chia* and *chiao* in Chinese thought and religion using the theories from Part 1. (See p. 263.)

3. Confucianism emphasizes the "ethical meaning of human relationships." Discuss how this is religious. (See p. 264.)

4. The emphasis in Taoism is different from that in Confucianism. Elaborate. (See pp. 270–71.)

5. Compare the role of ancestors in indigenous religions (or the role of Christian saints) with the role of ancestors in Chinese religions. (See p. 274.)

Selected Online Resources

▶ Confucius Publishing: English—a selection of texts translated into English; the website also provides translations in over twenty other languages
http://www.confucius.org/maine.htm

▶ Tao Te Ching—multiple translations with commentaries
http://www.centertao.org/tao-te-ching/

▶ Christians in China—personal accounts of the experiences of Christians living in China, including photos and video
http://www.christiansinchina.com/

Part 8: Korean and Japanese Religions

Chapter Summaries

51. Sinkyo: Korea's Traditional Religion

Called "the religion without a name," Sinkyo is a way of seeing the world and the person's sacred link with it. Its five "magnetic points" are between the self and the cosmos, the norm, destiny, salvation, and the Supreme Being. The opposite forces of Yin and Yang bring harmony when they are balanced and create geomancy. Ritual sacrifice is one tool in bringing harmony or restoring unity; another is the role played by Mudang, a female spiritual leader who can cure disease and ensure fertility.

Sinkyo was changed and strengthened through its contacts with Chinese religions as well as Christianity. New religious movements also have their roots in traditional Sinkyo beliefs.

52. Japanese Religions: A Tapestry of Traditions

Religion in Japan is deeply affected by the country's geography: strong influences on its traditions come from Korea and China. Shinto was first organized and defined in reaction to Buddhism and Confucianism. The island makeup of Japan has also been key: major temples and shrines are found on Honshu, while an important pilgrimage route is on Shikoku. Mountains often have shrines at their summits; Mount Fuji is a quasi-religious symbol for the country.

Animism is a strong thread in Shinto, as is the imperial cult. Shinto is based primarily in its individual shrines, which are established to honor a natural phenomenon, a historical event, or a personal devotion. Worship tends to be individual and simple, involving an offering, sounding a bell, clapping, and prayer. The beginning of the New Year is a popular time to visit shrines. Shinto festivals typically feature a procession or a fair; people drink *sake* while a portable shrine is taken from the main shrine to various locations, symbolizing the journey made by the *kami* (god).

Japanese Buddhism includes several different local sects. Bodhisattvas, or savior figures, are revered as protectors. Buddhist practices focus on home altars, funerals, and festivals. New Buddhist movements have arisen around the *Lotus Sutra*, while other new religions include the Religion of the Heavenly Wisdom (*Tenrikyo*), based on the revelations and healings of a nineteenth-century Japanese woman.

Key Personalities

Tangun (c. 2300 BCE)

The legendary founder of Korea, which was first called the Kingdom of Choson ("Land of the Morning Calm"). According to mythology his mother was a woman turned into a bear by his father. Tangun's birth story is commemorated in the Korean national holiday of Kaechonjol.

Sun Myung Moon (1920–2012)

Korean engineer, businessman, and founder of the Unification Church. He claimed to have authoritative visions of Jesus. Members of the federation accorded him a high, if publicly ill-defined, status.

"Today our world needs drastic change in order to become God-centered. I came to call for that change. The Divine Principle will bring about a revolution among humanity. The power of this truth is touching millions of human lives and igniting hundreds of thousands of them. It will bring about the true, lasting unification of the human family and the world."

("True Love Quote," Unification Reverend Moon's Teachings, http://www.reverendsunmyungmoon.org/rev_moon _teaching.html)

Kukai (Kobo-Daishi) (774–835 CE)

Japanese Buddhist teacher who tried to reconcile Buddhism with Shinto. He is sometimes regarded as a manifestation of the Buddha Vairocana. Some believe he exists in a deep trance from which he is able to perform miracles and that he will return one day as a savior.

Autumn day viewing Shinsen'en Garden.
Step with the left foot, step with the right foot, Shinsen seasonal things.
Mind confused cannot return.
High terrace god reached with non-human power.
Pond mirror clear deep pool containing radiant sunshine.
Crane sound reverberates heaven, tame in the imperial garden.

The snow-goose wings hesitate, folded up about to fly.
Swimming fish frolic in seaweed, their fate to swallow a hook.
Deer call, deep grass dew dampened clothes.
All that roam all abide, feeling the sovereign's virtue.
Autumn moon, autumn wind, the entry doors of emptiness ('ūnyatā).
Holding grass in their mouths, chewing the bridge to what non-existence?
Patter, patter, leading one another in dancing the profound mystery of existence.

("Autumn Day Viewing Shinsen'en Garden," http://ww2. coastal.edu/rgreen/kukaipoetry.htm)

ADDITIONAL RESOURCE

▶ Monk Kobo Daishi Kukai (biographical essay) http://templesofjapan.com/Kobo-Daishi -Kukai.html

Nichiren (1222–82)

Japanese Buddhist reformer who taught that the Lotus Sutra contained the ultimate truth and that it could be compressed into a sacred formula: *namu myoho renge kyo*. He denounced all other forms of Buddhism. When the Mongols threatened Japan he preached a fiery nationalism, urging the nation to convert to true Buddhism. His teachings have provided the inspiration for some modern Buddhist sects.

"If you wish to free yourself from the sufferings of birth and death you have endured through eternity and attain supreme enlightenment in this lifetime, you must awaken to the mystic truth which has always been within your life. This truth is Myohorenge-kyo. Chanting Myoho-renge-kyo will therefore enable you to grasp the mystic truth within you. Myoho-renge-kyo is the king of sutras, flawless in both letter and principle. Its words are the reality of life, and the reality of life is the Mystic Law (Myoho). It is called the Mystic Law because it explains the mutually inclusive relationship of life and all phenomena. That is why this sutra is the wisdom of all Buddhas."

(Nichiren, "On Attaining Buddhahood," in *Major Writings of Nichiren Daishonin* 1:3, http://nichiren.info/gosho/OnAttainingBuddhahood.htm)

Primary Source Readings

The following excerpted readings represent some of the important primary sources mentioned in the main text. Additional primary sources are available both in print and online, and students are encouraged to contact their instructors for further information.

VIII.1 The Kojiki (Shinto)

Source: *The Kojiki*, trans. B. H. Chamberlain, 1882, http://www.sacred-texts.com/shi/kojiki.htm

PART I. THE BIRTH OF THE DEITIES

The Beginning of Heaven and Earth

The names of the deities that were born in the Plain of High Heaven when the Heaven and Earth began were the deity Master-of-the-August-Center-of-Heaven; next, the High-August-Producing-Wondrous deity; next, the Divine-Producing-Wondrous deity. These three deities were all deities born alone, and hid their persons. The names of the deities that were born next from a thing that sprouted up like unto a reed-shoot when the earth, young and like unto floating oil, drifted about medusa-like, were the Pleasant-Reed-Shoot-Prince-Elder deity, next the Heavenly-Eternally-Standing deity. These two deities were likewise born alone, and hid their persons.

The five deities in the above list are separate Heavenly deities.

The Seven Divine Generations

The names of the deities that were born next were the Earthly-Eternally-Standing deity; next, the Luxuriant-Integrating-Master deity. These two

deities were likewise deities born alone, and hid their persons. The names of the deities that were born next were the deity Mud-Earth-Lord; next, his Younger sister the deity—Mud-Earth-Lady; next, the Germ-Integrating deity; next, his younger sister the Life-Integrating-Deity; next, the deity of Elder-of-the-Great-Place; next, his younger sister the deity Elder-Lady-of-the-Great-Place; next, the deity Perfect-Exterior; next, his younger sister the deity Oh-Awful-Lady; next, the deity Izanagi or the Male-Who-Invites; next, his younger sister Izanami or the deity the Female-Who-Invites.

From the Earthly-Eternally-Standing deity down to the deity the Female-Who-Invites in the previous list are what are termed the Seven Divine Generations.

Courtship of the Deities the Male-Who-Invites and the Female-Who-Invites

Having descended from Heaven on to this island, they saw to the erection of a heavenly august pillar, they saw to the erection of a hall of eight fathoms. Then Izanagi, the Male-Who-Invites, said to Izanami, the Female-Who-Invites, "We should create children"; and he said, "Let us go around the heavenly august pillar, and when we meet on the other side let us be united. Do you go around from the left, and I will go from the right." When they met, Her Augustness, the Female-Who-Invites, spake first, exclaiming, "Ah, what a fair and lovable youth!" Then His Augustness said, "Ah what a fair and lovable maiden!" But afterward he said, " It was not well that the woman should speak first!" The child which was born to them was Hiruko (the leech-child), which when three years old was still unable to stand upright. So they placed the leech-child in a boat of reeds and let it float away. Next they gave birth to the island of Aha. This likewise is not reckoned among their children.

Hereupon the two deities took counsel, saving: "The children to whom we have now given birth are not good. It will be best to announce this in the august place of the Heavenly deities." They ascended forthwith to Heaven and inquired of Their Augustnesses the Heavenly deities. Then the Heavenly deities commanded and found out by grand divination, and ordered them, saying: "they were not good because the woman spoke first. Descend back again and amend your words." So thereupon descending back, they again went round the heavenly august pillar. Thereupon his Augustness the Male-who-Invites spoke first: " Ah! what a fair and lovely maiden!" Afterward his younger sister Her Augustness the Female-Who-Invites spoke: " Ah! what a fair and lovely youth! " Next they gave birth to the Island of Futa-na in Iyo. This island has one body and four faces, and each face has a name. So the Land of Iyo is called Lovely-Princess; the Land of Sanuki is called Princess-Good-Boiled-Rice; the Land of Aha is called the Princess-of-Great-Food, the Land of Tosa is called Brave-Good-Youth. Next they gave birth to the islands of Mitsu-go near Oki, another name for which islands is Heavenly-Great-Heart-Youth. This island likewise has one body and four faces, and each face has a name. So the Land of Tsukushi is called White-Sun-Youth; the Land of Toyo is called Luxuriant-Sun-Youth; the Land of Hi is called Brave-Sun-Confronting-Luxuriant-Wondrous-Lord-Youth; the Land of Kumaso is called Brave-Sun-Youth. Next they gave birth to the Island of Iki, another name for which is Heaven's One-Pillar. Next they gave birth to the Island of Tsu, another name for which is Heavenly-Hand-Net-Good-Princess. Next they gave birth to the Island of Sado. Next they gave birth to Great-Yamato-the-Luxuriant-Island-of-the-Dragon-fly, another name for which is Heavenly-August-Sky-Luxuriant-Dragon-fly-Lord-Youth. The name of "Land-of-the-Eight-Great-Islands" therefore originated in these eight islands having been born first. After that, when they had returned, they gave birth to the Island of Koo-zhima in Kibi, another name for which island is Brave-Sun-Direction-Youth. Next they gave birth to the Island of Adzuki, another name for which is Oho-Nu-De-Hime. Next they gave birth to the Island of Oho-shima, another name for which is Oho-Tamaru-Wake.—Next they gave birth to the Island of Hime, another name for which is Heaven's-One-Root. Next they gave birth to the Island of Chika, another name for which is

Heavenly-Great-Male. Next they gave birth to the islands of Futa-go, another name for which is Heaven's Two-Houses. (Six islands in all from the Island of Ko in Kibi to the Island of Heaven's-Two-Houses.)

Birth of the Various Deities

When they had finished giving birth to countries, they began afresh giving birth to deities. So the name of the deity they gave birth to was the deity Great-Male-of-the-Great-Thing; next, they gave birth to the deity Rock-Earth-Prince; next, they gave birth to the deity Rock-Nest-Princess; next, they gave birth to the deity Great-Door-Sun-Youth; next, they gave birth to the deity Heavenly-Blowing-Male; next, they gave birth to the deity Great-House-Prince; next, they gave birth to the deity Youth-of-the-Wind-Breath-the-Great-Male; next, they gave birth to the sea-deity, whose name is the deity Great-Ocean-Possessor next, they gave birth to the deity of the Water-Gates, whose name is the deity Prince-of-Swift-Autumn ; next they gave birth to his younger sister the deity Princess-of-Swift-Autumn. (Ten deities in all from the deity Great-Male-of-the-Great-Thing to the deity Princess-of-Autumn.) The names of the deities given birth to by these two deities Prince-of-Swift-Autumn and Princess-of-Swift-Autumn from their separate dominions of river and sea were: the deity Foam-Calm; next, the deity Foam-Waves; next the deity Bubble-Calm; next, the deity Bubble-Waves; next the deity Heavenly-Water-Divider; next, the deity Earthly-Water-Divider; next, the deity Heavenly-Water-Drawing-Gourd-Possessor; next, the deity Earthly-Water-Drawing-Gourd-Possessor. (Eight deities in all from the deity Foam-Prince to the deity Earthly-Water-Drawing-Gourd-Possessor.) Next, they gave birth to the deity of Wind, whose name is the deity Prince-of-Long-Wind. Next, they gave birth to the deity of Trees, whose name is deity Stem-Elder; next, they gave birth to the deity of Mountains, whose name is the deity Great-Mountain-Possessor. Next, they gave birth to the deity of Moors, whose name is the deity Thatch-Moor-Princess, another name for whom is the deity Moor-Elder. (Four deities in all from the deity Prince-of-long-wind to Moor-Elder.) The names of the deities given birth to by these two deities, the deity Great-Mountain-Possessor and the deity, Moor-Elder from their separate dominions of mountain and moor were: the deity Heavenly-Elder-of-the Passes; next, the deity Earthly-Elder-of-the-Passes; next, the deity Heavenly-Pass-Boundary; next, the deity Earthly-Pass-Boundary; next, the deity Heavenly-Dark-Door; next, the deity Earthly-Dark-Door next, the deity Great-Vale-Prince; next, the deity Great-Vale-Princess. (Eight deities in all from the deity Heavenly-Elder-of-the-Passes to the deity Great-Vale-Princess.) The name of the deity they next gave birth to was the deity Bird's-Rock-Camphor-tree-Boat, another name for whom is the Heavenly-Bird-Boat. Next, they gave birth to the deity Princess-of-Great-Food. Next, they gave birth to the Fire-Burning-Swift-Male deity, another name for whom is the deity Fire-Shining-Prince, and another name is the deity Fire-Shining-Elder.

Part II. The Quarrel of Izanaga and Izanami

The Land of Hades

Thereupon His Augustness the Male-Who-Invites, wishing to meet and see his younger sister Her Augustness the Female-Who-Invites, followed after her to the Land of Hades. So when from the palace she raised the door and came out to meet him, His Augustness the Male-Who-Invites spoke, saying: "Thine Augustness, my lovely younger sister! the lands that I and thou made are not yet finished making; so come back! " Then Her Augustness the Female-Who-Invites answered, saying: " Lamentable indeed that thou camest not sooner! I have eaten of the furnace of Hades. Nevertheless, as I reverence the entry here of Thine Augustness, my lovely elder brother, I wish to return. Moreover, I will discuss it particularly with the deities of Hades. Look not at me!" Having thus spoken, she went back inside the palace; and as she tarried there very long, he could not wait. So having taken and broken off one of the end-teeth of the multitudinous and close-toothed comb stuck in the august left bunch of his hair, he lit one light and went in and looked. Maggots were

swarming, and she was rotting, and in her head dwelt the Great-Thunder, in her breast dwelt the Fire-Thunder, in her left hand dwelt the Young-Thunder, in her right hand dwelt the Earth-Thunder, in her left foot dwelt the Rumbling-Thunder, in her right foot dwelt the Couchant-Thunder—altogether eight Thunder-deities had been born and dwelt there. Hereupon His Augustness the Male-Who-Invites, overawed at the sight, fled back, whereupon his younger sister, "Her Augustness the Female-Who-Invites, said: "Thou hast put me to shame," and at once sent the Ugly-Female-of-Hades to pursue him. So His Augustness the Male-Who-Invites took his black august head-dress and cast it down, and it instantly turned into grapes. While she picked them up and ate them, he fled on; but as she still pursued him, he took and broke the multitudinous and close-toothed comb in the right bunch of his hair and cast it down, and it instantly turned into bamboo-sprouts. While she pulled them up and ate them, he fled on. Again, later, his younger sister sent the eight Thunder-deities with a thousand and five hundred warriors of Hades to pursue him. So he, drawing the ten-grasp saber that was augustly girded on him, fled forward brandishing it in his back hand;" and as they still pursued, he took, on reaching the base of the Even-Pass-of-Hades, three peaches that were growing at its base, and waited and smote his pursuers therewith, so that they all fled back. Then His Augustness the Male-Who-Invites announced to the peaches: "Like as ye have helped me, so must ye help all living people in the Central Land of Reed-Plains when they shall fall into troublous circumstances and be harassed! "—and he gave to the peaches the designation of Their Augustnesses Great-Divine-Fruit. Last of all, his younger sister, Her Augustness the Princess-Who-Invites, came out herself in pursuit. So he drew a thousand-draught rock, and with it blocked up the Even-Pass-of-Hades, and placed the rock in the middle; and they stood opposite to one another and exchanged leave-takings ; and Her Augustness the Female-Who-Invites said: "My lovely elder brother, thine Augustness! If thou do like this, I will in one day strangle to death a thousand of the folk of thy land." Then His Augustness the Male-Who-Invites replied: "My lovely younger sister, Thine Augustness! If thou do this, I will in one day set up a thousand and five hundred parturition-house. In this manner each day a thousand people would surely be born." So Her Augustness the Female-Who-Invites is called the Great-Deity-of-Hades. Again it is said that, owing to her having pursued and reached her elder brother, she is called the Road-Reaching-Great deity." ' Again, the rock with which he blocked up the Even-Pass-of-Hades is called the Great-Deity-of-the-Road-Turning-back, and again it is called the Blocking-Great-Deity-of-the-Door-of-Hades. So what was called the Even-Pass-of-Hades is now called the Ifuya-Pass in the Land of Idzumo.

VIII.2 Nihon Shoki: *Age of the Gods*

Source: *Nihon Shoki*, Scroll 1, http://nihonshoki.wikidot .com/scroll-1-age-of-the-gods-1

SECTION ONE, MAIN VERSION

Of old, heaven and earth were still unparted, yin and yang undivided, and they were mixed in chaos like an egg. The dark watery expanse contained a bud. From that clear and bright thing, frail fibers became sky, while a heavy and turbid thing, submerged and stagnant, became earth. The subtle essence easily collected into union, but the heavy and turbid thing hardened only with difficulty. Therefore, heaven took shape prior to earth. Afterwards, the gods were born from within.

Of old it is said, from the beginning of this opening [the separation of heaven and earth], the land floated about like fish upon the surface of the water. At some time, an object was born from within heaven and earth. Its form was like the bud of a reed. Then it changed to become a god. It was called Kunikotachi no Mikoto. It is called mikoto out of esteem. From here, it is also called mikoto. As well, it is also read mikoto. This applies to all the following. Next was Kuninosatsuchi no Mikoto. Next was Toyokumunu no Mikoto. Together there were three gods. They

were all in the way of Ame no Michi [Yin]. They were purely male.

SECTION ONE, VERSION TWO

One version says, when heaven and earth were first divided, one thing existed within the void. Its form was difficult to say. From within this it changed and a god was born. It was called Kunitokotachi no Mikoto. It was also called Kunisokotachi no Mikoto. Next was Kuninosatsuchi no Mikoto. It was also called Kuninosatsutachi no Mikoto. Next was Toyokuninushi no Mikoto. It was also called Toyokumino no Mikoto. It was also called Toyokafushino no Mikoto. It was also called Ukitsunenotoyoka no Mikoto. It was also called Toyokunino no Mikoto. It was also called Toyokamuno no Mikoto. It was also called Hakokunino no Mikoto. It was also called Mino no Mikoto.

SECTION ONE, VERSION THREE

One version says, of old the continent was young, like floating oil; a floating marsh. At some time, something was born from the continent. Its form was like a reed bud coming forth from the ground. Then this became a god. It was called Umashimehikoshu no Mikoto. Next was Kunitokotachi no Mikoto. Next was Kunisatsuchi no Mikoto. Hakokuni is read ha-ko-ku-ni. Umashi is read u-ma-shi.

SECTION ONE, VERSION FOUR

One version says, when heaven and earth were mixed together, the birth of a god began. It was called Kamiashimehikoji no Mikoto. Next was Kunisokotachi no Mikoto. Hikoji is read hi-ko-ji.

SECTION ONE, VERSION FIVE

One version says, at the first division of heaven and earth the birth of all the gods took place. The first was called Kunitokotachi no Mikoto. Next was Kunisatsuchi no Mikoto. It also says that high heaven was the origin for the birth of a kami, called Amagonakanushi no Mikoto. Next was Takakamimusuhi no Mikoto. Next was the god Kamimimusuhi no Mikoto. Mimusuhi is read mi-mu-su-hi.

Section One, Version Six

Another version says, when heaven and earth were still unborn, it was like clouds floating on the sea, without root or place. From within that a thing was born, like a reed's first budding out of the mud. Then it changed into a person. It was called Kunitokotachi no Mikoto.

Section One, Version Seven

Another version says, at the first division of heaven and earth a thing existed. It was like a young reed bud, birthed in the sky. Therefore, this became a god, called Amatokotachi no Mikoto. Next came Kami-ashimehikoshu no Mikoto. Another thing existed, like young floating grease, birthed in the sky. Therefore, this became a god, called Kunitokotachi no Mikoto.

Key Terms

butsu-dan　A Japanese domestic altar to the Buddha that contains images or objects of worship and memorial tablets to ancestors. There may be lights, flowers, and incense; it is the focus of daily prayer chanting and the offering of food and drink.

kami　Powers of nature that are venerated in Shinto. They are beneficent spirits who help in the processes of fertility and growth. They were generated by the gods and the Japanese people are descended from them according to Shinto mythology.

Lotus Sutra　Mahayana Buddhist scripture in the form of a sermon preached by the Buddha to a vast throng of gods, demons, rulers, and cosmic powers. It contains the essence of Mahayana teachings on the eternity of the Buddha, the universal capacity for Buddhahood, and the compassion and power of the bodhisattvas. It is especially revered in Japan and is the basic scripture of the Nichiren Buddhist new religions.

matsuri　Japanese name for a solemn celebration intended to invoke worship of the Shinto gods and obedience to their moral will. They take place at stated intervals in Shinto sanctuaries.

Nihon Shoki　One of the oldest Japanese literary works (circa 720 CE), containing myths and legends of gods, goddesses, emperors, and empresses. It continues to be honored in Japan, especially by followers of Shinto.

Shingon　"True Word" sect of Japanese Buddhism founded in the ninth century CE and characterized by a complex sacramental and magical ritual that may have been influenced by Tantrism and by indigenous Shinto practices.

Shinto　The indigenous nature religion of Japan, which has provided a focus for nationalistic aspirations.

Sinkyo　Traditional religion of Korea.

Tendai　Japanese Buddhist sect based on a former Chinese sect T'ien-t'ai, and founded in the ninth century CE. Tendai was an attempt at a synthesis between Mahayana teachings that stressed meditation and those that stressed devotion.

torii　Gateway to a Shinto shrine, consisting of two vertical posts supporting two horizontal bars, the higher of which is often curved at each end toward the sky.

Questions for Study and Discussion

1. How do Yin and Yang relate to the system called "geomancy"?
2. Describe the role of the Mudang in Sinkyo.
3. How does the geography of Japan affect the structure and practice of Shinto?
4. What are the three main types of Shinto shrines? What are their common features?
5. The author Michael Pye hypothesizes that Christianity has had little impact in Japan "probably because it is strongly identified with the West" (p. 293). Why do you think Christianity has had more overall success in China than in Japan?

Questions for Reflection

Write your personal reflections to each of these questions in the space provided.

1. How do the five magnetic points of Sinkyo address basic religious questions? (See pp. 280–81.)

2. Characterize the interaction between Sinkyo and other major religions present in East Asia. (See p. 281.)

3. How does the emperor cult in Shinto relate to ancestor worship in other traditions? How does it differ? (See p. 286.)

4. How is Buddhism connected with national culture in Japan? (See p. 291.)

5. What patterns do you notice in the historical development of indigenous religions like Sinkyo and Shinto and their relationships with religions introduced from outside? (Think across the chapter.)

Selected Online Resources

▶ Hidden Korea: Religion—brief essays on Korea's religious traditions with additional links, related to a public television program on Korean culture
http://www.pbs.org/hiddenkorea/religion.htm

▶ Sacred Places: Shrine at Ise, Japan—photographic essay by an art historian
http://witcombe.sbc.edu/sacredplaces/ise.html

▶ Kukai, Founder of Japanese Shingon Buddhism—excerpts from a biography of the Japanese monk by Ron Green
http://ww2.coastal.edu/rgreen/kukai.htm

Part 9: Judaism

Chapter Summaries

53. A Historical Overview

Judaism traces its roots to the days of King Nebuchadnezzar and the exile of the Judeans in Babylon and Egypt. The center of Judean religion was the Temple at Jerusalem; those living in exile did their best to visit Jerusalem and worship in obedience to the Torah. Once Cyrus II of Persia captured Babylon, the Hebrews were allowed to return to Jerusalem. Ultimately the community in Judah divided between Jews and non-Jews; the division was marked by circumcision, observance of *Shabbat*, and recognition of the Torah.

Under Alexander the Great the Judean community in Alexandria and elsewhere became Greek-speaking, while other Jewish peoples continued to speak Aramaic. The Jews resisted the Romans in the late second century BCE, and the Maccabees were ultimately victorious, able to cleanse the desecrated Temple and reclaim Jerusalem. Later Judea became a vassal of Rome, and after another revolt the Temple was destroyed in 70 CE—a watershed event in Jewish history.

Judaism began to branch into different schools and cultures, including Hellenistic Judaism (of which Philo was an important biblical interpreter) and rabbinic Judaism, dominated by the Pharisees and producer of the Mishnah. Meanwhile, Jewish revolts against the Roman Empire continued. Not long after Constantine made Christianity a legal religion, Jewish-Christian tensions built.

By the ninth century many Jews lived under Muslim rule and had relatively good living conditions. Jewish and Muslim scholars made many great advances in the sciences and other areas. In Babylon the heads of the academies, called Gaons, collected Talmudic laws and fixed and annotated the text of the Bible.

Alongside the rise of Jewish scholarship in Western Europe came anti-Semitism and the mass persecution of Jews during the Crusades. Later, the Ottoman Empire brought some improvement to Jewish people's lives, although hardships still continued under some rulers. Messianic movements arose during the late seventeenth century; in eighteenth-century Poland Hasidism developed as a popular movement.

The next century saw large numbers of Jews immigrating to the United States as well as the development of Reform Judaism.

54. Sacred Writings

The three major textual traditions are the Hebrew scriptures, or Tanakh; the Mishnah (Law); and the Talmud, which is the exposition of the Torah and the Mishnah. The Jewish concept of canon developed over centuries and became centered on the texts that spoke directly to the life of the community. The Mishnah is a collection of tractates that applies the Law to daily life; its authors saw themselves as part of an unbroken chain of tradition. The Talmud is a vast collection of rabbinical teachings; it is in fact two collections, the Palestinian or Jerusalem Talmud and the longer Babylonian Talmud. They contain many kinds of literature and cover a vast range of topics.

55. Beliefs

In Judaism, the belief in one God as the creator of the universe, including human beings in his image, means that there is one humanity and one world. God is both above his creation and actively involved in it. God is also all-powerful and all-knowing. While people have free will, they cannot understand the nature of God's knowledge or why his omniscience still allows free will. God gave the people of Israel (the Jews) the mission to bear divine truth to all humanity; the Torah lays out the responsibilities given to God's chosen people as part of this mission. The covenant between God and the Jewish people is the heart of Judaism. Jewish tradition also holds that a messiah will come at the end of time to redeem his people and usher in a messianic age. However, modern Judaism tends not to promote a particular eschatological view, and much of the faith was deeply affected by the events of the Holocaust.

56. Family and Society

According to Orthodox Jewish law, a Jewish boy must be circumcised at the age of eight days; his mother is responsible for his early religious education. He studies Hebrew and the scriptures so he can become a "son of the commandment," or Bar-Mitzvah, when he is of age (thirteen). In Orthodox tradition girls study Torah but not Talmud. A girl becomes a daughter of the commandment, or Bat-Mitzvah, at thirteen.

Orthodox Jewish men pray three times a day, typically with a prayer-shawl (*tallit*) and phylacteries (*tephillin*), which contain four passages of scripture. Women also pray but not under the same obligations as men.

Traditional Jewish households keep kosher—that is, follow rules of food purity set down in the Torah. Jews observe *Shabbat* every week, beginning at sunset on Friday, by lighting candles, attending synagogue, and eating a meal together with a blessing over bread and wine. No work is permitted on the Sabbath.

Marriage is considered a holy covenant, but divorce is permitted through a religious court. After death the *kaddish* prayer is said at the funeral, while family sit *shivah*, a mourning period that can last seven days. On the anniversary of their parent's death, the children light a candle and recite the *kaddish*.

57. Worship and Festivals

The Jewish calendar features a festival almost every month of the year, beginning with Rosh Hashanah (the New Year). Worship focuses on the synagogue, where the *Sefer* Torah is kept in an ark and taken out once during each service. Children are part of all major festivals; for example, the youngest child asks the questions about Passover during the Seder meal. Major festivals include Pesach (Passover), Shavuot (Pentecost), and Sukkot (Tabernacles). The holiest day of the year is Yom Kippur, the Day of Atonement. Another important day of observance is Yom HaShoah (Holocaust Day).

58. The Holocaust

More than six million Jews were killed during the Holocaust. Adolf Hitler and the Nazi Party came to power in 1933 and began a systematic oppression of Jewish people using legal means and military might. They set up concentration camps to imprison millions of Jewish men, women, and children as well as other "undesirables," including people with disabilities and gays and lesbians; prisoners were forced to labor at the camps, and some were made to participate in medical experiments. At Nazi death camps in Poland and Germany, thousands of prisoners were gassed to death every day. Jews and their allies resisted the Nazis using many different approaches, from spiritual resistance to physical fighting. The Holocaust is remembered today on Yom HaShoah and through museums and other memorial institutions as the most dire event in Jewish history.

59. Branches of Judaism

Most Jews today are descendants of either the Sephardim, from Spain, or the Ashkenazim, from central Europe. Some Jews are from other, smaller communities, like the Falasha of Ethiopia. In addition to cultural differences, the religion has several different branches. Orthodox Judaism considers itself the only true version of the faith. Orthodox Jews live their lives under the commandments and place a strong emphasis on education. Reform Judaism originated in Enlightenment Germany and expanded in the United States. Reform Jews do not necessarily follow dietary laws, and their worship services are not segregated by sex. The approach tends to be individualized and focused on ethical teachings rather than the ritual Law. Other, more radical branches include Reconstructionism and Renewal. Conservative Judaism is a response to the Reform branch and emphasizes historical elements of the tradition. Other sects, like the Hasidim and the Haredim, tend to be more traditional and even separatist in orientation.

60. Judaism in the Modern World

The question of who is a Jew is hotly debated within contemporary Judaism. While Orthodox Judaism maintains that a Jew must be born of a Jewish mother or a convert under strict criteria, Reform Judaism allows for anyone with a Jewish parent or raised in a Jewish community to be recognized as Jewish. The state of Israel since 1948 has been a focus of the Jewish world as well as a point of contention. Some Orthodox within Israel do not support its existence because they believe it contradicts the tradition and its values. The Zionist movement supports the view that Israel must exist to provide a safe haven for Jews all over the world.

Judaism is known for its capacity to adapt to changing times and circumstances. The traditions have been preserved despite centuries of violent oppression and the near genocide of the Holocaust. Social justice is a strong value for many modern Jews. Moreover, Jews are involved in interfaith dialogue and education to counter worldwide anti-Semitism and to build a better world for diverse peoples.

Key Personalities

Moses

The father of Judaism who received the Torah from God on Mount Sinai having led the people of Israel out of captivity in Egypt. The first five books of the Bible are traditionally ascribed to him.

"And Moses said unto the LORD: 'See, Thou sayest unto me: Bring up this people; and Thou hast not let me know whom Thou wilt send with me. Yet Thou hast said: I know thee by name, and thou hast also found grace in My sight. Now therefore, I pray Thee, if I have found grace in Thy sight, show me now Thy ways, that I may know Thee, to the end that I may find grace in Thy sight; and consider that this nation is Thy people.' And He said: 'My presence shall go with thee, and I will give thee rest.' And he said unto Him: 'If Thy presence go not with me, carry us not up hence. For wherein now shall it be known that I have found grace in Thy sight, I and Thy people? is it not in that Thou goest with us, so that we are distinguished, I and Thy people, from all the people that are upon the face of the earth?'

"And the LORD said unto Moses: 'I will do this thing also that thou hast spoken, for thou hast found grace in My sight, and I know thee by name.' And he said: 'Show me, I pray Thee, Thy glory.' And He said: 'I will make all My goodness pass before thee, and will proclaim the name of the LORD before thee; and I will be gracious to whom I will be gracious, and will show mercy on whom I will show mercy.' And He said: 'Thou canst not see My face, for man shall not see Me and live.' And the LORD said: 'Behold, there is a place by Me, and thou shalt stand upon the rock. And it shall come to pass, while My glory passeth by, that I will put thee in a cleft of the rock, and will cover thee with My hand until I have passed by. And I will take away My hand, and thou shalt see My back; but My face shall not be seen.'

(Exodus 33:12-23, Jewish Publication Society translation)

Judas Maacabeus (died 160 BCE)

Jewish revolutionary who opposed the Hellenizing Seleucid emperor Antiochus Epiphanes who had set up an image of Olympian Zeus in the Temple of Jerusalem. Under Judas, sporadic guerrilla revolt became full-scale war. In 165 BCE Antiochus was defeated, and in the following year the temple was rededicated. Though he achieved religious freedom, he failed to establish a free Jewish state.

Hillel

Pharisaic Jewish teacher of the first century CE. He was known for his humane and lenient interpretations of the Torah, in contrast to his chief opponent, the stern and rigorous Shammai.

"As President of the Sanhedrin, Hillel played his part in the foundation of the system developed by the Pharisaic sages by contributing to the development of general principles for interpretation and codification of the Oral Law. This was part of a process which culminated at the beginning of the third century CE in the compilation of the Mishnah. (lit. 'repetition') in Galilee. . . . Thus Hillel is credited, for example, with codifying the existing rules of scriptural interpretation, and producing what became known as the 'Seven Rules of Hillel.' These set out principles which judges or lawmakers can apply in a particular case where the Biblical law is ambiguous or silent. He is also credited with originating the division into the separate areas of law, the six 'Orders,' into which the Mishnah came to be organised."

(Ian Lacey, "Hillel the Elder," Israel & Judaism Studies, 2006, http://www.ijs.org.au/Hillel-the-Elder/default.aspx)

Philo of Alexandria (about 25 BCE–40 CE)

Jewish philosopher who tried to reconcile Greek philosophy with the Hebrew scriptures. His commentaries used allegorical devices to penetrate the meaning of scripture. He developed the Greek doctrine of the Logos or Word of God into the status of 'a second God'. His speculations were widely studied by the early Christians.

Rabbi Akiba (50–135 CE)

Jewish teacher who developed the Mishnah method of repetitive transmission of teachings. He began the work of systematizing the available interpretations of the Torah, laying the foundations for the work of Judah Hanasi. He was also famous for his use of Midrash, investing every detail of the Hebrew texts with significance.

Rabbi Moshe ben Maimon (Maimonides) (1135–1204 CE)

Jewish philosopher who lived in Spain and later Egypt and attempted a synthesis of Aristotelian and biblical teaching. He listed the thirteen principles of belief which have been treated in Judaism as a creed and are found in the *Jewish Daily Prayer Book.*

Abraham Geiger (1810–1874)

German rabbi who founded Reform Judaism.

"As Geiger saw it, the nationalistic and particularistic aspects of Judaism reflected no more than stages in Judaism's progress towards, universalism. He advocated, therefore, the substitution of German for the Hebrew of many prayers and the rejection of the idea of a return to Zion and the rebuilding of the Temple, in favor of the idea that Jews have a mission to all mankind; although he did believe in a version of the Chosen People idea according to which Jews had been especially gifted with the powerful religious sense that resulted in the emergence of ethical monotheism."

(Louis Jacobs, "Rabbi Abraham Geiger," in *The Jewish Religion: A Companion* [New York: Oxford University Press, 1995], http://www.myjewishlearning.com/history/Modern _History/1700-1914/Denominationalism/Reform /Abraham_Geiger.shtml)

Mordecai Kaplan (1881–1983)

The founder of Reconstructionism, which stresses Judaism as an evolving religious civilization and gives equal importance to religion, ethics, and culture.

"The Thirteen Wants"

1. We want Judaism to help us overcome temptation, doubt and discouragement.
2. We want Judaism to imbue us with a sense of responsibility for the righteous use of the blessings wherewith God endows us.
3. We want the Jew so to be trusted that his yea will be taken as yea, and his nay as nay.
4. We want to learn how to utilize our leisure to best advantage, physically, intellectually, and spiritually.
5. We want the Jewish home to live up to its traditional standards of virtue and piety.
6. We want the Jewish upbringing of our children to further their moral and spiritual growth, and to enable them to accept with joy their heritage as Jews.
7. We want the synagogue to enable us to worship God in sincerity and in truth.
8. We want our religious traditions to be interpreted in terms of understandable experience and to be made relevant to our present-day needs.
9. We want to participate in the upbuilding of *Eretz Yisrael* as a means to the renaissance of the Jewish spirit.
10. We want Judaism to find rich, manifold and ever new expression in philosophy, letters and the arts.
11. We want all forms of Jewish organization to make for spiritual purpose and ethical endeavor.
12. We want the unity of Israel throughout the world to be fostered through mutual help in time of need, and through cooperation in the furtherance of Judaism at all time.
13. We want Judaism to function as a potent influence for justice, freedom and peace in the life of men and nations.

(Mordecai M. Kaplan, "The Criteria of Jewish Loyalty," 1926, http://www.sacred-texts.com/jud/wants.htm)

Primary Source Readings

The following excerpted readings represent some of the important primary sources mentioned in the main text. Additional primary sources are available both in print and online, and students are encouraged to contact their instructors for further information.

The source for all biblical passages below is the New Revised Standard Version Bible.

IX.1 Creation of the World according to the Book of Genesis

Genesis 1:1—2:3

[1]In the beginning when God created the heavens and the earth, [2]the earth was a formless void and darkness covered the face of the deep, while a wind from God swept over the face of the waters. [3]Then God said, 'Let there be light'; and there was light. [4]And God saw that the light was good; and God separated the light from the darkness. [5]God called the light Day, and the darkness he called Night. And there was evening and there was morning, the first day.

[6]And God said, 'Let there be a dome in the midst of the waters, and let it separate the waters from the waters.' [7]So God made the dome and separated the waters that were under the dome from the waters that were above the dome. And it was so. [8]God called the dome Sky. And there was evening and there was morning, the second day.

[9]And God said, 'Let the waters under the sky be gathered together into one place, and let the dry land appear.' And it was so. [10]God called the dry land Earth, and the waters that were gathered together he called Seas. And God saw that it was good. [11]Then God said, 'Let the earth put forth vegetation: plants yielding seed, and fruit trees of every kind on earth that bear fruit with the seed in it.' And it was so. [12]The earth brought forth vegetation: plants yielding seed of every kind, and trees of every kind bearing fruit with the seed in it. And God saw that it was good. [13]And there was evening and there was morning, the third day.

[14]And God said, 'Let there be lights in the dome of the sky to separate the day from the night; and let them be for signs and for seasons and for days and years, [15]and let them be lights in the dome of the sky to give light upon the earth.' And it was so. [16]God made the two great lights—the greater light to rule the day and the lesser light to rule the night—and the stars. [17]God set them in the dome of the sky to give light upon the earth, [18]to rule over the day and over the night, and to separate the light from the darkness. And God saw that it was good. [19]And there was evening and there was morning, the fourth day.

[20]And God said, 'Let the waters bring forth swarms of living creatures, and let birds fly above the earth across the dome of the sky.' [21]So God created the great sea monsters and every living creature that moves, of every kind, with which the waters swarm, and every winged bird of every kind. And God saw that it was good. [22]God blessed them, saying, 'Be fruitful and multiply and fill the waters in the seas, and let birds multiply on the earth.' [23]And there was evening and there was morning, the fifth day.

[24]And God said, 'Let the earth bring forth living creatures of every kind: cattle and creeping things and wild animals of the earth of every kind.' And it was so. [25]God made the wild animals of the earth of every kind, and the cattle of every kind, and everything that creeps upon the ground of every kind. And God saw that it was good.

[26]Then God said, 'Let us make humankind in our image, according to our likeness; and let them have dominion over the fish of the sea, and over the birds of the air, and over the cattle, and over all the wild animals of the earth, and over every creeping thing that creeps upon the earth.'

[27]So God created humankind in his image,

in the image of God he created them;

male and female he created them.

[28]God blessed them, and God said to them, 'Be fruitful and multiply, and fill the earth and subdue it; and have dominion over the fish of the sea and over the birds of the air and over every living thing that moves upon the earth.' [29]God said, 'See, I have given you every plant yielding seed that is upon the face of all the earth, and every tree with seed in its fruit; you shall have them for food. [30]And to every beast of the earth, and to every bird of the air, and to everything that creeps on the earth, everything that has the breath of life, I have given every green plant for food.' And it was so. [31]God saw everything that he had made, and indeed, it was very good. And there was evening and there was morning, the sixth day.

[2:1]Thus the heavens and the earth were finished, and all their multitude. [2]And on the seventh day God finished the work that he had done, and he rested on the seventh day from all the work that he had done. [3]So God blessed the seventh day and hallowed it, because on it God rested from all the work that he had done in creation.

IX.3 God's Covenant with Abram (Abraham)

Genesis 17:1-8

[17:1]When Abram was ninety-nine years old, the Lord appeared to Abram, and said to him, 'I am God Almighty; walk before me, and be blameless. [2]And I will make my covenant between me and you, and will make you exceedingly numerous.' [3]Then Abram fell on his face; and God said to him, [4]'As for me, this is my covenant with you: You shall be the ancestor of a multitude of nations. [5]No longer shall your name be Abram, but your name shall be Abraham; for I have made you the ancestor of a multitude of nations. [6]I will make you exceedingly fruitful; and I will make nations of you, and kings shall come from you. [7]I will establish my covenant between me and you, and your offspring after you throughout their generations, for an everlasting covenant, to be God to you and to your offspring after you. [8]And I will give to you, and to your offspring after you, the land where you are now an alien, all the land of Canaan, for a perpetual holding; and I will be their God.'

IX.4 The First Passover and Exodus Out of Egypt

Exodus 12

[12:1]The Lord said to Moses and Aaron in the land of Egypt: [2]This month shall mark for you the beginning of months; it shall be the first month of the year for you. [3]Tell the whole congregation of Israel that on the tenth of this month they are to take a lamb for each family, a lamb for each household. [4]If a household is too small for a whole lamb, it shall join its closest neighbour in obtaining one; the lamb shall be divided in proportion to the number of people who eat of it. [5]Your lamb shall be without blemish, a year-old male; you may take it from the sheep or from the goats. [6]You shall keep it until the fourteenth day of this month; then the whole assembled congregation of Israel shall slaughter it at twilight. [7]They shall take some of the blood and put it on the two doorposts and the lintel of the houses in which they eat it. [8]They shall eat the lamb that same night; they shall eat it roasted over the fire with unleavened bread and bitter herbs. [9]Do not eat any of it raw or boiled in water, but roasted over the fire, with its head, legs, and inner organs. [10]You shall let none of it remain until the morning; anything that remains until the morning you shall burn. [11]This is how you shall eat it: your loins girded, your sandals on your feet, and your staff in your hand; and you shall eat it hurriedly. It is the passover of the Lord. [12]For I will pass through the land of Egypt that night, and I will strike down every firstborn in the land of Egypt, both human beings and animals; on all the gods of Egypt I will execute judgements: I am the Lord. [13]The blood shall be a sign for you on the houses where you live: when I see the blood, I will pass over you, and no plague shall destroy you when I strike the land of Egypt.

[14] This day shall be a day of remembrance for you. You shall celebrate it as a festival to the Lord; throughout your generations you shall observe it

as a perpetual ordinance. [15]Seven days you shall eat unleavened bread; on the first day you shall remove leaven from your houses, for whoever eats leavened bread from the first day until the seventh day shall be cut off from Israel. [16]On the first day you shall hold a solemn assembly, and on the seventh day a solemn assembly; no work shall be done on those days; only what everyone must eat, that alone may be prepared by you. [17]You shall observe the festival of unleavened bread, for on this very day I brought your companies out of the land of Egypt: you shall observe this day throughout your generations as a perpetual ordinance. [18]In the first month, from the evening of the fourteenth day until the evening of the twenty-first day, you shall eat unleavened bread. [19]For seven days no leaven shall be found in your houses; for whoever eats what is leavened shall be cut off from the congregation of Israel, whether an alien or a native of the land. [20]You shall eat nothing leavened; in all your settlements you shall eat unleavened bread.

[21] Then Moses called all the elders of Israel and said to them, 'Go, select lambs for your families, and slaughter the passover lamb. [22]Take a bunch of hyssop, dip it in the blood that is in the basin, and touch the lintel and the two doorposts with the blood in the basin. None of you shall go outside the door of your house until morning. [23]For the Lord will pass through to strike down the Egyptians; when he sees the blood on the lintel and on the two doorposts, the Lord will pass over that door and will not allow the destroyer to enter your houses to strike you down. [24]You shall observe this rite as a perpetual ordinance for you and your children. [25]When you come to the land that the Lord will give you, as he has promised, you shall keep this observance. [26]And when your children ask you, "What do you mean by this observance?" [27]you shall say, "It is the passover sacrifice to the Lord, for he passed over the houses of the Israelites in Egypt, when he struck down the Egyptians but spared our houses."' And the people bowed down and worshipped.

[28] The Israelites went and did just as the Lord had commanded Moses and Aaron.

[29] At midnight the Lord struck down all the firstborn in the land of Egypt, from the firstborn of Pharaoh who sat on his throne to the firstborn of the prisoner who was in the dungeon, and all the firstborn of the livestock. [30]Pharaoh arose in the night, he and all his officials and all the Egyptians; and there was a loud cry in Egypt, for there was not a house without someone dead. [31]Then he summoned Moses and Aaron in the night, and said, 'Rise up, go away from my people, both you and the Israelites! Go, worship the Lord, as you said. [32]Take your flocks and your herds, as you said, and be gone. And bring a blessing on me too!'

[33] The Egyptians urged the people to hasten their departure from the land, for they said, 'We shall all be dead.' [34]So the people took their dough before it was leavened, with their kneading-bowls wrapped up in their cloaks on their shoulders. [35]The Israelites had done as Moses told them; they had asked the Egyptians for jewellery of silver and gold, and for clothing, [36]and the Lord had given the people favour in the sight of the Egyptians, so that they let them have what they asked. And so they plundered the Egyptians.

[37] The Israelites journeyed from Rameses to Succoth, about six hundred thousand men on foot, besides children. [38]A mixed crowd also went up with them, and livestock in great numbers, both flocks and herds. [39]They baked unleavened cakes of the dough that they had brought out of Egypt; it was not leavened, because they were driven out of Egypt and could not wait, nor had they prepared any provisions for themselves.

[40] The time that the Israelites had lived in Egypt was four hundred and thirty years. [41]At the end of four hundred and thirty years, on that very day, all the companies of the Lord went out from the land of Egypt. [42]That was for the Lord a night of vigil, to bring them out of the land of Egypt. That same night is a vigil to be kept for the Lord by all the Israelites throughout their generations.

[43] The Lord said to Moses and Aaron: This is the ordinance for the passover: no foreigner shall eat of

it, ⁴⁴but any slave who has been purchased may eat of it after he has been circumcised; ⁴⁵no bound or hired servant may eat of it. ⁴⁶It shall be eaten in one house; you shall not take any of the animal outside the house, and you shall not break any of its bones. ⁴⁷The whole congregation of Israel shall celebrate it. ⁴⁸If an alien who resides with you wants to celebrate the passover to the Lord, all his males shall be circumcised; then he may draw near to celebrate it; he shall be regarded as a native of the land. But no uncircumcised person shall eat of it; ⁴⁹there shall be one law for the native and for the alien who resides among you.

⁵⁰ All the Israelites did just as the Lord had commanded Moses and Aaron. ⁵¹That very day the Lord brought the Israelites out of the land of Egypt, company by company.

IX.5 God's Covenant with Moses

Exodus 19–20; 24

¹⁹At the third new moon after the Israelites had gone out of the land of Egypt, on that very day, they came into the wilderness of Sinai. ²They had journeyed from Rephidim, entered the wilderness of Sinai, and camped in the wilderness; Israel camped there in front of the mountain. ³Then Moses went up to God; the Lord called to him from the mountain, saying, 'Thus you shall say to the house of Jacob, and tell the Israelites: ⁴You have seen what I did to the Egyptians, and how I bore you on eagles' wings and brought you to myself. ⁵Now therefore, if you obey my voice and keep my covenant, you shall be my treasured possession out of all the peoples. Indeed, the whole earth is mine, ⁶but you shall be for me a priestly kingdom and a holy nation. These are the words that you shall speak to the Israelites.'

⁷ So Moses came, summoned the elders of the people, and set before them all these words that the Lord had commanded him. ⁸The people all answered as one: 'Everything that the Lord has spoken we will do.' Moses reported the words of the people to the Lord. ⁹Then the Lord said to Moses, 'I am going to come to you in a dense cloud, in order that the

people may hear when I speak with you and so trust you ever after.'

When Moses had told the words of the people to the Lord, ¹⁰the Lord said to Moses: 'Go to the people and consecrate them today and tomorrow. Have them wash their clothes ¹¹and prepare for the third day, because on the third day the Lord will come down upon Mount Sinai in the sight of all the people. ¹²You shall set limits for the people all around, saying, "Be careful not to go up the mountain or to touch the edge of it. Any who touch the mountain shall be put to death. ¹³No hand shall touch them, but they shall be stoned or shot with arrows; whether animal or human being, they shall not live." When the trumpet sounds a long blast, they may go up on the mountain.' ¹⁴So Moses went down from the mountain to the people. He consecrated the people, and they washed their clothes. ¹⁵And he said to the people, 'Prepare for the third day; do not go near a woman.'

¹⁶ On the morning of the third day there was thunder and lightning, as well as a thick cloud on the mountain, and a blast of a trumpet so loud that all the people who were in the camp trembled. ¹⁷Moses brought the people out of the camp to meet God. They took their stand at the foot of the mountain. ¹⁸Now Mount Sinai was wrapped in smoke, because the Lord had descended upon it in fire; the smoke went up like the smoke of a kiln, while the whole mountain shook violently. ¹⁹As the blast of the trumpet grew louder and louder, Moses would speak and God would answer him in thunder. ²⁰When the Lord descended upon Mount Sinai, to the top of the mountain, the Lord summoned Moses to the top of the mountain, and Moses went up. ²¹Then the Lord said to Moses, 'Go down and warn the people not to break through to the Lord to look; otherwise many of them will perish. ²²Even the priests who approach the Lord must consecrate themselves or the Lord will break out against them.' ²³Moses said to the Lord, 'The people are not permitted to come up to Mount Sinai; for you yourself warned us, saying, "Set limits around the mountain and keep it holy." ' ²⁴The Lord said to him, 'Go down, and come up bringing Aaron with you; but do not let either the priests or

the people break through to come up to the Lord; otherwise he will break out against them.' ²⁵So Moses went down to the people and told them.

^{20:1}Then God spoke all these words:

² I am the Lord your God, who brought you out of the land of Egypt, out of the house of slavery; ³you shall have no other gods before me.

⁴ You shall not make for yourself an idol, whether in the form of anything that is in heaven above, or that is on the earth beneath, or that is in the water under the earth. ⁵You shall not bow down to them or worship them; for I the Lord your God am a jealous God, punishing children for the iniquity of parents, to the third and the fourth generation of those who reject me, ⁶but showing steadfast love to the thousandth generation of those who love me and keep my commandments.

⁷ You shall not make wrongful use of the name of the Lord your God, for the Lord will not acquit anyone who misuses his name.

⁸ Remember the sabbath day, and keep it holy. ⁹For six days you shall labour and do all your work. ¹⁰But the seventh day is a sabbath to the Lord your God; you shall not do any work—you, your son or your daughter, your male or female slave, your livestock, or the alien resident in your towns. ¹¹For in six days the Lord made heaven and earth, the sea, and all that is in them, but rested the seventh day; therefore the Lord blessed the sabbath day and consecrated it.

¹² Honour your father and your mother, so that your days may be long in the land that the Lord your God is giving you.

¹³ You shall not murder.

¹⁴ You shall not commit adultery.

¹⁵ You shall not steal.

¹⁶ You shall not bear false witness against your neighbour.

¹⁷ You shall not covet your neighbour's house; you shall not covet your neighbour's wife, or male or female slave, or ox, or donkey, or anything that belongs to your neighbour.

¹⁸ When all the people witnessed the thunder and lightning, the sound of the trumpet, and the mountain smoking, they were afraid and trembled and stood at a distance, ¹⁹and said to Moses, 'You speak to us, and we will listen; but do not let God speak to us, or we will die.' ²⁰Moses said to the people, 'Do not be afraid; for God has come only to test you and to put the fear of him upon you so that you do not sin.' ²¹Then the people stood at a distance, while Moses drew near to the thick darkness where God was. . . .

^{24:1}Then he said to Moses, 'Come up to the Lord, you and Aaron, Nadab, and Abihu, and seventy of the elders of Israel, and worship at a distance. ²Moses alone shall come near the Lord; but the others shall not come near, and the people shall not come up with him.'

³ Moses came and told the people all the words of the Lord and all the ordinances; and all the people answered with one voice, and said, 'All the words that the Lord has spoken we will do.' ⁴And Moses wrote down all the words of the Lord. He rose early in the morning, and built an altar at the foot of the mountain, and set up twelve pillars, corresponding to the twelve tribes of Israel. ⁵He sent young men of the people of Israel, who offered burnt-offerings and sacrificed oxen as offerings of well-being to the Lord. ⁶Moses took half of the blood and put it in basins, and half of the blood he dashed against the altar. ⁷Then he took the book of the covenant, and read it in the hearing of the people; and they said, 'All that the Lord has spoken we will do, and we will be obedient.' ⁸Moses took the blood and dashed it on the people, and said, 'See the blood of the covenant that the Lord has made with you in accordance with all these words.'

⁹ Then Moses and Aaron, Nadab, and Abihu, and seventy of the elders of Israel went up, ¹⁰and they saw the God of Israel. Under his feet there was something like a pavement of sapphire stone, like the very heaven for clearness. ¹¹God did not lay his hand on

the chief men of the people of Israel; also they beheld God, and they ate and drank.

[12] The Lord said to Moses, 'Come up to me on the mountain, and wait there; and I will give you the tablets of stone, with the law and the commandment, which I have written for their instruction.' [13]So Moses set out with his assistant Joshua, and Moses went up into the mountain of God. [14]To the elders he had said, 'Wait here for us, until we come to you again; for Aaron and Hur are with you; whoever has a dispute may go to them.'

[15] Then Moses went up on the mountain, and the cloud covered the mountain. [16]The glory of the Lord settled on Mount Sinai, and the cloud covered it for six days; on the seventh day he called to Moses out of the cloud. [17]Now the appearance of the glory of the Lord was like a devouring fire on the top of the mountain in the sight of the people of Israel. [18]Moses entered the cloud, and went up on the mountain. Moses was on the mountain for forty days and forty nights.

IX.6 Psalms of David

PSALM 8: DIVINE MAJESTY AND HUMAN DIGNITY (A PSALM OF PRAISE)

1 O Lord, our Sovereign,
how majestic is your name in all the earth!
You have set your glory above the heavens.
2 Out of the mouths of babes and infants
you have founded a bulwark because of your foes,
to silence the enemy and the avenger.
3 When I look at your heavens, the work of your
	fingers,
the moon and the stars that you have established;
4 what are human beings that you are mindful of
	them,
mortals that you care for them?
5 Yet you have made them a little lower than God,
and crowned them with glory and honour.
6 You have given them dominion over the works of
	your hands;
you have put all things under their feet,

7 all sheep and oxen,
and also the beasts of the field,
8 the birds of the air, and the fish of the sea,
whatever passes along the paths of the seas.
9 O Lord, our Sovereign,
how majestic is your name in all the earth!

PSALM 20: PRAYER FOR VICTORY (A ROYAL PSALM)

To the leader. A Psalm of David.
1 The Lord answer you in the day of trouble!
The name of the God of Jacob protect you!
2 May he send you help from the sanctuary,
and give you support from Zion.
3 May he remember all your offerings,
and regard with favour your burnt sacrifices.
4 May he grant you your heart's desire,
and fulfil all your plans.
5 May we shout for joy over your victory,
and in the name of our God set up our banners.
May the Lord fulfil all your petitions.
6 Now I know that the Lord will help his anointed;
he will answer him from his holy heaven
with mighty victories by his right hand.
7 Some take pride in chariots, and some in horses,
but our pride is in the name of the Lord our God.
8 They will collapse and fall,
but we shall rise and stand upright.
9 Give victory to the king, O Lord;
answer us when we call.

PSALM 32: THE JOY OF FORGIVENESS (A TEACHING, OR DIDACTIC PSALM)

1 Happy are those whose transgression is forgiven,
whose sin is covered.
2 Happy are those to whom the Lord imputes no
	iniquity,
and in whose spirit there is no deceit.
3 While I kept silence, my body wasted away
through my groaning all day long.
4 For day and night your hand was heavy upon me;
my strength was dried up as by the heat of summer.
Selah
5 Then I acknowledged my sin to you,

and I did not hide my iniquity;

I said, 'I will confess my transgressions to the Lord',
and you forgave the guilt of my sin.
Selah

6 Therefore let all who are faithful
offer prayer to you;
at a time of distress, the rush of mighty waters
shall not reach them.

7 You are a hiding-place for me;
you preserve me from trouble;
you surround me with glad cries of deliverance.
Selah

8 I will instruct you and teach you the way you
should go;
I will counsel you with my eye upon you.

9 Do not be like a horse or a mule, without
understanding,

whose temper must be curbed with bit and bridle,
else it will not stay near you.

10 Many are the torments of the wicked,
but steadfast love surrounds those who trust in the
Lord.

11 Be glad in the Lord and rejoice, O righteous,
and shout for joy, all you upright in heart.

IX.7 The Rambam's Thirteen Principles of Faith

Source: Orthodox Union, http://www.ou.org/torah
/rambam.htm

Note: "'G-d' is a manner of referring to God that
respects the idea of God being beyond human
understanding and prevents anyone from 'destroying' the name of God, given that God's name is not
actually 'written' when it appears as 'G-d.'"

THE RAMBAM'S THIRTEEN PRINCIPLES OF JEWISH FAITH

1. I believe with perfect faith that G-d is the Creator
   and Ruler of all things. He alone has made, does
   make, and will make all things.

2. I believe with perfect faith that G-d is One. There
   is no unity that is in any way like His. He alone
   is our G-d He was, He is, and He will be.

3. I believe with perfect faith that G-d does not have
   a body. physical concepts do not apply to Him.
   There is nothing whatsoever that resembles
   Him at all.

4. I believe with perfect faith that G-d is first and last.

5. I believe with perfect faith that it is only proper
   to pray to G-d. One may not pray to anyone or
   anything else.

6. I believe with perfect faith that all the words of the
   prophets are true.

7. I believe with perfect faith that the prophecy of
   Moses is absolutely true. He was the chief of all
   prophets, both before and after Him.

8. I believe with perfect faith that the entire Torah
   that we now have is that which was given to
   Moses.

9. I believe with perfect faith that this Torah will not
   be changed, and that there will never be another
   given by G-d.

10. I believe with perfect faith that G-d knows all
    of man's deeds and thoughts. It is thus writ-
    ten (Psalm 33:15), "He has molded every heart
    together, He understands what each one does."

11. I believe with perfect faith that G-d rewards
    those who keep His commandments, and pun-
    ishes those who transgress Him.

12. I believe with perfect faith in the coming of the
    Messiah. How long it takes, I will await His
    coming every day.

13. I believe with perfect faith that the dead will be
    brought back to life when G-d wills it to happen.

IX.8 The Mishnah

Source: D. A. Sola and M. J. Raphall, *Eighteen Treatises
from the Mishna*, 1843, http://www.sacred-texts.com/jud
/etm/index.htm

THE METHOD OF LEGAL PROCEDURE IN NON-CAPITAL CASES

M.III. 6a. How were witnesses examined? They
were brought in and admonished; they were then
sent out, leaving behind the chief one of them. He is
asked, "How do you know that A is indebted to B?"
If he answers, "A acknowledged the indebtedness to

me," or "C told me that A was indebted to B," his statement is valueless. His evidence is valueless until he can say, "In our presence A acknowledged that he owed B two hundred zuzim."

T. V. 5b. The evidence of witnesses is not regarded as valid unless they have actually seen what they assert; and R. Jehoshua, the son of Karha, maintains that it is likewise invalid when the two witnesses do not agree. Their evidence is only regarded as upheld when the two are as one.

R. Shimeon says: They hear the words of the first witness one day, and when the other comes on the morrow they hear his words.

VI. 1. If the witnesses say, "We testify against A that he slew the ox of B," or "cut the plants of C," and the accused say, "I do not know," he is guilty. If they were to say, "Thou didst intend to slay it," or "Thou didst intend to cut them," it is merely a matter of suspicion. If a man say, "Hast thou slain my ox?" or "Hast thou cut my plants?" the other may answer "No" or "Yes" with the intent of mystifying his questioner. For there is a nay that is a yea, and a yea that is a nay.

M.III. 6b. If after the second witness has been brought in and examined their statements are found to agree, the matter is then discussed. Should two of the judges pronounce the accused innocent and one guilty, he is declared innocent. Should two pronounce him guilty and one innocent, he is declared to be guilty. Should one pronounce him innocent and one guilty, or even if two pronounce him innocent or guilty, while the third declares himself to be in doubt, the number of judges must be increased.

7. After the matter has been discussed, the contending parties are brought in. The chief judge then announces, "A, thou art innocent," or "A, thou art guilty." And whence do we know that when one of the judges goes out he must not say, "It was I who acquitted and my colleagues who convicted; but what can I do when they are in the majority"? Of such a one as this it is said: HE THAT GOETH ABOUT AS A TALE-BEARER, REVEALETH SECRETS; BUT HE THAT IS OF A FAITHFUL SPIRIT CONCEALETH THE MATTER.

T. VI. 2. Men must stand when they pronounce sentence, or bear witness, or ask for absolution from vows, or when they remove any one from the status of priesthood or of Israelitish citizenship. The judges may not show forbearance to one man and strictness to another, nor suffer one to stand and another to sit; for it is written: IN RIGHTEOUSNESS SHALT THOU JUDGE THY NEIGHBOUR. R. Jehuda said, "I have heard a tradition that if they wish to let them both sit, they can do so; yet this is of no importance. But where is it forbidden that one sit and another stand?" They replied in the name of R. Ishmael: "It has been said: Be clothed as he is clothed, or: Clothe him as thou art clothed."

3. After what fashion do they conduct the trial? The judges remain seated with the contending parties standing before them; and the one who brings the charge states his case first. When there are witnesses, these are brought in and admonished. All of them except the chief witness are then sent out, and the judges hear what he has to say and then dismiss him. Afterwards they bring in the two contending parties who state their case in each other's presence. If all the judges decide that the accused is innocent, he is adjudged innocent; and if all the judges decide that he is guilty, he is adjudged guilty. The same applies to non-capital and capital cases.

Non-capital cases are tried by three judges. If two convict or acquit and the other declares that he is in doubt, the number of judges is increased. Of more worth is the decision of one who says "guilty" than that of one who declares himself in doubt. To what extent do they add to the judges? Gradually, adding two at a time. If both (the new judges) declare him innocent, he is adjudged innocent; and if guilty, he is adjudged guilty. If one of them convicts while the other declares himself in doubt, the number of the judges must be increased, for up to that point the court has not come to a decision. If one says innocent, and another guilty, and another declares himself in doubt, the number of judges is increased, for up to that point they have but added one (to either side).

4a. They must go on adding to the judges until the trial is completed.

M.III. 8. So long as the accused can bring forward evidence, it may undo the decision. If he have been told to bring forward all his evidence within M. thirty days, and he do so within the thirty days, it may undo the decision. But after thirty days it may not undo the decision.

Rabban Shimeon, the son of Gamaliel, asked: "What happens if he have not found it within thirty days, but find it after thirty days?" It was answered: "If they have said to him, 'Bring witnesses,' and he say 'I have no witnesses'; or 'Bring evidence,' and he say 'I have no evidence'; yet after the stated time he find both witnesses and evidence, it shall not avail him."

Rabban Shimeon, the son of Gamaliel, asked: "What happens if he did not know that he had witnesses, then found witnesses; or did not know that he had evidence, then found evidence?" It was answered: "If they have said to him, 'Bring witnesses,' and he say 'I have none'; or 'Bring evidence,' and he say 'I have none'; and then, seeing himself about to be condemned, he say: 'Bring in such and such men and let them bear witness,' or if he bring out some evidence from his girdle, it shall not avail him."

T. VI. 4b. Evidence and proofs can always be brought to the court until the trial is completed. The witnesses cannot withdraw their statements until the trial is completed, or until such time as that to which the trial has been deferred. If the judges fix a time limit for the accused, and he bring forward further evidence within that time, it is accepted from him; after that time it is not accepted from him,—so R. Meir; but the majority hold that even if he bring it after three years it is accepted from him, and may annul the former decision. But if they say "Have you other witnesses?" and he say "I have but these"; or "Have you further proofs?" and he say "None but these," yet after that time he have found other witnesses and other proofs, they cannot be accepted from him unless he bring evidence to the fact that he never knew of them.

5. The witnesses can always withdraw their statements before they are investigated by the court. But after they have been investigated by the court they cannot withdraw them. And that is the general rule on this question. Witnesses who give evidence in cases of clean and unclean, of family relationships, of what is forbidden or allowed, of guilt or innocence,—if before their testimony has been investigated they say, "We were inventing," they are to be believed. If they say this after their testimony has been investigated they are not to be believed.

6. Witnesses cannot be adjudged perjurers until the trial has been completed. They cannot be scourged, fined, or put to death, until the trial has been completed. One of the witnesses cannot be adjudged a perjurer without the other; and one cannot be scourged without the other, or put to death without the other, or fined without the other. Said R. Jehuda, the son of Tabbai: "May I not live to see the consolation, if I did not once put to death a perjured witness in order to root out the opinion of the Boethuseans, who used to say that a perjured witness could not be put to death till after the accused had been put to death." Shimeon, the son of Shatah, said to him: "May I not live to see the consolation, if thou hast not shed innocent blood! For the Law says: AT THE MOUTH OF TWO WITNESSES OR THREE WITNESSES SHALL HE THAT IS TO DIE BE PUT TO DEATH. Just as there are two witnesses, so there must be two perjurers." At that time Jehuda, the son of Tabbai, agreed that he would never utter a legal decision except in agreement with Shimeon, the son of Shatah. . . .

IX. 9 Babylonian Talmud

Source: *The Babylonian Talmud, Book 1: Tract Sabbath*, trans. Michael L. Rodkinson, 1903, http://www.sacred-texts.com/jud/t01/t0115.htm

CHAPTER VII. THE GENERAL RULE CONCERNING THE PRINCIPAL ACTS OF LABOR OF SABBATH

MISHNA I.: A general rule was laid down respecting the Sabbath. One who has entirely forgotten the principle of (keeping) the Sabbath and performed many kinds of work on many Sabbath days, is liable to bring but one sin-offering. He, however, who was aware of the principle of Sabbath, but (forgetting the day) committed many acts of labor on Sabbath days, is liable to bring a separate sin-offering for each and every Sabbath day (which he has violated). One who knew that it was Sabbath and performed many kinds of work on different Sabbath days (not knowing that such work was prohibited), is liable to bring a separate sin-offering for every principal act of labor committed. One who committed many acts all emanating from one principal act is liable for but one sin-offering.

GEMARA: What is the reason that the Mishna uses the expression "a general rule"? Shall we assume that it means to teach us a subordinate rule in the succeeding Mishna, and the same is the case with the Mishna concerning the Sabbatical year, where at first a general rule is taught and the subsequent Mishnas teach a subordinate rule? Why does the Mishna relating to tithes teach one rule and the succeeding Mishna another, but does not call the first rule a "general rule"? Said R. Jose b. Abbin: Sabbath and the Sabbatical years, in both of which there are principals and derivatives, he expresses a general rule; tithes, however, in which there are no principals and derivatives, no general rule was laid down. But did not Bar Kapara teach us a general rule also in tithes? It must be therefore explained thus: The subject of Sabbath is greater than Sabbatical, as the first applies to attached and detached things, while the Sabbatical applies only to attached ones. The subject of the latter, however, is greater than tithes, as it applies to human and cattle food; while tithes applies only to human food. And Bar Kapara teaches a general rule in tithes also, because it is greater than *peah* (corner tithe), as the former applies also to figs and herbs, which is not the case with *peah*.

It was taught concerning the statement of the Mishna: He who forgot, etc., that Rabh and Samuel both said: Even a child that was captured by idolaters or a proselyte who remained among idolaters is regarded as one who was aware of the principle, but forgot it and is liable; and both R. Johanan and Resh

Lakish said that the liability falls only upon him who was aware, but subsequently forgot; the child and the proselyte in question are considered as if they were never aware, and are free.

An objection was raised from the following: A general rule was laid down concerning the observation of the Sabbath. One who had entirely forgotten the principle of Sabbath, and had performed many kinds of work on many Sabbath days, is liable for but one sin-offering. How so? A child which was captured by idolaters and a proselyte remaining with idolaters, who had performed many acts of labor on different Sabbaths, are liable for but one sin-offering; and also for the blood or (prohibited) fats which he has consumed during the whole time, and even for worshipping idols during the whole time, he is liable for only one sin-offering. Munbaz, however, frees them entirely. And thus did he discuss before R. Aqiba: Since the intentional transgressor and the unintentional are both called sinners, I may say: As an intentional one cannot be called so unless he was aware that it is a sin, the same is the case with an unintentional, who cannot be called sinner unless he was at some time aware that this is a sin (it is true, then, the above must be considered as never having been aware of it). Said R. Aqiba to, him: "I will make an amendment to your decree, as the intentional transgressor cannot be considered as such unless he is cognizant of his guilt at the time of action, so also should not the unintentional transgressor be considered as such unless he is cognizant at the time of action." Answered Munbaz: "So it is, and the more so after your amendment." Thereupon R. Aqiba replied: "According to your reasoning, one could not be called an unintentional transgressor, but an intentional." Hence it is plainly stated: "How so? A child," etc. This is only in accordance with Rabh and Samuel, and it contradicts R. Johanan and R. Simeon b. Lakish. They may say: "Is there not a Tana Munbaz, who freed them? We hold with him and with his reason, namely: It is written [Numb. xv. 29]: "A law shall be for you, for him that acteth through ignorance, and the next verse says [ibid. 30], "but the person that doeth aught with a high hand." The verse compares then the ignorant to him who has acted intentionally; and as the latter cannot be guilty unless he was aware of his sin, the same is the case with the ignorant, who cannot be considered guilty unless he was at some time aware of the sin.

Another objection was raised from a Mishna farther on: "Forty less one are the principal acts of labor." And deliberating for what purpose the number is taught, said R. Johanan: For that, if one performed them all through forgetfulness, he is liable for each of them. How is such a thing (as utter forgetfulness) to be imagined? We must assume that although cognizant of the (day being) Sabbath, one forgot which acts of labor (were prohibited). And this is correct only in accordance with R. Johanan, who holds: "If one is ignorant of what acts of labor constitute (sin punishable with) Karath (being 'cut off'), and commits one of those acts even intentionally, he is bound to bring a sin-offering only." And such an instance can be found in case one knows that those acts of labor were prohibited, at the same time being ignorant of that punishment which is Karath. But according to R. Simeon b. Lakish, who holds that one must be totally ignorant of both the punishment of Karath and what acts are prohibited on Sabbath, how can the above case be found? He was aware that Sabbath must be kept. But what was he aware of in the observance of Sabbath? He only knew of the law governing the going outside of the boundaries of the city. . . .

Rabha said (referring to the traveller who forgot the Sabbath): "On every day, except the one on which he realizes that he has missed the Sabbath, he may perform enough labor to sustain himself." But one that should do nothing and die (of hunger)? Nay; only in case he provided himself with his necessaries on the preceding day. Perhaps the preceding day was Sabbath. Therefore read: he may labor even on that day to sustain himself. In what respects is that day, then, to be distinguished from other days? By means of Kiddush and Habhdalah.

Said Rabha again: "If he only recollects the number of days he has been travelling, he may labor all day

on the eighth day of his journey, in any event" (for he surely did not start on his journey on a Sabbath). Is this not self-evident? Lest one say that one would not only not start out on the Sabbath, but also not on the day before Sabbath; hence, if he went out on the fifth day of the week, he is permitted to work on both the eighth and ninth days of his journey. Therefore he comes to teach us that only on the eighth day of his journey would he be permitted to work, for frequently one comes upon a caravan on Friday and starts out even on that day. "One who has entirely forgotten," etc. Whence is this deduced? Said R. Na'hman in the name of Rabba b. Abuhu: "There are two verses in the Scripture, viz. [Exod. xxxi. 16]: 'And the children of Israel shall keep the Sabbath,' and [Lev. xix. 3]: 'And my Sabbaths shall ye keep.' How is this to be explained?" The first means the observance of the commandment of Sabbath generally, and the second means one observance of the commandment for each Sabbath.

"One who knew (the principle of) Sabbath." What is the reason of a difference between the former and the latter part of the Mishna? Said R. Na'hman: For what transgression does the Scripture make one liable for a sin-offering? For what is done through ignorance? In the former part of the Mishna the case of one who was not aware that it was Sabbath is dealt with, and hence only one sin-offering is imposed, while in the latter the case dealt with is of one who was aware that it was Sabbath, but ignorant as to the acts of labor, hence a sin-offering for each act is prescribed. . . .

MISHNA II.: The principal acts of labor (prohibited on the Sabbath) are forty less one—viz.: Sowing, ploughing, reaping, binding into sheaves, threshing, winnowing, fruit-cleaning, grinding, sifting, kneading, baking, wool-shearing, bleaching, combing, dyeing, spinning, warping, making two spindle-trees, weaving two threads, separating two threads (in the warp), tying a knot, untying a knot, sewing on with two stitches, tearing in order to sew together with two stitches, hunting deer, slaughtering the same, skinning them, salting them, preparing the hide, scraping the hair off, cutting it, writing two (single) letters (characters), erasing in order to write two letters, building, demolishing (in order to rebuild), kindling, extinguishing (fire), hammering, transferring from one place into another. These are the principal acts of labor—forty less one.

GEMARA: For what purpose is the number (so distinctly) given? (They are enumerated.) Said R. Johanan: If one labored through total ignorance of the (laws governing the) Sabbath, he must bring a sin-offering for every act of labor performed.

Sowing, ploughing." Let us see: Ploughing being always done before sowing, let it be taught first, The Tana (who taught as in the Mishna) is a Palestinian, and in his country they sow first and then plough. Some one taught that sowing, pruning, planting, transplanting, and grafting are all one and the same kind of labor. What would he inform us thereby? That if one performs many acts of labor, all of the same class, he is liable for but one sin-offering.

Said R. Aha in the name of R. Hyya b. Ashi, quoting R. Ami: "One who prunes is guilty of planting, and one who plants, transplants, or grafts is guilty of sowing." Of sowing and not of planting? I mean to say of sowing also.

Said R. Kahana: One who prunes and uses the branches for fuel is liable for two sin-offerings, one for reaping and one for planting. Said R. Joseph: One who mows alfalfa (hay) is guilty of mowing and planting both. Said Abayi: One who mows clover hay (which sheds its seed when mowed) is liable (for a sin-offering) for mowing and sowing. . . .

The rabbis taught: If there are several kinds of food before a man on the Sabbath, he may select such as he desires and even set it aside, but he must not separate the good from the spoilt. If he does this, he is liable for a sin-offering. How is this to be understood? R. Hamnuna explained it thus: "One may select the good from the spoilt for immediate or later consumption, but he must not pick out the spoilt, leaving the good for later consumption. If he does this, he is liable." Abayi opposed: "Is there anything mentioned (in the Mishna) about separating the good from the spoilt?" He therefore explained the Boraitha as follows: "Food may be selected for immediate consumption and setting aside, but not for later consumption. If this is done, it is considered the same as storing it, and involves the liability." This was reported to Rabha by the rabbis, and he said: Na'hmeni (Abayi) has explained it correctly.

Key Terms

Ashkenazim   One of the two main cultural groups in Judaism which emerged in the Middle Ages. Their tradition is from Palestinian Jewry and they live in central northern and eastern Europe. They developed Yiddish as their language, which is a mixture of Hebrew, Slav, and German.

circumcision   The cutting off of the prepuce in males or the internal labia in females as a religious rite. It is widely practiced in traditional African religion, either shortly after birth or at puberty. In Judaism boys are circumcised at eight days of age in commemoration of Abraham's covenant with God. Male converts to Judaism undergo this rite. Circumcision is also practiced in Islam.

Conservative Judaism   Movement which tries to stand midway between Orthodox and Progressive Judaism. It claims to accept the Talmudic tradition but to interpret the Torah in the light of modern needs.

covenant   A bargain or agreement. In Judaism the chief reference is to that made with Moses at Sinai: God, having liberated his people from Egypt, promises them the land of Israel and his blessing and protection as long as they keep the Torah. This confirms the earlier covenants with Abraham and with Noah. The term is also used of God's special relationship with the house of David. With the defeat of the Kingdom of Judah in 586 BCE, Jeremiah's prophecy of a new covenant written on the people's hearts came into its own.

Hasidim   ("The pious") (1) The group of Jewish quietist ascetics who were the forerunners of the Pharisees. (2) A group of medieval mystics who were particularly important for the development of Judaism in Germany. (3) Followers of Baal Shem Tov, who taught a new kind of Hasidism in the eighteenth century CE.

Hanukkah   ("Dedication") Eight-day Jewish festival marked by the lighting of ritual candles which celebrates the rededication of the Temple OF Jerusalem by Judas Maccabeus in 164 BCE.

Holocaust   (From the Latin Bible's word for "whole burnt offering") The name given to Hitler's extermination of 6 million Jews in the Nazi death camps in Europe 1941–45. Mass destruction was envisaged as the "final solution" to the "problem" of the Jews. The memory of the Holocaust is the key to modern Jewish theology and made the founding of the state of Israel an event of profound significance.

Jerusalem   Fortified city captured by David in the tenth century BCE which became the capital and principal sanctuary for the people of Israel. It has remained the focus of Jewish religious aspirations and ideals. It is a holy city for Christians because of its association with the passion, death, and resurrection of Jesus of Nazareth. For Muslims it is the holiest city after Mecca. The Mosque of the Dome of the Rock stands over the site of Muhammad's night journey.

Kabbalah   Jewish mystical tradition that flourished in the teaching of two schools: the practical school based in Germany, which concentrated in prayer and meditation; the speculative school in France and Spain in the thirteenth and fourteenth centuries. The tradition originates in Talmudic speculation on the themes of the work of creation and the divine chariot mentioned in the biblical book of Ezekiel. The most famous Kabbalistic book is *Zohar* ("splendor"), a Midrash on the Pentateuch.

Mishnah   A compilation of Jewish oral teachings undertaken by Rabbi Judah Hanasi in around 200 CE. It quickly became second in authority only to the Hebrew Bible and formed the basis of the Talmud. The Mishnah helped Jewish teaching to survive in a period of persecution when the future of the Sanhedrin was in doubt.

Orthodox Judaism   Traditional Judaism which is Talmudic in belief and practice. It is the largest of the modern groupings and it is the form of religion accepted as authentic in Israel.

Passover (*Pesach*)   Seven-day Jewish spring festival marking the deliverance from Egypt. Since Talmudic times the festival has begun with a service in the home where unleavened bread, wine and bitter herbs symbolize the joys and sorrows of the exodus. There is a meal and the evening concludes with psalms and hymns which look to God's final redemption of Israel.

Progressive Judaism   Term covering the Liberal and Reform movements which emerged in Judaism in nineteenth-century Europe. Both movements are critical of the Talmudic fundamentalism of Orthodox Judaism and welcome scientific research on the Bible. They also tend to use the vernacular in worship and interpret the dietary laws more liberally than do the Orthodox.

rabbi   ("My master") Jewish religious teacher and interpreter of the Torah. In modern Judaism he or she is a minister to the community, a preacher, and a leader of synagogue worship.

rabbinic Judaism   The religion of the medieval rabbis who expanded the interpretation of the Talmud and produced authoritative codes of laws, responses, views and judgments, mostly in the form of correspondence with particular communities.

Sanhedrin   Jewish supreme council of seventy which organized religious life during the period of independence following the revolt of the Maccabees. Under Herod the Great the Sanhedrin was divided: the Sadducees dealt with political matters; the Pharisees concentrated on the interpretation of the Torah.

Sephardim   One of the two main cultural groups in Judaism which emerged during the Middle Ages. Sephardic Jews lived in Spain and Portugal and their traditions go back to Babylonian Jewry. They developed Ladino as their language.

Shabbat   (Sabbath) Jewish day of worship and rest lasting from Friday sunset to Saturday sunset. The Sabbath is holy because it commemorates God's rest on the seventh day of creation and reminds Jews (2) of the deliverance from Egypt.

Shema   The Jewish confession of faith, recited in the morning and evening service. *Shema* is the opening word in Hebrew of the confession: 'Hear, O Israel, the Lord our God, the Lord is One . . .'. Three passages from the Torah confirm that there is one God and that Israel is chosen to witness to him.

Talmud   The written interpretation and development of the Hebrew scriptures. It is based on the Mishnah of Judah Hanasi, with the addition of some excluded teachings and commentary recorded from the debates and controversies of the Schools of Babylon on Palestine. There are two versions: the Palestinian, compiled while the Jews were under duress from the Christian Church, and the Babylonian which is more detailed and complete.

Temple of Jerusalem   The temple first built by Solomon on a site bequeathed by David. It was divided into the Holy Place and the Holy of Holies where dwelt the presence of YHWH. This temple was destroyed in 586 BCE. The second temple was dedicated in 515 BCE. It was desecrated by the Hellenistic Seleucid king Antiochus Epiphanes but rededicated by Judas Maccabeus. Rebuilding was begun under Herod the Great in 20 BCE. The temple was virtually completed in 62 CE, but destroyed by Titus in 70 CE.

Torah   (1) The five books of the Law (the Pentateuch) revealed to Moses; the first division of the Hebrew Bible. (2) "The teaching," the correct response of Israel to God, outlined in the rules for purity and social justice. It is God's gift to Israel and the way for Israel to fulfill God's call for holiness. (3) The cosmological principle of order which embraces moral and religious instruction as well as the physical ordering of the universe by God.

Zionism   The movement to establish a national and permanent homeland for Jews. In 1897 the first Zionist Congress was organized in Basle by Theodor Herzl in the wake of a wave of European anti-Semitism. Gradually the movement became determined that Palestine was the only realistic place to establish the Jewish state and Jews were encouraged to emigrate and acquire property there. The majority of Jews today support Zionism to the extent that it is manifested in the modern state of Israel.

Questions for Study and Discussion

1.   What was the significance of the Temple in Jerusalem to early Judaism? What were some of the consequences of its destruction?
2.   Explain the main differences among Orthodox, Conservative, and Reform Judaism.

3.   What was the role of covenant in pre-modern Judaism? Give an example of a covenant described in biblical writings.
4.   What are the three meanings of the word *torah*? What is the Tanakh?
5.   What is Zionism? What is its significance in today's world?
6.   Name two major Jewish thinkers who lived before the twentieth century and describe their impact on the development of the faith.
7.   The Holocaust forever changed the nature of Jewish theology. What aspects of Judaism would you say were most affected by the Holocaust?

Questions for Reflection

Write your personal reflections to each of these questions in the space provided.

1.   Discuss the role of history in the consciousness of Judaism. (See pp. 296–308.)

2.   Consider the evolution of the scriptures of Judaism. (See pp. 309–12.)

3.   What does it mean that the Jewish people have been elected by God? (See pp. 315–16.)

4.   Describe the role of the covenant in Judaism and Jewish history. (See pp. 318–19.)

5.   Draw from sociological and critical theories of religion to analyze the nation of Israel's dilemma in the modern world. (See pp. 338–39.)

Selected Online Resources

▶ Jerusalem 3000: Three Millennia of History—an online catalog of a 1996 exhibition of maps of Jerusalem from medieval to modern times, with explanatory text
http://oshermaps.org/exhibitions/jerusalem-3000/i-maps-and-history-jerusalem

▶ Judaism and Jewish Resources—an extensive, categorized list of web links
http://shamash.org/trb/judaism.html

▶ United States Holocaust Memorial Museum—many different and changing online exhibitions as well as other resources
http://www.ushmm.org

Part 10: Christianity

Chapter Summaries

61. A Historical Overview

Early Christianity had three centers of growth: Jerusalem, Asia Minor, and Alexandria. At first a Jewish sect, it spread rapidly through the house church movement despite facing persecution by the Roman Empire as well as local leaders. Once Constantine recognized the Christian faith as a legitimate religion, the church began to experience tensions over fundamental doctrines like the identity of Jesus and the nature of God. Eventually the church divided between East and West. Later, the Renaissance supported expanded study of scripture and work on translations. The Reformation then brought new ideas as well as upheaval among clergy and laity alike. Modern Christianity was developed through missionary contact as well as political developments like the rise of communism. Today Christianity can be seen as primarily a faith of the developing world.

62. Jesus

The historical Jesus was a Palestine-born Jew and a prophet born in Bethlehem and raised in Galilee. According to the accounts in the New Testament Gospels, he was famed for his preaching, teaching, and healing. Because he questioned authority, both Jewish and imperial, and crossed societal barriers, he faced serious opposition quickly. Ultimately he was tried on charges of blasphemy and sentenced to death by the Roman governor Pontius Pilate as a political rebel. Some of his followers claimed that he was resurrected three days after death and appeared to them, urging them to spread his message about the kingdom of God, the need for repentance, and the hope of salvation for all who believed.

63. Sacred Writings

The Christian Bible encompasses the Hebrew Bible, or Old Testament, and the New Testament—together a collection of writings from a thousand-year period. The Gospels are four accounts of the life of Jesus; the New Testament includes these, letters from the Apostle Paul as well as later writers using his name, and Revelation (an apocalyptic story). The Bible is considered "inspired," meaning that the writers were directed by God. Different strands of Christianity interpret the Bible in various ways and consider different translations more authoritative than others.

64. Beliefs

Christianity's Jewish roots can be seen in its basic belief in God the Creator and Lord of the universe. Its unique beliefs are based in a Trinitarian view of God as Father, Son, and Holy Spirit, with Jesus the Son of God who was resurrected from the dead and fulfilled the prophecy of the Old Testament. Jesus's death has been seen as cancelling sin—God's gift to humanity. Early Christians were also Jews, but ultimately, the belief that Jesus's life, death, and resurrection superseded the Law meant that Jewish beliefs and practices were not seen as essential to Christian belief. The Christian message to all people is that everyone faces God's judgment but that all can be saved through belief in Jesus Christ. Christianity as a world religion has developed in multiple ways with many sects and schismatic groups, so that it contains conflicting views on many fundamental doctrines, including salvation and biblical authority.

65. Worship and Festivals

The Eucharist, also called the Lord's Supper, is the heart of Christian worship. It originally commemorated Jesus's death and resurrection, with the sacramental bread and wine signifying his body and blood. Baptism is the ritual in which believers enter Christian community; churches vary on whether baptism is for infants or for adults only. Christian worship developed over the centuries from its roots as a house-church movement into a church-based faith with clergy, creeds, liturgy, and rituals. The Reformation brought criticism of what some saw as corruption among the church leadership and a return to simpler forms of worship as well as the development of new sects and traditions.

66. Family and Society

For the Apostle Paul, the church is the body of Christ and stands above one's family. Yet Christianity grew because of married couples joining the church and raising children within the faith. It was Protestant Christianity in particular that valued the family as equal to the church; Roman Catholicism followed suit after the Reformation. While modern churches lost some power in political and educational institutions, they held sway in the domestic arena. Tensions within the church over what constitutes unbreakable tradition and what values are supreme reflect general societal changes that Christians, like all people, must confront.

67. Contemporary Christianity

Christianity has always been capable of translation into different languages and cultural forms. Today, while it appears to be on the decline in many Western and developed nations, it is on the rise in Africa, Latin America, and some parts of Asia. Western missions were key to the spread of Christianity in the nineteenth century and into the twentieth; now it is local Christians who continue to grow the church in their communities. As Christianity continues to grow and change, pluralism is a common theme, as well as the struggle for social and economic justice on a global scale.

Key Personalities

Jesus of Nazareth (first century CE)

Teacher, prophet and worker of miracles in first-century Palestine and founder of Christianity. He taught the coming of the kingdom of God with forgiveness and new life for all who believed. Claims that he was the promised messiah (or Christ) roused opposition from the religious authorities, and he was put to death by crucifixion. But after his death his followers claimed that he was risen from the dead and he was seen alive by many. Christians believe him to be fully divine and fully human, and await his promised second coming, which will bring the fulfillment of the kingdom of God.

"As he was setting out on a journey, a man ran up and knelt before him, and asked him, 'Good Teacher, what must I do to inherit eternal life?' Jesus said to him, 'Why do you call me good? No one is good but God alone. You know the commandments: "You shall not murder; You shall not commit adultery; You shall not steal; You shall not bear false witness; You shall not defraud; Honor your father and mother."' He said to him, 'Teacher, I have kept all these things since my youth.' Jesus, looking at him, loved him and said, 'You lack one thing; go, sell what you own, and give the money to the poor, and you will have treasure in heaven; then come, follow me.' When he heard this, he was shocked and went away grieving, for he had many possessions."

(Mark 10:17-22, New Revised Standard Version translation)

Thomas Aquinas (1225–74)

Dominican theologian and philosopher whose teachings form the basis of official Roman Catholic theology. He taught a fundamental distinction between faith and reason, asserting that God's existence can be proved, but that the doctrines of the trinity and the incarnation are revealed and must be accepted on faith.

"The natural dictates of reason must certainly be quite true: it is impossible to think of their being

otherwise. Nor a gain is it permissible to believe that the tenets of faith are false, being so evidently confirmed by God. Since therefore falsehood alone is contrary to truth, it is impossible for the truth of faith to be contrary to principles known by natural reason. . . . The knowledge of principles naturally known is put into us by God, seeing that God Himself is the author of our nature. Therefore these principles also are contained in the Divine Wisdom. Whatever therefore is contrary to these principles is contrary to Divine Wisdom, and cannot be of God. . . . What is natural cannot be changed while nature remains. But contrary opinions cannot be in the same mind at the same time: therefore no opinion or belief is sent to man from God contrary to natural knowledge."

(Thomas Aquinas, "Of God and His Creatures," in *Summa Contra Gentiles*, trans. Joseph Rickaby [London; Burns and Oates, 1905], http://www2.nd.edu/Departments /Maritain/etext/gc.htm)

Martin Luther (1483–1546)

Founder of the German Reformation. He held that people could only be justified before God by faith in Jesus Christ, not by any works of religion, so the priesthood and the mediating role of the church are unnecessary.

"We find many who pray, fast, establish endowments, do this or that, lead a good life before men, and yet if you should ask them whether they are sure that what they do pleases God, they say, 'No'; they do not know, or they doubt. And there are some very learned men, who mislead them, and say that it is not necessary to be sure of this; and yet, on the other hand, these same men do nothing else but teach good works. Now all these works are done outside of faith, therefore they are nothing and altogether dead. For as their conscience stands toward God and as it believes, so also are the works which grow out of it. Now they have no faith, no good conscience toward God, therefore the works lack their head, and all their life and goodness is nothing. Hence it comes that when I exalt faith and reject such works done without faith, they accuse me of forbidding good works, when in truth I am trying hard to teach real good works of faith."

(Martin Luther, *A Treatise on Good Works*, http://www .iclnet.org/pub/resources/text/wittenberg/luther/work -02a.txt)

John Calvin (1509–64)

French theologian who organized the Reformation from Geneva. He emphasized justification by faith and the sole authority of the Bible and in particular that each person's eternal destiny was decided irrevocably by God and only those destined for salvation would come to faith.

"When we attribute foreknowledge to God, we mean that all things have ever been, and perpetually remain, before His eyes, so that to His knowledge nothing in future or past, but all things are present; and present in such a manner, that He does not merely conceive of them from ideas formed in His mind, as things remembered by us appear present to our minds, but really beholds and sees them as if actually placed before Him. And this foreknowledge extends to the whole world, and to all the creatures. Predestination we call the eternal decree of God, by which He has determined in Himself what would have to become of every individual of mankind. For they are not all created with a similar destiny; but eternal life is fore-ordained for some, and eternal damnation for others. Every man, therefore, being created for one or the other of these ends, we say, he is predestinated either to life or to death. This God has not only testified in particular persons, but has given a specimen of it in the whole posterity of Abraham, which should evidently show the future condition of every nation to depend upon His decision."

(John Calvin, *Institutes of the Christian Religion*, http:// www.fordham.edu/halsall/mod/calvin-predest.html)

Primary Source Readings

The following excerpted readings represent some of the important primary sources mentioned in the main text. Additional primary sources are available both in print and online, and students are encouraged to contact their instructors for further information.

The source for all biblical passages below is the New Revised Standard Version Bible.

X.1 Infancy Narratives from the Gospels of Matthew and Luke

MATTHEW 1:18-25—THE BIRTH OF JESUS THE MESSIAH

18 Now the birth of Jesus the Messiah took place in this way. When his mother Mary had been engaged to Joseph, but before they lived together, she was found to be with child from the Holy Spirit. [19]Her husband Joseph, being a righteous man and unwilling to expose her to public disgrace, planned to dismiss her quietly. [20]But just when he had resolved to do this, an angel of the Lord appeared to him in a dream and said, 'Joseph, son of David, do not be afraid to take Mary as your wife, for the child conceived in her is from the Holy Spirit. [21]She will bear a son, and you are to name him Jesus, for he will save his people from their sins.' [22]All this took place to fulfil what had been spoken by the Lord through the prophet:

[23] 'Look, the virgin shall conceive and bear a son,

and they shall name him Emmanuel,'

which means, 'God is with us.' [24]When Joseph awoke from sleep, he did as the angel of the Lord commanded him; he took her as his wife, [25]but had no marital relations with her until she had borne a son; and he named him Jesus.

LUKE 1:26-56, 2:1-21—THE BIRTH OF JESUS FORETOLD

26 In the sixth month the angel Gabriel was sent by God to a town in Galilee called Nazareth, [27]to a virgin engaged to a man whose name was Joseph, of the house of David. The virgin's name was Mary. [28]And he came to her and said, 'Greetings, favoured one!

The Lord is with you.' [29]But she was much perplexed by his words and pondered what sort of greeting this might be. [30]The angel said to her, 'Do not be afraid, Mary, for you have found favour with God. [31]And now, you will conceive in your womb and bear a son, and you will name him Jesus. [32]He will be great, and will be called the Son of the Most High, and the Lord God will give to him the throne of his ancestor David. [33]He will reign over the house of Jacob for ever, and of his kingdom there will be no end.' [34]Mary said to the angel, 'How can this be, since I am a virgin?' [35]The angel said to her, 'The Holy Spirit will come upon you, and the power of the Most High will overshadow you; therefore the child to be born will be holy; he will be called Son of God. [36]And now, your relative Elizabeth in her old age has also conceived a son; and this is the sixth month for her who was said to be barren. [37]For nothing will be impossible with God.' [38]Then Mary said, 'Here am I, the servant of the Lord; let it be with me according to your word.' Then the angel departed from her.

Mary Visits Elizabeth

39 In those days Mary set out and went with haste to a Judean town in the hill country, [40]where she entered the house of Zechariah and greeted Elizabeth. [41]When Elizabeth heard Mary's greeting, the child leapt in her womb. And Elizabeth was filled with the Holy Spirit [42]and exclaimed with a loud cry, 'Blessed are you among women, and blessed is the fruit of your womb. [43]And why has this happened to me, that the mother of my Lord comes to me? [44]For as soon as I heard the sound of your greeting, the child in my womb leapt for joy. [45]And blessed is she who believed that there would be a fulfilment of what was spoken to her by the Lord.'

Mary's Song of Praise

46 And Mary said,

'My soul magnifies the Lord,

[47] and my spirit rejoices in God my Saviour,

[48] for he has looked with favour on the lowliness of his servant.

Surely, from now on all generations will call me blessed;

[49] for the Mighty One has done great things for me,

and holy is his name.

[50] His mercy is for those who fear him

from generation to generation.

[51] He has shown strength with his arm;

he has scattered the proud in the thoughts of their hearts.

[52] He has brought down the powerful from their thrones,

and lifted up the lowly;

[53] he has filled the hungry with good things,

and sent the rich away empty.

[54] He has helped his servant Israel,

in remembrance of his mercy,

[55] according to the promise he made to our ancestors,

to Abraham and to his descendants for ever.'

56 And Mary remained with her for about three months and then returned to her home.

The Birth of Jesus

2In those days a decree went out from Emperor Augustus that all the world should be registered. [2]This was the first registration and was taken while Quirinius was governor of Syria. [3]All went to their own towns to be registered. [4]Joseph also went from the town of Nazareth in Galilee to Judea, to the city of David called Bethlehem, because he was descended from the house and family of David. [5]He went to be registered with Mary, to whom he was engaged and who was expecting a child. [6]While they were there, the time came for her to deliver her child. [7]And she gave birth to her firstborn son and wrapped him in bands of cloth, and laid him in a manger, because there was no place for them in the inn.

The Shepherds and the Angels

8 In that region there were shepherds living in the fields, keeping watch over their flock by night. [9]Then an angel of the Lord stood before them, and the glory of the Lord shone around them, and they were terrified. [10]But the angel said to them, 'Do not be afraid; for see—I am bringing you good news of great joy for all the people: [11]to you is born this day in the city of David a Saviour, who is the Messiah, the Lord. [12]This will be a sign for you: you will find a child wrapped in bands of cloth and lying in a manger.' [13]And suddenly there was with the angel a multitude of the heavenly host, praising God and saying,

[14] 'Glory to God in the highest heaven,

and on earth peace among those whom he favours!'

15 When the angels had left them and gone into heaven, the shepherds said to one another, 'Let us go now to Bethlehem and see this thing that has taken place, which the Lord has made known to us.' [16]So they went with haste and found Mary and Joseph, and the child lying in the manger. [17]When they saw this, they made known what had been told them about this child; [18]and all who heard it were amazed at what the shepherds told them. [19]But Mary treasured all these words and pondered them in her heart. [20]The shepherds returned, glorifying and praising God for all they had heard and seen, as it had been told them.

Jesus Is Named

21 After eight days had passed, it was time to circumcise the child; and he was called Jesus, the name given by the angel before he was conceived in the womb.

X.2 The Sermon on the Mount

MATTHEW 5–7—THE BEATITUDES

5When Jesus saw the crowds, he went up the mountain; and after he sat down, his disciples came to him. [2]Then he began to speak, and taught them, saying:

3 'Blessed are the poor in spirit, for theirs is the kingdom of heaven.

4 'Blessed are those who mourn, for they will be comforted.

5 'Blessed are the meek, for they will inherit the earth.

6 'Blessed are those who hunger and thirst for righteousness, for they will be filled.

7 'Blessed are the merciful, for they will receive mercy.

8 'Blessed are the pure in heart, for they will see God.

9 'Blessed are the peacemakers, for they will be called children of God.

10 'Blessed are those who are persecuted for righteousness' sake, for theirs is the kingdom of heaven.

11 'Blessed are you when people revile you and persecute you and utter all kinds of evil against you falsely on my account. [12]Rejoice and be glad, for your reward is great in heaven, for in the same way they persecuted the prophets who were before you.

Salt and Light

13 'You are the salt of the earth; but if salt has lost its taste, how can its saltiness be restored? It is no longer good for anything, but is thrown out and trampled under foot.

14 'You are the light of the world. A city built on a hill cannot be hidden. [15]No one after lighting a lamp puts it under the bushel basket, but on the lampstand, and it gives light to all in the house. [16]In the same way, let your light shine before others, so that they may see your good works and give glory to your Father in heaven.

The Law and the Prophets

17 'Do not think that I have come to abolish the law or the prophets; I have come not to abolish but to fulfil. [18]For truly I tell you, until heaven and earth pass away, not one letter, not one stroke of a letter, will pass from the law until all is accomplished. [19]Therefore, whoever breaks one of the least of these commandments, and teaches others to do the same, will be called least in the kingdom of heaven; but

whoever does them and teaches them will be called great in the kingdom of heaven. [20]For I tell you, unless your righteousness exceeds that of the scribes and Pharisees, you will never enter the kingdom of heaven.

Concerning Anger

21 'You have heard that it was said to those of ancient times, "You shall not murder"; and "whoever murders shall be liable to judgement." [22]But I say to you that if you are angry with a brother or sister, you will be liable to judgement; and if you insult a brother or sister, you will be liable to the council; and if you say, "You fool," you will be liable to the hell of fire. [23]So when you are offering your gift at the altar, if you remember that your brother or sister has something against you, [24]leave your gift there before the altar and go; first be reconciled to your brother or sister, and then come and offer your gift. [25]Come to terms quickly with your accuser while you are on the way to court with him, or your accuser may hand you over to the judge, and the judge to the guard, and you will be thrown into prison. [26]Truly I tell you, you will never get out until you have paid the last penny.

Concerning Adultery

27 'You have heard that it was said, "You shall not commit adultery." [28]But I say to you that everyone who looks at a woman with lust has already committed adultery with her in his heart. [29]If your right eye causes you to sin, tear it out and throw it away; it is better for you to lose one of your members than for your whole body to be thrown into hell. [30]And if your right hand causes you to sin, cut it off and throw it away; it is better for you to lose one of your members than for your whole body to go into hell.

Concerning Divorce

31 'It was also said, "Whoever divorces his wife, let him give her a certificate of divorce." [32]But I say to you that anyone who divorces his wife, except on the ground of unchastity, causes her to commit adultery; and whoever marries a divorced woman commits adultery.

Concerning Oaths

33 'Again, you have heard that it was said to those of ancient times, "You shall not swear falsely, but carry out the vows you have made to the Lord." [34]But I say to you, Do not swear at all, either by heaven, for it is the throne of God, [35]or by the earth, for it is his footstool, or by Jerusalem, for it is the city of the great King. [36]And do not swear by your head, for you cannot make one hair white or black. [37]Let your word be "Yes, Yes" or "No, No"; anything more than this comes from the evil one.

Concerning Retaliation

38 'You have heard that it was said, "An eye for an eye and a tooth for a tooth." [39]But I say to you, Do not resist an evildoer. But if anyone strikes you on the right cheek, turn the other also; [40]and if anyone wants to sue you and take your coat, give your cloak as well; [41]and if anyone forces you to go one mile, go also the second mile. [42]Give to everyone who begs from you, and do not refuse anyone who wants to borrow from you.

Love for Enemies

43 'You have heard that it was said, "You shall love your neighbour and hate your enemy." [44]But I say to you, Love your enemies and pray for those who persecute you, [45]so that you may be children of your Father in heaven; for he makes his sun rise on the evil and on the good, and sends rain on the righteous and on the unrighteous. [46]For if you love those who love you, what reward do you have? Do not even the tax-collectors do the same? [47]And if you greet only your brothers and sisters, what more are you doing than others? Do not even the Gentiles do the same? [48]Be perfect, therefore, as your heavenly Father is perfect.

Concerning Almsgiving

6'Beware of practising your piety before others in order to be seen by them; for then you have no reward from your Father in heaven.

2 'So whenever you give alms, do not sound a trumpet before you, as the hypocrites do in the

synagogues and in the streets, so that they may be praised by others. Truly I tell you, they have received their reward. ³But when you give alms, do not let your left hand know what your right hand is doing, ⁴so that your alms may be done in secret; and your Father who sees in secret will reward you.

Concerning Prayer

5 'And whenever you pray, do not be like the hypocrites; for they love to stand and pray in the synagogues and at the street corners, so that they may be seen by others. Truly I tell you, they have received their reward. ⁶But whenever you pray, go into your room and shut the door and pray to your Father who is in secret; and your Father who sees in secret will reward you.

7 'When you are praying, do not heap up empty phrases as the Gentiles do; for they think that they will be heard because of their many words. ⁸Do not be like them, for your Father knows what you need before you ask him.

9 'Pray then in this way:

Our Father in heaven,

hallowed be your name.

¹⁰ Your kingdom come.

Your will be done,

on earth as it is in heaven.

¹¹ Give us this day our daily bread.

¹² And forgive us our debts,

as we also have forgiven our debtors.

¹³ And do not bring us to the time of trial,

but rescue us from the evil one.

¹⁴For if you forgive others their trespasses, your heavenly Father will also forgive you; ¹⁵but if you do not forgive others, neither will your Father forgive your trespasses.

Concerning Fasting

16 'And whenever you fast, do not look dismal, like the hypocrites, for they disfigure their faces so as to show others that they are fasting. Truly I tell you, they have received their reward. ¹⁷But when you fast, put oil on your head and wash your face, ¹⁸so that your fasting may be seen not by others but by your Father who is in secret; and your Father who sees in secret will reward you.

Concerning Treasures

19 'Do not store up for yourselves treasures on earth, where moth and rust consume and where thieves break in and steal; ²⁰but store up for yourselves treasures in heaven, where neither moth nor rust consumes and where thieves do not break in and steal. ²¹For where your treasure is, there your heart will be also.

The Sound Eye

22 'The eye is the lamp of the body. So, if your eye is healthy, your whole body will be full of light; ²³but if your eye is unhealthy, your whole body will be full of darkness. If then the light in you is darkness, how great is the darkness!

Serving Two Masters

24 'No one can serve two masters; for a slave will either hate the one and love the other, or be devoted to the one and despise the other. You cannot serve God and wealth.

Do Not Worry

25 'Therefore I tell you, do not worry about your life, what you will eat or what you will drink, or about your body, what you will wear. Is not life more than food, and the body more than clothing? ²⁶Look at the birds of the air; they neither sow nor reap nor gather into barns, and yet your heavenly Father feeds them. Are you not of more value than they? ²⁷And can any of you by worrying add a single hour to your span of life? ²⁸And why do you worry about clothing? Consider the lilies of the field, how they grow; they neither toil nor spin, ²⁹yet I tell you, even Solomon

in all his glory was not clothed like one of these. [30]But if God so clothes the grass of the field, which is alive today and tomorrow is thrown into the oven, will he not much more clothe you—you of little faith? [31]Therefore do not worry, saying, "What will we eat?" or "What will we drink?" or "What will we wear?" [32]For it is the Gentiles who strive for all these things; and indeed your heavenly Father knows that you need all these things. [33]But strive first for the kingdom of God and his righteousness, and all these things will be given to you as well.

34 'So do not worry about tomorrow, for tomorrow will bring worries of its own. Today's trouble is enough for today.

Judging Others

7[1]'Do not judge, so that you may not be judged. [2]For with the judgement you make you will be judged, and the measure you give will be the measure you get. [3]Why do you see the speck in your neighbour's eye, but do not notice the log in your own eye? [4]Or how can you say to your neighbour, "Let me take the speck out of your eye", while the log is in your own eye? [5]You hypocrite, first take the log out of your own eye, and then you will see clearly to take the speck out of your neighbour's eye.

Profaning the Holy

6 'Do not give what is holy to dogs; and do not throw your pearls before swine, or they will trample them under foot and turn and maul you.

Ask, Search, Knock

7 'Ask, and it will be given to you; search, and you will find; knock, and the door will be opened for you. [8]For everyone who asks receives, and everyone who searches finds, and for everyone who knocks, the door will be opened. [9]Is there anyone among you who, if your child asks for bread, will give a stone? [10]Or if the child asks for a fish, will give a snake? [11]If you then, who are evil, know how to give good gifts to your children, how much more will your Father in heaven give good things to those who ask him!

The Golden Rule

12 'In everything do to others as you would have them do to you; for this is the law and the prophets.

The Narrow Gate

13 'Enter through the narrow gate; for the gate is wide and the road is easy that leads to destruction, and there are many who take it. [14]For the gate is narrow and the road is hard that leads to life, and there are few who find it.

A Tree and Its Fruit

15 'Beware of false prophets, who come to you in sheep's clothing but inwardly are ravenous wolves. [16]You will know them by their fruits. Are grapes gathered from thorns, or figs from thistles? [17]In the same way, every good tree bears good fruit, but the bad tree bears bad fruit. [18]A good tree cannot bear bad fruit, nor can a bad tree bear good fruit. [19]Every tree that does not bear good fruit is cut down and thrown into the fire. [20]Thus you will know them by their fruits.

Concerning Self-Deception

21 'Not everyone who says to me, "Lord, Lord", will enter the kingdom of heaven, but only one who does the will of my Father in heaven. [22]On that day many will say to me, "Lord, Lord, did we not prophesy in your name, and cast out demons in your name, and do many deeds of power in your name?" [23]Then I will declare to them, "I never knew you; go away from me, you evildoers."

Hearers and Doers

24 'Everyone then who hears these words of mine and acts on them will be like a wise man who built his house on rock. [25]The rain fell, the floods came, and the winds blew and beat on that house, but it did not fall, because it had been founded on rock. [26]And everyone who hears these words of mine and does not act on them will be like a foolish man who built his house on sand. [27]The rain fell, and the floods came, and the winds blew and beat against that house, and it fell—and great was its fall!'

28 Now when Jesus had finished saying these things, the crowds were astounded at his teaching, [29]for he taught them as one having authority, and not as their scribes.

X.3 The Trial, Crucifixion, and Resurrection of Jesus

MARK 14:43-16:8—THE BETRAYAL AND ARREST OF JESUS

43 Immediately, while he was still speaking, Judas, one of the twelve, arrived; and with him there was a crowd with swords and clubs, from the chief priests, the scribes, and the elders. [44]Now the betrayer had given them a sign, saying, 'The one I will kiss is the man; arrest him and lead him away under guard.' [45]So when he came, he went up to him at once and said, 'Rabbi!' and kissed him. [46]Then they laid hands on him and arrested him. [47]But one of those who stood near drew his sword and struck the slave of the high priest, cutting off his ear. [48]Then Jesus said to them, 'Have you come out with swords and clubs to arrest me as though I were a bandit? [49]Day after day I was with you in the temple teaching, and you did not arrest me. But let the scriptures be fulfilled.' [50]All of them deserted him and fled.

51 A certain young man was following him, wearing nothing but a linen cloth. They caught hold of him, [52]but he left the linen cloth and ran off naked.

Jesus before the Council

53 They took Jesus to the high priest; and all the chief priests, the elders, and the scribes were assembled. [54]Peter had followed him at a distance, right into the courtyard of the high priest; and he was sitting with the guards, warming himself at the fire. [55]Now the chief priests and the whole council were looking for testimony against Jesus to put him to death; but they found none. [56]For many gave false testimony against him, and their testimony did not agree. [57]Some stood up and gave false testimony against him, saying, [58]'We heard him say, "I will destroy this temple that is made with hands, and in three days I will build another, not made with hands."' [59]But even on this

point their testimony did not agree. [60]Then the high priest stood up before them and asked Jesus, 'Have you no answer? What is it that they testify against you?' [61]But he was silent and did not answer. Again the high priest asked him, 'Are you the Messiah, the Son of the Blessed One?' [62]Jesus said, 'I am; and

"you will see the Son of Man

seated at the right hand of the Power,"

and "coming with the clouds of heaven."'

[63]Then the high priest tore his clothes and said, 'Why do we still need witnesses? [64]You have heard his blasphemy! What is your decision?' All of them condemned him as deserving death. [65]Some began to spit on him, to blindfold him, and to strike him, saying to him, 'Prophesy!' The guards also took him over and beat him.

Peter Denies Jesus

66 While Peter was below in the courtyard, one of the servant-girls of the high priest came by. [67]When she saw Peter warming himself, she stared at him and said, 'You also were with Jesus, the man from Nazareth.' [68]But he denied it, saying, 'I do not know or understand what you are talking about.' And he went out into the forecourt. Then the cock crowed. [69]And the servant-girl, on seeing him, began again to say to the bystanders, 'This man is one of them.' [70]But again he denied it. Then after a little while the bystanders again said to Peter, 'Certainly you are one of them; for you are a Galilean.' [71]But he began to curse, and he swore an oath, 'I do not know this man you are talking about.' [72]At that moment the cock crowed for the second time. Then Peter remembered that Jesus had said to him, 'Before the cock crows twice, you will deny me three times.' And he broke down and wept.

Jesus before Pilate

15As soon as it was morning, the chief priests held a consultation with the elders and scribes and the whole council. They bound Jesus, led him away, and handed him over to Pilate. [2]Pilate asked him, 'Are you the King of the Jews?' He answered him, 'You say so.' [3]Then the chief priests accused him of many things.

[4]Pilate asked him again, 'Have you no answer? See how many charges they bring against you.' [5]But Jesus made no further reply, so that Pilate was amazed.

Pilate Hands Jesus over to Be Crucified

6 Now at the festival he used to release a prisoner for them, anyone for whom they asked. [7]Now a man called Barabbas was in prison with the rebels who had committed murder during the insurrection. [8]So the crowd came and began to ask Pilate to do for them according to his custom. [9]Then he answered them, 'Do you want me to release for you the King of the Jews?' [10]For he realized that it was out of jealousy that the chief priests had handed him over. [11]But the chief priests stirred up the crowd to have him release Barabbas for them instead. [12]Pilate spoke to them again, 'Then what do you wish me to do with the man you call the King of the Jews?' [13]They shouted back, 'Crucify him!' [14]Pilate asked them, 'Why, what evil has he done?' But they shouted all the more, 'Crucify him!' [15]So Pilate, wishing to satisfy the crowd, released Barabbas for them; and after flogging Jesus, he handed him over to be crucified.

The Soldiers Mock Jesus

16 Then the soldiers led him into the courtyard of the palace (that is, the governor's headquarters); and they called together the whole cohort. [17]And they clothed him in a purple cloak; and after twisting some thorns into a crown, they put it on him. [18]And they began saluting him, 'Hail, King of the Jews!' [19]They struck his head with a reed, spat upon him, and knelt down in homage to him. [20]After mocking him, they stripped him of the purple cloak and put his own clothes on him. Then they led him out to crucify him.

The Crucifixion of Jesus

21 They compelled a passer-by, who was coming in from the country, to carry his cross; it was Simon of Cyrene, the father of Alexander and Rufus. [22]Then they brought Jesus to the place called Golgotha (which means the place of a skull). [23]And they offered him wine mixed with myrrh; but he did not take it. [24]And they crucified him, and divided his clothes among them, casting lots to decide what each should take.

25 It was nine o'clock in the morning when they crucified him. [26]The inscription of the charge against him read, 'The King of the Jews.' [27]And with him they crucified two bandits, one on his right and one on his left. [29]Those who passed by derided him, shaking their heads and saying, 'Aha! You who would destroy the temple and build it in three days, [30]save yourself, and come down from the cross!' [31]In the same way the chief priests, along with the scribes, were also mocking him among themselves and saying, 'He saved others; he cannot save himself. [32]Let the Messiah, the King of Israel, come down from the cross now, so that we may see and believe.' Those who were crucified with him also taunted him.

The Death of Jesus

33 When it was noon, darkness came over the whole land until three in the afternoon. [34]At three o'clock Jesus cried out with a loud voice, 'Eloi, Eloi, lema sabachthani?' which means, 'My God, my God, why have you forsaken me?' [35]When some of the bystanders heard it, they said, 'Listen, he is calling for Elijah.' [36]And someone ran, filled a sponge with sour wine, put it on a stick, and gave it to him to drink, saying, 'Wait, let us see whether Elijah will come to take him down.' [37]Then Jesus gave a loud cry and breathed his last. [38]And the curtain of the temple was torn in two, from top to bottom. [39]Now when the centurion, who stood facing him, saw that in this way he breathed his last, he said, 'Truly this man was God's Son!'

40 There were also women looking on from a distance; among them were Mary Magdalene, and Mary the mother of James the younger and of Joses, and Salome. [41]These used to follow him and provided for him when he was in Galilee; and there were many other women who had come up with him to Jerusalem.

The Burial of Jesus

42 When evening had come, and since it was the day of Preparation, that is, the day before the sabbath,

[43]Joseph of Arimathea, a respected member of the council, who was also himself waiting expectantly for the kingdom of God, went boldly to Pilate and asked for the body of Jesus. [44]Then Pilate wondered if he were already dead; and summoning the centurion, he asked him whether he had been dead for some time. [45]When he learned from the centurion that he was dead, he granted the body to Joseph. [46]Then Joseph bought a linen cloth, and taking down the body, wrapped it in the linen cloth, and laid it in a tomb that had been hewn out of the rock. He then rolled a stone against the door of the tomb. [47]Mary Magdalene and Mary the mother of Joses saw where the body was laid.

The Resurrection of Jesus

16When the sabbath was over, Mary Magdalene, and Mary the mother of James, and Salome bought spices, so that they might go and anoint him. [2]And very early on the first day of the week, when the sun had risen, they went to the tomb. [3]They had been saying to one another, 'Who will roll away the stone for us from the entrance to the tomb?' [4]When they looked up, they saw that the stone, which was very large, had already been rolled back. [5]As they entered the tomb, they saw a young man, dressed in a white robe, sitting on the right side; and they were alarmed. [6]But he said to them, 'Do not be alarmed; you are looking for Jesus of Nazareth, who was crucified. He has been raised; he is not here. Look, there is the place they laid him. [7]But go, tell his disciples and Peter that he is going ahead of you to Galilee; there you will see him, just as he told you.' [8]So they went out and fled from the tomb, for terror and amazement had seized them; and they said nothing to anyone, for they were afraid.

X.4 Paul on the Distinction between Judaism and Christianity

GALATIANS 1:6-23, 2:1-21

6 I am astonished that you are so quickly deserting the one who called you in the grace of Christ and are turning to a different gospel—[7]not that there is another gospel, but there are some who are confusing you and want to pervert the gospel of Christ. [8]But even if we or an angel from heaven should proclaim to you a gospel contrary to what we proclaimed to you, let that one be accursed! [9]As we have said before, so now I repeat, if anyone proclaims to you a gospel contrary to what you received, let that one be accursed!

10 Am I now seeking human approval, or God's approval? Or am I trying to please people? If I were still pleasing people, I would not be a servant of Christ.

Paul's Vindication of His Apostleship

11 For I want you to know, brothers and sisters, that the gospel that was proclaimed by me is not of human origin; [12]for I did not receive it from a human source, nor was I taught it, but I received it through a revelation of Jesus Christ.

13 You have heard, no doubt, of my earlier life in Judaism. I was violently persecuting the church of God and was trying to destroy it. [14]I advanced in Judaism beyond many among my people of the same age, for I was far more zealous for the traditions of my ancestors. [15]But when God, who had set me apart before I was born and called me through his grace, was pleased [16]to reveal his Son to me, so that I might proclaim him among the Gentiles, I did not confer with any human being, [17]nor did I go up to Jerusalem to those who were already apostles before me, but I went away at once into Arabia, and afterwards I returned to Damascus.

18 Then after three years I did go up to Jerusalem to visit Cephas and stayed with him for fifteen days; [19]but I did not see any other apostle except James the Lord's brother. [20]In what I am writing to you, before God, I do not lie! [21]Then I went into the regions of Syria and Cilicia, [22]and I was still unknown by sight to the churches of Judea that are in Christ; [23]they only heard it said, 'The one who formerly was persecuting us is now proclaiming the faith he once tried to destroy.'

Then after fourteen years I went up again to Jerusalem with Barnabas, taking Titus along with me.

[2]I went up in response to a revelation. Then I laid before them (though only in a private meeting with the acknowledged leaders) the gospel that I proclaim among the Gentiles, in order to make sure that I was not running, or had not run, in vain. [3]But even Titus, who was with me, was not compelled to be circumcised, though he was a Greek. [4]But because of false believers secretly brought in, who slipped in to spy on the freedom we have in Christ Jesus, so that they might enslave us—[5]we did not submit to them even for a moment, so that the truth of the gospel might always remain with you. [6]And from those who were supposed to be acknowledged leaders (what they actually were makes no difference to me; God shows no partiality)—those leaders contributed nothing to me. [7]On the contrary, when they saw that I had been entrusted with the gospel for the uncircumcised, just as Peter had been entrusted with the gospel for the circumcised [8](for he who worked through Peter making him an apostle to the circumcised also worked through me in sending me to the Gentiles), [9]and when James and Cephas and John, who were acknowledged pillars, recognized the grace that had been given to me, they gave to Barnabas and me the right hand of fellowship, agreeing that we should go to the Gentiles and they to the circumcised. [10]They asked only one thing, that we remember the poor, which was actually what I was eager to do.

Paul Rebukes Peter at Antioch

11 But when Cephas came to Antioch, I opposed him to his face, because he stood self-condemned; [12]for until certain people came from James, he used to eat with the Gentiles. But after they came, he drew back and kept himself separate for fear of the circumcision faction. [13]And the other Jews joined him in this hypocrisy, so that even Barnabas was led astray by their hypocrisy. [14]But when I saw that they were not acting consistently with the truth of the gospel, I said to Cephas before them all, 'If you, though a Jew, live like a Gentile and not like a Jew, how can you compel the Gentiles to live like Jews?'

Jews and Gentiles Are Saved by Faith

15 We ourselves are Jews by birth and not Gentile sinners; [16]yet we know that a person is justified not by the works of the law but through faith in Jesus Christ. And we have come to believe in Christ Jesus, so that we might be justified by faith in Christ, and not by doing the works of the law, because no one will be justified by the works of the law. [17]But if, in our effort to be justified in Christ, we ourselves have been found to be sinners, is Christ then a servant of sin? Certainly not! [18]But if I build up again the very things that I once tore down, then I demonstrate that I am a transgressor. [19]For through the law I died to the law, so that I might live to God. I have been crucified with Christ; [20]and it is no longer I who live, but it is Christ who lives in me. And the life I now live in the flesh I live by faith in the Son of God, who loved me and gave himself for me. [21]I do not nullify the grace of God; for if justification comes through the law, then Christ died for nothing.

X.5 Two Christian Creeds

Source: Apostles' Creed and Nicene Creed, http://www .sacred-texts.com/chr/apocreed.htm, http://www.sacred -texts.com/chr/nicene.htm

THE APOSTLE'S CREED

1. I believe in God the Father, Almighty, Maker of heaven and earth:
2. And in Jesus Christ, his only begotten Son, our Lord:
3. Who was conceived by the Holy Ghost, born of the Virgin Mary:
4. Suffered under Pontius Pilate; was crucified, dead and buried: He descended into hell:
5. The third day he rose again from the dead:
6. He ascended into heaven, and sits at the right hand of God the Father Almighty:
7. From thence he shall come to judge the quick and the dead:
8. I believe in the Holy Ghost:
9. I believe in the holy catholic church: the communion of saints:

10. The forgiveness of sins:

11. The resurrection of the body:

12. And the life everlasting. Amen.

THE NICENE CREED

I believe in one God, the Father Almighty, Maker of heaven and earth, and of all things visible and invisible.

And in one Lord Jesus Christ, the only-begotten Son of God, begotten of the Father before all worlds; God of God, Light of Light, very God of very God; begotten, not made, being of one substance with the Father, by whom all things were made.

Who, for us men for our salvation, came down from heaven, and was incarnate by the Holy Spirit of the virgin Mary, and was made man; and was crucified also for us under Pontius Pilate; He suffered and was buried; and the third day He rose again, according to the Scriptures; and ascended into heaven, and sits on the right hand of the Father; and He shall come again, with glory, to judge the quick and the dead; whose kingdom shall have no end.

And I believe in the Holy Ghost, the Lord and Giver of Life; who proceeds from the Father *and the Son*; who with the Father *and the Son* together is worshipped and glorified; who spoke by the prophets.

And I believe [sic] one holy catholic and apostolic Church. I acknowledge one baptism for the remission of sins; and I look for the resurrection of the dead, and the life of the world to come. Amen.

Key Terms

charismatic movement   Renewal movement in Catholic and Protestant Churches stressing the work and manifestation of the Holy Spirit in the life of the church and of the individual believer.

ecumenical movement   Movement for the recovery of unity among the Christian Churches. It dates from the Edinburgh World Missionary Conference of 1910 and today focuses in the World Council of Churches.

Eucharist   ("Thanksgiving") The central act of Christian worship instituted by Christ on the night before his death. It involves sharing bread and wine which are sacramentally associated with the body and blood of Christ

evangelicals   Christians of all denominations who emphasize the centrality of the Bible, justification by faith and the need for personal conversion. In Germany and Switzerland, the term refers to members of the Lutheran as opposed to the Calvinist churches.

Gospel   (1) One of the four accounts of the "good news" about Jesus in the New Testament. (2) The Christian message, proclamation of "good news," referring especially to Jesus' teaching about the kingdom of God and to the preaching of the church about Jesus. (3) The ritual reading of a set portion from the Gospels (1) in the context of the Eucharist. (4) A partial account of the life and teaching of Jesus, usually ascribed to a New Testament figure but not included in the canon (authoritative version) of the Bible.

Holy Spirit   The third person of the Christian trinity. In the Bible the Holy Spirit is the instrument of divine action and is portrayed as fire or wind. In this sense the Spirit is acknowledged in Judaism and Islam. The divinity of the Holy Spirit was agreed at the Council of Constantinople in 381 CE. The Holy Spirit is the source of faith and new life in the believer and the church, giving "spiritual gifts," guidance, and holiness.

Jerusalem   Fortified city captured by David in the tenth century BCE which became the capital and principal sanctuary for the people of Israel. It has remained the focus of Jewish religious aspirations and ideals. It is a holy city for Christians because of its association with the passion, death, and resurrection of Jesus of Nazareth. For Muslims it is the holiest city after Mecca. The Mosque of the Dome of the Rock stands over the site of Muhammad's night journey.

messiah   ("Anointed one") A Hebrew word referring to the person chosen by God to be king. (1) After the end of the Israelite monarchy it came to refer to a figure who would restore Israel, gathering the tribes together and ushering in the kingdom of God. Judaism has known several false messiahs. Modern Jews are divided as to whether the messiah is a symbolic or a representative figure and whether the founding of the Jewish state is in any way a prelude to his coming. (2) In the Christian New Testament, Jesus of Nazareth is described by messianic titles, e.g. messiah, Christ, the King, the One who Comes. The account of Jesus' entry into Jerusalem is deliberately phrased in messianic terms. Jesus himself was cautious about claiming to be messiah, probably because of its political overtones.

Protestant Reformation   The movement within Western Christianity between the fourteenth and the seventeenth centuries which led to the separation of the Protestant Churches from Rome. The main issue was the authority of the pope but doctrinal issues such as the precise meaning of the Eucharist and the authority and accessibility of Scripture were also important.

New Testament   The second division of the Christian Bible, comprising the Gospels, the Acts of the Apostles, the Revelation of John and various Epistles.

Old Testament   The Hebrew Bible as treated as the first division of the Christian Bible.

Orthodox Churches   Christianity as practiced by the Eastern Churches after the Great Schism. Orthodox Christians are found mostly in Eastern Europe, the Balkan States and Russia.

Pentecostal churches   Churches that have formed from a renewal movement which started in the United States in 1906. They teach the experience of "baptism in the Holy Spirit," which shows itself in speaking in tongues and other "spiritual gifts."

resurrection   (1) The Christian belief that Jesus of Nazareth was raised from death by God the Father who thus vindicated him as messiah and revealed his defeat of death and sin. (2) The raising of all the dead for judgment as taught in Judaism, Christianity and Islam.

trinity   Christian doctrine of God as three Persons, equally God: the Father, the Son and the Holy Spirit, constituting the divine unity.

Questions for Study and Discussion

1.   Describe the relationship of the early church to its surrounding culture, the Roman empire.
2.   Briefly describe the criticisms of the church made by the Reformers of the sixteenth century.
3.   What are the core messages contained in the Beatitudes of Jesus' Sermon on the Mount? (See sidebar on page 353.)
4.   What was the "good news" that Jesus preached?

5. Name three Jewish beliefs that are also found in Christianity. Name two Christian festivals that are related to Jewish tradition and explain their significance to Christians.
6. Select two photographs or illustrations from the chapter and explain how they demonstrate core Christian beliefs or values or give evidence of changes in modern Christianity.
7. Compare Jason Hood's story ("I am a Christian," p. 376–77) to that of one other person from a previous chapter of your choosing (for example, "I am a Sikh," p. 449–50, or "I am a Jew," p. 330–31). What common themes do you see? Do the writers demonstrate any similar values or concerns?

Questions for Reflection

Write your personal reflections to each of these questions in the space provided.

1. Explain the tension between 'imperial cult' and Christianity in the early church. (See p. 344.)

2. How has Christianity been affected by the theorists covered in Part 1? (See p. 348–50.)

3. Explain what it means to belong to Orthodox Christianity. (See p. 359.)

4. Consider the variety of branches of the church and reflect on the factors that create such variety. (See pp. 359–62.)

5. Discuss the relationship between the Hebrew Scriptures and Christian Scriptures. (See p. 363.)

6. Discuss the relationship of Christianity to Judaism in a thematic and historic context. (See pp. 365–66.)

Selected Online Resources

▶ Frontline: From Jesus to Christ—extensive supportive materials related to a public television program on the historical Jesus
http://www.pbs.org/wgbh/pages/frontline/shows/religion
▶ What Orthodox Christians Believe—collection of links to articles on Orthodox beliefs and history, including sacraments, saints, and the structure of the church
http://aggreen.net/beliefs/beliefs.html
▶ Religion in Latin America—discussion of evangelical Christian, Catholic, and indigenous religious movements, among others; also includes statistics, photographs, and recommended reading
http://www.utexas.edu/cola/depts/rs/religion-in-Latin-America/about.php

Part 11: Islam

Chapter Summaries

68. A Historical Overview

Islam began among the merchants of seventh-century Mecca. The prophet Muhammad began to receive messages from God around 610 and believed he was to convey these revelations to his fellow Meccans. Later they were collected and became the holy book of Islam, the Qur'an. Once he and his followers began to be persecuted, they emigrated to Medina in an event called the Hijrah. There Islam began to take shape under Muhammad's direction, involving prayer, almsgiving, fasting, and pilgrimage. When the prophet died, he left behind both a religion and a state, headed by a caliph. Islam quickly expanded through North Africa and then Western Europe, as well as into the Near East and central Asia. Under 'Abbasid rule, Islam was consolidated; its law was elaborated, becoming Shari'a, the basis of Muslim society. The Ottoman Empire, beginning around 1500, expanded Islam's power and influence throughout much of Europe and the Mediterranean. In turn, European influence on the Islamic world was multilevel, involving politics, intellectual pursuits, and even religion. In many Muslim countries today there are two education systems, one religious and one secular. After the colonial era in the Middle East, oil has become a wealth-producing resource for a number of Islamic governments. Meanwhile, divisions have arisen within Muslim communities, with fundamentalism playing a significant role in religious growth.

69. The Unity and Variety of Islam

The question of Muhammad's successor led to the main division in Islam: Sunni and Shi'a. The Sunnis believed that Muhammad did not have a true successor and that future leaders (caliphs) would be selected by community consensus. Today the Sunni believe that if Shari'a law is observed, the transnational role of the caliph is not needed. Shi'a Muslims view the imam as the principal religious authority who inherits his position as a successor to Muhammad. The first imam was a member of Muhammad's family and was infallible in his interpretation of the Qur'an; he was also martyred. Most Shi'a await the messianic return of the twelfth imam.

Sufism is the mystical arm of Islam. Sufis can be Sunnis or Shi'as who seek intimacy with God through spiritual purification. Sufis will describe themselves as ones who seek to be Sufis. They follow a spiritual master and practice self-mortification.

70. Sacred Writings

The Qur'an is considered the supreme revelation of God's word in written form. It is divided into 114 chapters, each one (*surah*) typically based on a key word or theme. The text includes moral instruction as well as descriptions of ecstatic revelation. While ultimately translations of the Qur'an have been permitted by Muslim authorities, they are officially seen as commentaries, not as true Qur'ans. The supplementary sacred text, the Hadith, or Prophetic Traditions, is divided into two groups of accounts, one of God's words and the other of Muhammad's.

71. Beliefs

Muslims are strict monotheists who believe in the oneness of Allah, the supreme, eternal, omnipotent God of creation. They also believe that God is served by angels, who may serve as messengers between God and his prophets. Islam recognizes many sacred scriptures, with only four having survived: the Jewish Torah, the Psalms, the Gospel revealed to Jesus, and the Qur'an, which is the last and definitive revelation. The Day of Resurrection and Judgment is unknown to all except God, but the Hadith mention signs of its approach. Heaven is the reward for those who earn favor from God, while hell awaits those who did not follow God's law or hold right belief.

72. Worship and Festivals

Muslim worship brings together inward spirituality and outward devotion. The code of conduct, *shahadah*, is a commitment to obey God and follow the prophet, the first of seven pillars of the faith. For the second pillar, Muslims are to pray five times a day in the ritual of *salah*, preceded by ritual washing. On Fridays *salah* is performed communally. The third pillar is almsgiving; the fourth is fasting, which marks the holy month of Ramadan. The fifth is *Hajj*, or pilgrimage to Mecca.

73. The Law of Islam

The sacred law, Shari'a, is derived from four main sources: the Qur'an, the *sunnah* (the sayings and actions of the prophet Muhammad), the *ijma'* (community consensus), and the *qiyas* (deductions from the first three sources). Shari'a covers every aspect of life; it has been developed and elaborated over generations. In the modern world many Muslim countries have displaced Shari'a with new codes of law, typically Western in derivation, with the typical exception of family law.

74. Science, Art, and Culture

Muslim philosophers and naturalists laid the foundations of modern science between the ninth and the fourteenth centuries. Books by the eleventh-century philosopher Avicenna were used in European universities until the seventeenth century. Muslim Arabs made great astronomical and mathematical discoveries. The knowledge of Muslims spread throughout the West beginning in the tenth century. Muslim music, architecture, and other fine arts were introduced to many European countries.

75. Family and Society

The family is the cornerstone of Islamic society, regulated by the Qur'an and Hadith, which strongly recommend marriage. The Qur'an permits a man to marry up to four wives if he is able to care for all of them adequately. Divorce is permitted but considered by the prophet Muhammad as hateful to God. The Qur'an shows serious concern for widows and orphans, while in general children are considered a gift from God and the first responsibility of parents.

76. Islam in the Modern World

Two important figures in Islamic history are the Indian Sufi Wali Allah and the Arab al-Wahhab. They both emphasized the importance of the Qur'an and the prophet as example; Wali Allah saw God as potentially immanent, while al-Wahhab believed God was solely transcendent and unknowable.

For many Muslims in the early twentieth century, modernism was equivalent to colonial oppression. Sunni modernist reformers focused on education and encouraged Muslims to interpret scriptures for themselves. They believed that Muslims should endeavor to shape their communal destiny. Radical, or fundamentalist, reformers stressed the need to follow God's law in every facet. They tended to strongly critique secular Western societies. Although extremists have become more visible to the wider world since 9/11, most Muslims reject such violent beliefs. Meanwhile, political corruption is an ongoing issue in many Muslim countries, and it is complicated by the support of Western governments. Modernist Muslim thinkers have begun to change beliefs and Muslim laws to give more rights to women and reduce male privileges with the goal of better family life and community stability.

Key Personalities

Muhammad (about 570–632 CE)

Prophet and apostle of Islam, the final messenger of God whose message, the Qur'an, sums up and completes the previous revelations to the Jews and Christians. Muhammad saw the expansion of Islam in terms of military conquest and political organization and he was outstandingly successful as a commander and ruler in Medina and later Mecca.

"Like many of the Biblical prophets, Muhammad described the experience of revelation as wrenching. He felt as if his 'soul was being ripped away.' He doubted its validity at first, until reassured first by his wife, then by a Christian ascetic, and eventually by the revelations themselves. All his life he distinguished between his personal opinions and the words conveyed to him in revelation. . . . Once he began to hear messages and convey them, nothing would ever be the same for him, or for the world. From a humble merchant and family man, the experience transformed him into a spiritual teacher, lawgiver, and ultimately leader of the tribes of the Arabian Peninsula. The book he delivered grew in stature from a text that was first reviled and ridiculed by many, to become the most memorized text in the world, a spiritual comfort to hundreds of millions, and the scripture for a global religion of more than 1.2 billion followers."

(Michael Wolfe et al., "Muhammad and Qur'an," *Muhammad: Legacy of a Prophet*, PBS, 2002, http://www.pbs.org/muhammad/ma_quran.shtml)

Ibn Sina (Avicenna) (980–1037)

Iranian scholar, philosopher, and government administrator who trained in medicine and wrote important medical and scientific texts as well as works of philosophy.

"Avicenna wrote 99 books, almost all in Arabic, the language of religious and scientific expression in the entire Muslim world at that time. However, two of his works, the 'Daneshnameh-e-Alai' (Encyclopedia of philosophical sciences) and a small treatise on the pulse, were written in Farsi, his native language. He wrote about natural philosophy and astronomy, theology and metaphysics, medicine, psychology, music, mathematics, and physical sciences and he is also the reported author of Persian quatrains and short poems: 'Up from Earth's Centre through the Seventh Gate I rose, and on the Throne of Saturn sate, And many a knot unraveled by the Road, But not the Master-knot of Human Fate.'"

(Chris Marvin, "Ibn Sina [Avicenna]," *The Window: Philosophy on the Internet*, 1995–2000, http://www.trincoll .edu/depts/phil/philo/phils/muslim/sina.html)

Ibn Rushd (1126–98)

Muslim philosopher, known in the West as Averroes, who was greatly influenced by Plato and Aristotle. He believed that the Greek heritage was compatible with Islam. His synthesis, however, seemed suspicious to the orthodox, and he was banished and his books burnt.

"To Ibn Rushd, the supremacy of the human intellect did not allow for the possible contradiction between science and revelation. He gives religion an important role in the life of the state, considering that the scriptures when philosophically understood are far more superior to the religion of pure reason. Striving to bring the two together, he wrote that in case of differences, provided scriptural language does not violate the principles of reason, that is, it does not commit a contradiction, science should give way. . . . He contended that philosophy is nothing more than the systematic probing into the phenomenon of creation, revealing God's wisdom and might. Hence, revelation dictates the study of philosophy. Ibn Rushd tried to reconcile the Aristotelian precept of the eternity, which seemingly denied the creation of the world, to the creationism in Jewish, Christian and Muslim theology."

(Habeeb Salloum, "Averroës: The Great Muslim Philosopher Who Planted the Seeds of the European Renaissance," Al-Hewar Center, 2001, http://www.alhewar.com /habib_saloum_averroes.htm)

Shah Wali Allah (1703–62)

Indian Sufi who stressed the Qur'an and the *sunnah* as binding forces for faith and law but also believed in the possible vision of an immanent God.

"He emphasized a direct approach to the Qur'an. Prior to Shah Wali Allah, because of the notion that the Qur'an may not be translated, Qur'anic scholarship had been an exclusive domain of specialists. Shah Wali Allah took a bold initiative and translated the Qur'an into Persian, the *lingua franca* of the Muslim literati in the sub-continent. Thereafter it became increasingly possible for ordinary people to understand the teachings of the Qur'an. . . . 'Ubayd Allah Sindhi . . . expressed the view that after being imbued with the philosophy of Shah Wali Allah, one can understand the overall message of the Qur'an directly from its text and can be satisfied with it without being compelled to seek any external aid."

("Shah Wali Allah," adapted from Muhammad al-Ghazali, *The Socio-Political Thought of Shah Wali Allah*, International Institute of Islamic Thought, 2001, http://www.cis-ca .org/voices/s/shahwaliAllah.htm)

Sayyid Qutb (1906–1966)

Egyptian writer whose works influence contemporary radical Islamic groups, including al Qaeda. A leader of the Muslim Brotherhood, he was executed after being found guilty of plotting to overthrow the Egyptian government.

"Qutb advocated violent Jihad. Qutb's innovation is that he provided a theological basis for violent Jihad against Muslim governments as well. . . . Jihad must be carried out in all countries that do not obey Sharia law: 'Any place where the Islamic Shari'ah is not enforced and where Islam is not dominant becomes the Home of Hostility (*Dar-ul-Harb*). . . . A Muslim will remain prepared to fight against it, whether it be his birthplace or a place where his relatives reside or where his property or any other material interest are located. The homeland of the Muslim, in which he lives and [upon] which he depends, is not a piece of land; the nationality of the Muslim, by which he is identified, is not the nationality determined by a government. . . . Striving is purely for the sake of God, for the success of His religion and His law.' "

(Ami Isseroff, "Sayyid Qutb," *Encyclopedia of the Middle East*, December 7, 2008, http://www.mideastweb.org/Middle -East-Encyclopedia/sayyid_qutb.htm)

Primary Source Reading

In addition to the excerpts from the Qur'an below, Islam-related primary sources are available both in print and online, and students are encouraged to contact their instructors for further information.

XI.1 The Qur'an

Source: *The Holy Quran*, trans. Yusuf Ali, 1934, http://www.sacred-texts.com/isl/yaq/

SŪRA 96—IQRAA, OR READ! OR PROCLAIM!

In the name of God, Most Gracious,
Most Merciful.
1. Proclaim! (or Read!)
In the name
Of thy Lord and Cherisher,
Who created—
2. Created man, out of
A (mere) clot
Of congealed blood:
3. Proclaim! And thy Lord
Is Most Bountiful,—
4. He Who taught
(The use of) the Pen,—
5. Taught man that
Which he knew not.
6. Nay, but man doth
Transgress all bounds,
7. In that he looketh
Upon himself as self-sufficient.

8. Verily, to thy Lord
Is the return (of all).
9. Seest thou one
Who forbids—
10. A votary when he
(Turns) to pray?
11. Seest thou if
He is on (the road
Of) Guidance?—
12. Or enjoins Righteousness?
13. Seest thou if he
Denies (Truth) and turns away?
14. Knoweth he not
That God doth see?
15. Let him beware! If he
Desist not, We will
Drag him by the forelock,—
16. A lying, sinful forelock!
17. Then, let him call
(For help) to his council
(Of comrades):
18. We will call
On the angels of punishment
(To deal with him)!
19. Nay, heed him not:
But bow down in adoration,
And bring thyself
The closer (to God)!

SŪRA 97—QADR, OR THE NIGHT OF POWER

In the name of God, Most Gracious,
Most Merciful.
1. We have indeed revealed
This (Message)
In the Night of Power:
2. And what will explain
To thee what the Night
Of Power is?
3. The Night of Power
Is better than
A thousand Months,
4. Therein come dawn
The angels and the Spirit
By God's permission,

On every errand:
5. Peace! . . . This
Until the rise of Morn!

Sūra 10—Evils of Idolatry

26. To those who do right
Is a goodly (reward)—
Yea, more (than in measure)!
No darkness nor shame
Shall cover their faces!
They are Companions of the Garden;
They will abide therein
(For aye)!
27. But those who have earned
Evil will have a reward
Of like evil: ignominy
Will cover their (faces):
No defender will they have
From (the wrath of) God:
Their faces will be covered,
As it were, with pieces
From the depth of the darkness
Of Night: they are Companions
Of the Fire: they will
Abide therein (for aye)!
28. One Day shall We gather them
All together. Then shall We say
To those who joined gods (with Us):
"To your place! ye and those
Ye joined as "partners.""
We shall separate them,
And their "partners" shall say:
"It was not us
That ye worshipped!
29. "Enough is God for a witness
Between us and you: we
Certainly knew nothing
Of your worship of us!"
30. There will every soul prove
(The fruits of) the deeds
It sent before : they will
Be brought back to God
Their rightful Lord,
And their invented falsehoods

Will leave them in the lurch.
31. Say: "Who is it that
Sustains you (in life)
From the sky and from the earth?
Or who is it that
Has power over hearing
And sight? And who
Is it that brings out
The living from the dead
And the dead from the living?
And who is it that
Rules and regulates all affairs?"
They will soon say, "God".
Say, "Will ye not then
Show piety (to Him)?"
32. Such is God, your real
Cherisher and Sustainer:
Apart from Truth,
What (remains) but error?
How then are ye turned away?
33. Thus is the Word
Of thy Lord proved true
Against those who rebel:
Verily they will not believe.
34. Say: "Of your 'partners',
Can any originate creation
And repeat it?" Say:
"It is God Who originates
Creation and repeats it:
Then how are ye deluded
Away (from the truth)?"
35. Say: "Of your "partners"
Is there any that
Can give any guidance
Towards Truth?" Say: "It is God
Who gives guidance
Towards Truth. Is then He
Who gives guidance to Truth
More worthy to be followed,
Or he who finds not guidance
(Himself) unless he is guided?
What then is the matter
With you? How judge ye?"
36. But most of them follow
Nothing but fancy: truly

Fancy can be of no avail
Against Truth. Verily God
Is well aware of all
That they do.
37. This Qur-ān is not such
As can be produced
By other than God;
On the contrary it is
A confirmation of (revelations)
That went before it,
And a fuller explanation
Of the Book—wherein
There is no doubt
From the Lord of the Worlds.

SŪRA 2—ON LAWS

219. They ask thee
Concerning wine and gambling.
Say: "In them is great sin,
And some profit, for men;
But the sin is greater
Than the profit."
They ask thee how much
They are to spend;
Say: "What is beyond
Your needs."
Thus doth God
Make clear to you
His Signs: in order that
Ye may consider—
220. (Their bearings) on
This life and the Hereafter.
They ask thee
Concerning orphans.
Say: "The best thing to do
Is what is for their good;
If ye mix
Their affairs with yours,
They are your brethren;
But God knows
The man who means mischief
From the man who means good.
And if God had wished,
He could have put you

Into difficulties: He is indeed
Exalted in Power, Wise.
221. Do not marry
Unbelieving women (idolaters),
Until they believe:
A slave woman who believes
Is better than an unbelieving woman,
Even though she allure you.
Nor marry (your girls)
To unbelievers until
They believe:
A man slave who believes
Is better than an unbeliever,
Even though he allure you.
Unbelievers do (but)
Beckon you to the Fire.
But God beckons by His Grace
To the Garden (of Bliss)
And forgiveness,
And makes His Signs
Clear to mankind:
That they may
Celebrate His praise.
222. They ask thee
Concerning women's courses.
Say: They are
A hurt and a pollution:
So keep away from women
In their courses, and do not
Approach them until
They are clean.
But when they have
Purified themselves,
Ye may approach them
In any manner, time, or place
Ordained for you by God.
For God loves those
Who turn to Him constantly
And He loves those
Who keep themselves pure and clean,
223. Your wives are
As a tilth unto you;
So approach your tilth
When or how ye will;
But do some good act

For your souls beforehand;
And fear God,
And know that ye are
To meet Him (in the Hereafter),
And give (these) good tidings
To those who believe.
224. And make not
God's (name) an excuse
In your oaths against
Doing good, or acting rightly,
Or making peace
Between persons;
For God is One
Who heareth and knoweth
All things.
225. God will not
Call you to account
For thoughtlessness
In your oaths,
But for the intention
In your hearts;
And He is
Oft-forgiving
Most Forbearing.
226. For those who take
An oath for abstention
From their wives,
A waiting for four months
Is ordained;
If then they return,
God is Oft-forgiving,
Most Merciful.
227. But if their intention
Is firm for divorce,
God heareth
And knoweth all things.
228. Divorced women
Shall wait concerning themselves
For three monthly periods.
Nor is it lawful for them
To hide what God
Hath created in their wombs,
If they have faith
In God and the Last Day.
And their husbands

Have the better right
To take them back
In that period, if
They wish for reconciliation.
And women shall have rights
Similar to the rights
Against them, according
To what is equitable;
But men have a degree
(Of advantage) over them.
And God is Exalted in Power, Wise.
229. A divorce is only
Permissible twice: after that,
The parties should either hold
Together on equitable terms,
Or separate with kindness.
It is not lawful for you,
(Men), to take back
Any of your gifts (from your wives)
Except when both parties
Fear that they would be
Unable to keep the limits
Ordained by God.
If ye (judges) do indeed
Fear that they would be
Unable to keep the limits
Ordained by God,
There is no blame on either
Of them if she give
Something for her freedom.
These are the limits
Ordained by God;
So do not transgress them
If any do transgress
The limits ordained by God,
Such persons wrong
(Themselves as well as others).
230. So if a husband
Divorces his wife (irrevocably),
He cannot, after that,
Re-marry her until
After she has married
Another husband and
He has divorced her.
In that case there is

No blame on either of them
If they re-unite, provided
They feel that they
Can keep the limits
Ordained by God.
Such are the limits
Ordained by God,
Which He makes plain
To those who understand.
231. When ye divorce
Women, and they fulfil
The term of their (*Iddat*),
Either take them back
On equitable terms
Or set them free
On equitable terms;
But do not take them back
To injure them, (or) to take
Undue advantage;
If any one does that,
He wrongs his own soul.
Do not treat God's Signs
As a jest,
But solemnly rehearse
God's favours on you,
And the fact that He
Sent down to you
The Book
And Wisdom,
For your instruction.
And fear God,
And know that God
Is well acquainted
With all things.
232. When ye divorce
Women, and they fulfil
The term of their (*Iddat*),
Do not prevent them
From marrying
Their (former) husbands,
If they mutually agree
On equitable terms.
This instruction
Is for all amongst you,
Who believe in God

And the Last Day.
That is (the course
Making for) most virtue
And purity amongst you,
And God knows,
And ye know not.
233. The mothers shall give suck
To their offspring
For two whole years,
If the father desires
To complete the term.
But he shall bear the cost
Of their food and clothing
On equitable terms.
No soul shall have
A burden laid on it
Greater than it can bear.
No mother shall be
Treated unfairly
On account of her child.
Nor father
On account of his child,
An heir shall be chargeable
In the same way.
If they both decide
On weaning,
By mutual consent,
And after due consultation,
There is no blame on them.
If ye decide
On a foster-mother
For your offspring,
There is no blame on you,
Provided ye pay (the mother)
What ye offered,
On equitable terms.
But fear God and know
That God sees well
What ye do.
234. If any of you die
And leave widows behind,
They shall wait concerning themselves
Four months and ten days:
When they have fulfilled
Their term, there is no blame

On you if they dispose
Of themselves in a just
And reasonable manner.
And God is well acquainted
With what ye do.
235. There is no blame
On you if ye make
An offer of betrothal
Or hold it in your hearts.
God knows that ye
Cherish them in your hearts:
But do not make a secret contract
With them except in terms
Honourable, nor resolve on the tie
Of marriage till the term
Prescribed is fulfilled.
And know that God
Knoweth what is in your hearts,
And take heed of Him;
And know that God is
Oft-forgiving, Most Forbearing.
236. There is no blame on you
If ye divorce women
Before consummation
Or the fixation of their dower;
But bestow on them
(A suitable gift),
The wealthy
According to his means,
And the poor
According to his means;—
A gift of a reasonable amount
Is due from those
Who wish to do the right thing.
237. And if ye divorce them
Before consummation,
But after the fixation
Of a dower for them,
Then the half of the dower
(Is due to them), unless
They remit it
Or (the man's half) is remitted
By him in whose hands
Is the marriage tie;
And the remission

(Of the man's half)
Is the nearest to righteousness.
And do not forget
Liberality between yourselves.
For God sees well
All that ye do.
238. Guard strictly
Your (habit of) prayers,
Especially the Middle Prayer;
And stand before God
In a devout (frame of mind).
239. If ye fear (an enemy),
Pray on foot, or riding,
(As may be most convenient),
But when ye are
In security, celebrate
God's praises in the manner
He has taught you,
Which ye knew not (before).
240. Those of you
Who die and leave widows
Should bequeath
For their widows
A year's maintenance
And residence;
But if they leave
(The residence),
There is no blame on you
For what they do
With themselves,
Provided it is reasonable.
And God is Exalted in Power, Wise.
241. For divorced women
Maintenance (should be provided)
On a reasonable (scale).
This is a duty
On the righteous.
242. Thus doth God
Make clear His Signs
To you: in order that
Ye may understand.

SŪRA 5—JESUS THE PROPHET

109. One day will God

Gather the apostles together,
And ask: "What was
The response ye received
(From men to your teaching)?"
They will say: "We
Have no knowledge: it is Thou
Who knowest in full
All that is hidden."
110. When will God say:
"O Jesus the son of Mary!
Recount My favour"'
To thee and to thy mother.
Behold! I strengthened thee
With the holy spirit,
So that thou didst speak
To the people in childhood
And in maturity.
Behold! I taught thee
The Book and Wisdom,
The Law and the Gospel.
And behold! thou makest
Out of clay, as it were,
The figure of a bird,
By My leave,
And thou breathest into it,
And it becometh a bird
By My leave,
And thou healest those
Born blind, and the lepers,
By My leave.
And behold! thou
Bringest forth the dead
By My leave.
And behold! I did
Restrain the Children of Israel
From (violence to) thee
When thou didst show them
The Clear Signs,
And the unbelievers among them
Said: 'This is nothing
But evident magic.
111. "And behold! I inspired
The Disciples to have faith
In Me and Mine Apostle:
They said, 'We have faith,

And do thou bear witness
That we bow to God
As Muslims."
112. Behold! the Disciples said:
"O Jesus the son of Mary!
Can thy Lord send down to us
A Table set (with viands)
From heaven?" Said Jesus:
"Fear God, if ye have faith."
113. They said: "We only wish
To eat thereof and satisfy
Our hearts, and to know
That thou hast indeed
Told us the truth; and
That we ourselves may be
Witnesses to the miracle."
114. Said Jesus the son of Mary:
"O God our Lord!
Send us from heaven
A Table set (with viands),
That there may be for us
For the first and the last of us—
A solemn festival
And a Sign from Thee;
And provide for our sustenance,
For Thou art the best
Sustainer (of our needs)."
115. God said: "I will
Send it down unto you:
But if any of you
After that resisteth faith,
I will punish him
With a penalty such
As I have not inflicted
On any one among
All the peoples."
116. And behold! God will say:
"O Jesus the son of Mary!
Didst thou say unto men,
Worship me and my mother
As gods in derogation of God'?"
He will say: "Glory to Thee!
Never could I say
What I had no right
(To say). Had I said

Such a thing, Thou wouldst
Indeed have known it.
Thou knowest what is
In my heart, though I
Know not what is
In Thine. For Thou
Knowest in full
All that is hidden.
117. "Never said I to them
Aught except what Thou
Didst command me
To say, to wit, 'Worship
God, my Lord and your Lord';
And I was a witness
Over them whilst I dwelt
Amongst them; when thou
Didst take me up
Thou wast the Watcher
Over them, and Thou
Art a witness to all things.
118. "If Thou dost punish them,
They are Thy servants:
If Thou dost forgive them,
Thou art the Exalted in power,
The Wise."
119. God will say: "This is
A day on which
The truthful will profit
From their truth: theirs
Are Gardens, with rivers
Flowing beneath,—their eternal
Home: God well-pleased
With them, and they with God:
That is the great Salvation,
(The fulfilment of all desires).
120. To God doth belong the dominion
Of the heavens and the earth,
And all that is therein,
And it is He who hath power
Over all things.

SŪRA 2—FIVE PILLARS OF ISLAM

144. We see the turning
Of thy face (for guidance)
To the heavens: now
Shall We turn thee
To a Qibla that shall
Please thee. Turn then
Thy face in the direction
Of the sacred Mosque:
Wherever ye are, turn
Your faces in that direction.
The people of the Book
Know well that that is
The truth from their Lord.
Nor is God unmindful
Of what they do.
145. Even if thou wert to bring
To the people of the Book
All the Signs (together),
They would not follow
Thy Qibla; nor art thou
Going to follow their Qibla;
Nor indeed will they follow
Each other's Qibla. If thou
After the knowledge hath reached thee,
Wert to follow their (vain)
Desires,—then wert thou
Indeed (clearly) in the wrong.
146. The people of the Book
Know this as they know
Their own sons; but some
Of them conceal the truth
Which they themselves know.
147. The Truth is from thy Lord;
So be not at all in doubt.
148. To each is a goal
To which God turns him;
Then strive together (as in a race)
Towards all that is good.
Wheresoever ye are,
God will bring you
Together, For God
Hath power over all things.
149. From whencesoever
Thou startest forth, turn
Thy face in the direction
Of the Sacred Mosque;
That is indeed the truth

From thy Lord. And God
Is not unmindful
Of what ye do.
150. So from whencesoever
Thou startest forth, turn
Thy face in the direction
Of the Sacred Mosque;
And wheresoever ye are,
Turn your face thither:
That there be no ground
Of dispute against you
Among the people,
Except those of them that are
Bent on wickedness; so fear
Them not, but fear Me;
And that I may complete
My favours on you, and ye
May (consent to) be guided;
183. O ye who believe!
Fasting is prescribed to you
As it was prescribed
To those before you,
That ye may (learn)
Self-restraint,—
184. (Fasting) for a fixed
Number of days;
But if any of you is ill,
Or on a journey,
The prescribed number
(Should be made up)
From days later.
For those who can do it
(With hardship), is a ransom,
The feeding of one
That is indigent.
But he that will give
More, of his own free will,—
It is better for him.
And it is better for you
That ye fast,
If ye only knew.
185. Ramadhān is the (month)
In which was sent down
The Qur-ān, as a guide
To mankind, also clear (Signs)

For guidance and judgment
(Between right and wrong).
So every one of you
Who is present (at his home)
During that month
Should spend it in fasting,
But if any one is ill,
Or on a journey,
The prescribed period
(Should be made up)
By days later.
God intends every facility
For you; He does not want
To put you to difficulties.
(He wants you) to complete
The prescribed period,
And to glorify Him
In that He has guided you;
And perchance ye shall be grateful.
186. When My servants
Ask thee concerning Me,
I am indeed
Close (to them): I listen
To the prayer of every
Suppliant when he calleth on Me:
Let them also, with a will,
Listen to My call,
And believe in Me:
That they may walk
In the right way.
187. Permitted to you,
On the night of the fasts,
Is the approach to your wives.
They are your garments
And ye are their garments.
God knoweth what ye
Used to do secretly among yourselves;
But He turned to you
And forgave you;
So now associate with them,
And seek what God
Hath ordained for you,
And eat and drink,
Until the white thread
Of dawn appear to you

Distinct from its black thread;
Then complete your fast
Till the night appears;
But do not associate
With your wives
While ye are in retreat
In the mosques. Those are
Limits (set by) God:
Approach not nigh thereto.
Thus doth God make clear
His Signs to men: that
They may learn self-restraint.
195. And spend of your substance
In the cause of God,
And make not your own hands
Contribute to (your) destruction;
But do good;
For God loveth those
Who do good.
196. And complete
The *Ḥajj* or *'umra*
In the service of God.
But if ye are prevented
(From completing it),
Send an offering
For sacrifice,
Such as ye may find,
And do not shave your heads
Until the offering reaches
The place of sacrifice.
And if any of you is ill,
Or has an ailment in his scalp,
(Necessitating shaving),
(He should) in compensation
Either fast, or feed the poor,
Or offer sacrifice;
And when ye are
In peaceful conditions (again),
If any one wishes
To continue the *'umra*
On to the *ḥajj*,
He must make an offering,
Such as he can afford,
But if he cannot afford it,
He should fast

Three days during the *ḥajj*
And seven days on his return,
Making ten days in all.
This is for those
Whose household
Is not in (the precincts
Of) the Sacred Mosque.
And fear God,
And know that God.
Is strict in punishment?
197. For *Ḥajj*
Are the months well known.
If any one undertakes
That duty therein,
Let there be no obscenity,
Nor wickedness,
Nor wrangling
In the *Ḥajj*.
And whatever good
Ye do, (be sure)
God knoweth it.
And take a provision
(With you) for the journey,
But the best of provisions
Is right conduct.
So fear Me,
O ye that are wise.
198. It is no crime in you
If ye seek of the bounty
Of your Lord (during pilgrimage).
Then when ye pour down
From (Mount) 'Arafāt,
Celebrate the praises of God
At the Sacred Monument,
And celebrate His praises
As He has directed you,
Even though, before this,
Ye went astray.
199. Then pass on
At a quick pace from the place
Whence it is usual
For the multitude
So to do, and ask
For God's forgiveness.
For God is Oft-forgiving,

Most Merciful.
200. So when ye have
Accomplished your holy rites,
Celebrate the praises of God,
As ye used to celebrate
The praises of your fathers,—
Yea, with far more
Heart and soul.
There are men who say:
"Our Lord! Give us
(Thy bounties) in this world!"
But they will have
No portion in the Hereafter.

SŪRA 4—JIHAD

94. O ye who believe!
When ye go abroad
In the cause of God,
Investigate carefully,
And say not to any one
Who offers you a salutation:
"Thou art none of a Believer!"
Coveting the perishable goods
Of this life: with God
Are profits and spoils abundant.
Even thus were ye yourselves
Before, till God conferred
On you His favours: therefore
Carefully investigate.
For God is well aware
Of all that ye do.
95. Not equal are those
Believers who sit (at home)
And receive no hurt,
And those who strive
And fight in the cause
Of God with their goods
And their persons.
God hath granted
A grade higher to those
Who strive and fight
With their goods and persons
Than to those who sit (at home).

Unto all (in Faith)
Hath God promised good:
But those who strive and fight
Hath He distinguished
Above those who sit (at home)
By a special reward,—
96. Ranks specially bestowed
By Him. And Forgiveness
And Mercy. For God is
Oft forgiving, Most Merciful.
97. When angels take
The souls of those
Who die in sin
Against their souls,
They say: "In what (plight)
Were ye?" They reply:
"Weak and oppressed
Were we in the earth."
They say: "Was not
The earth of God
Spacious enough for you
To move yourselves away
(From evil)?" Such men
Will find their abode
In Hell,—What an evil
Refuge!—
98. Except those who are
(Really) weak and oppressed—
Men, women, and children—
Who have no means
In their power, nor (a guide-post)
To direct their way.
99. For these, there is hope
That God will forgive:
For God doth blot out (sins)
And forgive again and again.
100. He who forsakes his home
In the cause of God,
Finds in the earth
Many a refuge,
Wide and spacious:
Should he die
As a refugee from home
For God and His Apostle,
His reward becomes due

And sure with God:
And God is Oft-forgiving,
Most Merciful.
101. When ye travel
Through the earth,
There is no blame on you
If ye shorten your prayers,
For fear the Unbelievers
May attack you:
For the Unbelievers are
Unto you open enemies.
102. When thou (O Apostle)
Art with them, and standest
To lead them in prayer,
Let one party of them
Stand up (in prayer) with thee,
Taking their arms with them:
When they finish
Their prostrations, let them
Take their position in the rear.
And let the other party come up
Which hath not yet prayed—
And let them pray with thee,
Taking all precautions,
And bearing arms:
The Unbelievers wish,
If ye were negligent
Of your arms and your baggage,
To assault you in a single rush.
But there is no blame on you
If ye put away your arms
Because of the inconvenience

Of rain or because ye are ill;
But take (every) precaution
For yourselves. For the
Unbelievers
God hath prepared
A humiliating punishment.
103. When ye pass
(Congregational) prayers,
Celebrate God's praises,
Standing, sitting down,
Or lying down on your sides;
But when ye are free
From danger, set up
Regular Prayers:
For such prayers
Are enjoined on Believers
At stated times.
104. And slacken not
In following up the enemy:
If ye are suffering hardships,
They are suffering similar
Hardships; but ye have
Hope from God, while they
Have none. And God
Is full of knowledge and wisdom.
105. We have sent down
To thee the Book in truth,
That thou might test judge
Between men, as guided
By God: so be not (used)
As an advocate by those
Who betray their trust.

Key Terms

ayatollahs   ("Sign of God") Iranian term for a great mujtahid who has authority in the Shi'a Muslim community.

caliph   ("Deputy" or "representative") Title of the leaders of the Muslim community after the death of Muhammad. The first three caliphs ruled from Medina; the Ummayads from Damascus, and the 'Abbasids from Baghdad. Sunni Muslims revere only four Caliphs. From 1517 the caliph was based at Istanbul. Kemal Ataturk abolished the caliphate in 1923.

five pillars of Islam   Five duties enjoined on every Muslim as an appropriate response to God. They are: *salah* (ritual prayer); *zakah* (almsgiving); *sawm* (fasting in the month of Ramadan); *hajj* (pilgrimage to Mecca); and jihad (crusade).

Hajj   Pilgrimage to Mecca which is one of the five pillars of Islam and which Muslims are obliged to make at least once in a lifetime. *Hajj* must be performed in Dhu al-Hijjah (the last month of the Hijrah calendar). Umra (*Hajj* in miniature) can be performed at any time. On arrival at Mecca, pilgrims make a circuit of the Ka'ba and kiss the Black Stone.

Hadith   Traditions of Muhammad's words and actions, many of which complement or elucidate the directions of the Qur'an. There are many spurious Hadith; one of the major tasks of Muslim lawyers has been to categorize Hadith into likely degrees of authenticity.

Hijrah   ("Going forth") The migration of Muhammad, preceded by some of his followers, from Mecca to Medina in 622 CE. This was the decisive event for the development of Islam for it was in Medina that Muhammad established himself as a religious and political leader and organized his followers as an Islamic community. The Muslim calendar counts years after *Hijrah*.

ijma   The consensus of opinion of the Muslim community. It is an important principle of Islamic law-making.

imam   Meaning "model" or "example," the term refers to three types of leader within Islam. (1) The leader of ritual prayer in the local community. He is also a Quranic scholar and is therefore respected and often fulfills a leadership function within the local community. (2) Used in a more exalted sense, the term refers to leaders of particular Islamic schools of thought. For example, the founders of the schools of Islamic law are referred to as imams. Similarly, it is an honorific title given to great Islamic scholars (e.g. Al-Ghazali). (3) It has a special significance in the Shi'ite community. The term refers to a unique intercessor with exceptional spiritual authority, knowledge, and charisma. Imams are agents of divine illumination, indispensable for understanding the relevance of divine revelation for the contemporary community.

jihad   ("Striving") A much misunderstood concept. The relentless fight against worldly lust. Muslims are exhorted to wage holy war only in their defense against the infidel.

Ka'ba   ("Cube") The sanctuary in Mecca to which all Muslims turn in prayer. Set in its eastern corner is the Black Stone. A pre-Islamic holy place, all its religious images were removed in 630 CE by Muhammad when he purified it to be the central sanctuary of Islam. The Qur'an associates Abraham and Ishmael with the building of the Ka'ba.

Mecca   Holy city of Islam, in Saudi Arabia, the birthplace of Muhammad, and later the base for his Muslim state after its conquest in 630 CE. Pilgrimage to Mecca, *hajj*, is one of the five pillars of Islam and all Muslims are required to face Mecca to perform ritual prayer five times a day.

Medina   Formerly Yathrib, city 100 miles/169 kilometers north of Mecca, the political base for Muhammad from 622 CE until his conquest of Mecca. Pilgrims from Medina were among the first to accept and spread Muhammad's message. The city contains the site of Muhammad's tomb.

muezzin   Person who calls the Muslim faithful to prayer.

mujtahid   Muslim teacher who gives a ruling, legal decision or deduction on the basis of his own learning or authority. In Shi'a Islam, the *mujtahidun* have great authority.

Qur'an   The holy scripture of Islam. Muslims believe it was revealed to the prophet Muhammad, piecemeal, by God and written in Arabic. All Muslims believe the Qur'an to be divine in origin. It is literally divine thought and law in words. It forms part of the Mother of the Book (also called "the well-preserved Tablet") inscribed in heaven. The Qur'an descended to the lowest of the seven heavens to the House of Protection during the Night of Power. From there it was revealed bit by bit to Muhammad.

Ramadan   Islamic lunar month in which Muslims are obliged to fast from food and water between sunrise and sunset. The old and sick, pregnant women and nursing mothers are exempt, though they are expected, if possible, to make it up later.

Shari'a   ("The path") Body of law for the Muslim community which derives from the Qur'an, the Sunnah, and other sources, the legitimacy of which is debated in the different schools of law. Shari'a is regarded as divinely authoritative.

Shi'a/Shi'ites   The minority group in Islam, comprising 15 percent of Muslims. They reject the first three caliphs, believing 'Ali to be Muhammad's true successor. They also hold that authority resides in the imams, who are the infallible messengers of God in every age. The Shi'a live mostly in Iraq, Iran, Lebanon, Pakistan and India. The two main Shi'a divisions are the Isma'ilis and the Twelvers.

Sufism   Islamic mystical movement originating in the eighth century CE as a reaction to the worldliness of the Ummayad Dynasty. Sufis claimed direct experience of Allah through ascetic practices. The orthodox rejected them at first, but today Sufi orders are accepted among Sunnis and Shi'as.

sunnah   ("Trodden path") The source of authority in Islamic lawmaking which is second only to the Qur'an. It refers to the words and actions of Muhammad and, in a lesser degree, to the words and actions of the first four caliphs.

Sunnis   The majority group in Islam, comprising about 85 percent of Muslims. They accept the authority of the four rightly guided Caliphs and the developed process of lawmaking guided by the community's legal experts. Sunni Muslims live in the Arab states in North, West and East Africa and in India and Indonesia.

ummah   The Muslim community, those who have received God's revelation through Muhammad and live in submission to it.

Questions for Study and Discussion

1.   What characterized Muhammad's role as a prophet? What were the differences between his reception in Mecca and his reception in Medina by the respective communities there?

2. Briefly describe the main religious differences between Sunni Muslims and the Shi'a Muslims. Explain the significance of *ijma'* to the Sunni and the imam to the Shi'a.
3. Why would a true Sufi or Suffiya never use that term to describe himself or herself? What is the role of the individual versus the role of God in the spiritual life of a *mutasawwif*?
4. Briefly describe the structure of the Qur'an. What is the importance of the abrogation principle?
5. Name the five pillars of Islam (give the Arabic name and the English equivalent) and briefly define them.
6. How does Mohammed A. Khan's view of himself and his religion ("I am a Muslim," pp. 422–23) reflect the situation of Islam in the world today? What insights do you gain from his essay about the dilemmas faced by contemporary Muslims?
7. From your knowledge of the media and from any other relevant sources, how would you characterize the typical Western—and particularly the typical American—view of Muslims after September 11? What specific truths about Islam, if they were more widely understood, do you believe could improve Westerners' relationship with Muslims, both domestically and internationally?

Questions for Reflection

Write your personal reflections to each of these questions in the space provided.

1. Explain how Islam integrated politics and the state into its core beliefs, reflecting on today's political world in the Middle East. (See pp. 339–91.)

2. Explain the concept of *tawhid*, or oneness of God, and its function in Islam. (See p. 404.)

3. What is the Islamic view of Scripture? (See p. 401.)

4. Consider the global role of Islam over the centuries and its relationship to the spread of knowledge in the world. (See pp. 418–19.)

5. How does architecture reflect Islamic belief? (Think across the chapter.)

Selected Online Resources

▶ Islam and Islamic Studies Resources—extensive, categorized resources for the study of Islam and Islamic culture
http://www.uga.edu/islam

▶ Hajj Information Center—aimed primarily at Muslims who wish to plan a *Hajj*, this site features "Hajj: Step by Step Guide," which includes photographs and hypertext explaining the terms used
http://www.islamicity.com/mosque/hajj

▶ Islamic Art at the Los Angeles County Museum of Art—photographs of items from the museum's collection with accompanying information and architectural context, plus a glossary of terms
http://www.lacma.org/islamic_art/islamic.htm

Part 12: Sikhism

Chapter Summaries

77. A Historical Overview

Sikhism originated in the Punjab, a region in the northwest of India, about five hundred years ago. It evolved within the context of being a minority community surrounded by much larger Hindu and Muslim populations.

Its first Guru was Nank, who was born a Hindu but underwent spiritual transformation at age thirty. He was the first to create a community of Sikhs, and his teachings are the heart of the Sikh scriptures. He preached that salvation was dependent on devotion to the Formless One. The Sikh Panth (path) was led by a line of Gurus until the death of the tenth in 1708. Guru Arjan codified the scriptures, which have a central place in the ritual of the *gurdwara*, or temple. The last Guru, Gobind, adopted the role of ruler and reestablished the Guru's authority over the Panth. The Sikhs acted as guerrilla fighters in the resistance to Muslim invasion during the eighteenth century. They captured Lahore and made it the center of their kingdom until it was overtaken by the British Empire in 1849.

78. Sacred Writings

The principle scripture is the *Adi Granth* (eternal book). Its contents are referred to as *bani* (voice) and *gurbani* (utterance of the Guru). Since the time of Guru Nank it has been used in devotional singing as part of congregational worship; its presence is mandatory in all religious ceremonies. The second scriptural book is the *Dasam Granth*, which contains the compositions of the tenth Guru and other poets.

79. Beliefs

Sikh belief emphasizes the oneness of God; as they say, "*Ek Onkar.*" Sikhism is strictly monotheistic and forbids the worship of idols. In the divine order (*hukam*) human life is a gift, and people must submit to God's will. Humans are endowed with the ability to choose between good and evil. The soul (*atma*) is immortal and continues through cycles of death and rebirth. Only by working toward becoming

Guru-oriented can a person eventually attain spiritual liberation and be called *jivan-mukta*. They must be active in the practice of righteousness (*dharmsal*), affirming the grace and blessing (*gurparsad*) that come from God.

80. Worship and Festivals

Daily worship involves ritual bathing and reciting hymns, usually in the person's home. Congregational worship at the *gurdwara* involves hymn singing followed by a communal meal. Holy days, or *gurpurbs*, are days commemorating birthdays and martyrdoms of the Gurus. Festivals include Baisakhi, the birthday of Khalsa, and Hola, related to the Hindu festival of Holi.

81. Family and Society

While Sikh teachings reject the doctrine of caste, it still influences Sikh community. The basic unit of Sikh society is the joint family, typically with a traditional occupation. Marriage is the foundation of Sikh community and is seen as the alliance between two families. Singing hymns from the Adi Granth is part of the wedding ceremony. Children are seen as divine gifts. Boys begin to wear the turban (*pag*), a symbol of honor, when they are considered able to take care of it.

82. Sikhism Today

Reform movements in Sikhism arose as a response to the British takeover of the Punjab as well as the dominance of Hinduism. Reformers preached a return to the age of the Gurus and a devout lifestyle. Their efforts were assisted by new editions of the scriptures with extensive commentaries and additional reformist writings. Sikhs actively sought control over the major *gurdwaras* and established a major political party to help establish Sikhs as an ethno-religious minority. Ultimately a separatist movement led to armed conflict, the assassination of Indira Gandhi, and the loss of support for separatism from most Sikhs in India. Today the Sikh diaspora is involved in reformulating some of the earlier Sikh reformers' work.

Key Personalities

Guru Nanak (1469–1539)

Indian religious teacher and founder of the Sikh religion. He intended to reconcile Hindus and Muslims, and traveled widely preaching a monotheistic faith that was influenced by Bhakti and Sufism. He appointed a successor to continue his teachings.

"At Nanakmata, the Master [Guru Nanak] sat . . . under an old dry *peepal* tree. . . . The tree grew fresh sprouts and became green. This attracted notice, and some of the Yogis came and accosted the Master. . . . The Yogis enquired who he was, whose disciple, and wherefrom he had come. He had revived the tree that used to be dry, what further powers he possessed, the Yogis questioned. The Master replied that he was the disciple of the True Lord, than whom none greater existed or could exist, that from Him he had received instruction in the True Word, which had led to his emancipation from all bonds, but that he was a humble man, claiming no supernatural powers, and was roaming about to see the condition of God's creation."

(Sewaram Singh, *The Divine Master: Life and Teachings of Guru Nanak Dev* [reprint, New Delhi: Gian Publishing, 1989 (1904)], 182–83)

Guru Gobind Singh (1675–1708)

The tenth guru of the Sikh community. He militarized the Sikhs, requiring them to adopt a distinctive name and dress. He also shifted the focus of authority from the gurus to the sacred scripture, the *Adi Granth*.

"The Guru had donned white garments. Approaching the place of assembly, he took his seat on an impressive throne. To one side a contingent of five hundred mighty warriors sat armed and at the ready. After pouring water from the Satluj river into a large iron vessel the Guru gave instructions for the Cherished Five [warriors selected the previous day] to be clad in white garments (including breeches) together with a sword and other symbolic items. He then had them stand before him and commanded them to repeat the divine name 'Vahiguru,' fixing their minds on God as they did so. This they were to continue doing while he stirred the sanctified water (*amrit*) in the iron vessel with a double-edged sword held vertically."

(*Textual Sources for the Study of Sikhism*, ed. and trans. W. H. McLeod [Manchester, UK: Manchester University Press, 1984], 36

Guru Arjan (or Arjun) (1581–1606)

Founder of the Golden Temple, considered the heart of Sikhism, and the codifier of the Sikh scriptures, the *Adi Granth*.

"*Sangrand* [first day of every lunar month in the Hindu calendar] is regarded as an auspicious day. . . . Guru Arjun Dev composed the hymn of *Bara Maha* (literally the hymn of twelve months). It comprises twelve hymns. . . . Each hymn illustrates the stages of life and the journey of the soul while directing the Sikhs to conform to a specific code of discipline during each month. Sikhs visit gurdwaras on this festival day before setting off to work."

(Sewa Singh Kalsi, *Simple Guide to Sikhism* [Folkestone, Kent, UK: Global Books, 1999], 78)

Bhai Gurdas

The scribe who wrote the *Adi Granth* under the direction of Guru Arjan. His collected writings are called *varan*, or ballads, which are sung by Sikh musicians and preachers at the *gurdwaras*.

"Bhai Gurdas, the noted scholar and poet, came to Guru Ram Das seeking his blessings and requesting his formal initiation as a Sikh. Greatly moved by his devotion and humility, the Guru asked Bhai Gurdas to proceed to Agra and look after the spiritual needs of the Sikhs there.

"Bhai Gurdas undertook to prepare the master copy of the compilation. He was also invited by the Guru [Arjan] to contribute his own verses for inclusion in the *Holy Granth*, but his modesty of a disciple would not permit it. The compilation of the *Holy Granth* was completed in 1604."

(K. S. Duggal, *Sikh Gurus: Their Lives and Teachings* [New Delhi: UBS Publishing, 1993], 95, 116)

Maharaja Ranjit Singh (1790–1839)

Made crown prince (hence the title "Maharaja") by the Sikhs of Punjab after he seized power from the Mongols, he ruled from Lahore and built many Sikh temples still standing today.

"Maharaja Ranjit Singh was a striking figure. Dressed always in white, he habitually wore on his arm the Koh-i-noor diamond, at the time the largest and most valuable gem in the world and now one of the British Crown Jewels. He had lost an eye early in life, and his one-eyed stare was penetrating. Under his rule, new gurdwaras were built and many old ones renovated. He strictly enforced Sikh rules, demanding that even foreigners in his court refrain from cutting their hair and beards, eating beef, or smoking tobacco in public."

(Nikky-Guninder Kaur Singh, *Sikhism: World Religions* [New York: Facts on File, 1993], 114)

Primary Source Readings

The following excerpted readings represent some of the important primary sources mentioned in the main text. Additional primary sources are available both in print and online, and students are encouraged to contact their instructors for further information.

XII.1 Shri Guru Granth Sahib: Jup

Source: *Shri Guru Granth Sahib*, http://www.sacred-texts.com/skh/granth/gr01.htm

SECTION 1, PART 1

One Universal Creator God. The Name Is Truth. Creative Being Personified. No Fear. No Hatred. Image Of The Undying, Beyond Birth, Self-Existent. By Guru's Grace ~

Chant And Meditate:

True In The Primal Beginning. True Throughout The Ages.

True Here And Now. O Nanak, Forever And Ever True.

By thinking, He cannot be reduced to thought, even by thinking hundreds of thousands of times.

By remaining silent, inner silence is not obtained, even by remaining lovingly absorbed deep within.

The hunger of the hungry is not appeased, even by piling up loads of worldly goods.

Hundreds of thousands of clever tricks, but not even one of them will go along with you in the end.

So how can you become truthful? And how can the veil of illusion be torn away?

O Nanak, it is written that you shall obey the Hukam of His Command, and walk in the Way of His Will.

By His Command, bodies are created; His Command cannot be described.

By His Command, souls come into being; by His Command, glory and greatness are obtained.

By His Command, some are high and some are low; by His Written Command, pain and pleasure are obtained.

Some, by His Command, are blessed and forgiven; others, by His Command, wander aimlessly forever.

Everyone is subject to His Command; no one is beyond His Command.

O Nanak, one who understands His Command, does not speak in ego.

Some sing of His Power—who has that Power?

Some sing of His Gifts, and know His Sign and Insignia.

Some sing of His Glorious Virtues, Greatness and Beauty.

Some sing of knowledge obtained of Him, through difficult philosophical studies.

Some sing that He fashions the body, and then again reduces it to dust.

Some sing that He takes life away, and then again restores it.

Some sing that He seems so very far away.

SECTION 1, PART 2

Some sing that He watches over us, face to face, ever-present.

There is no shortage of those who preach and teach.

Millions upon millions offer millions of sermons and stories.

The Great Giver keeps on giving, while those who receive grow weary of receiving.

Throughout the ages, consumers consume.

The Commander, by His Command, leads us to walk on the Path.

O Nanak, He blossoms forth, Carefree and Untroubled.

True is the Master, True is His Name—speak it with infinite love.

People beg and pray, "Give to us, give to us", and the Great Giver gives His Gifts.

So what offering can we place before Him, by which we might see the Darbaar of His Court?

What words can we speak to evoke His Love?

In the Amrit Vaylaa, the ambrosial hours before dawn, chant the True Name, and contemplate His Glorious Greatness.

By the karma of past actions, the robe of this physical body is obtained. By His Grace, the Gate of Liberation is found.

O Nanak, know this well: the True One Himself is All.

He cannot be established, He cannot be created.

He Himself is Immaculate and Pure.

Those who serve Him are honored.

O Nanak, sing of the Lord, the Treasure of Excellence.

Sing, and listen, and let your mind be filled with love.

Your pain shall be sent far away, and peace shall come to your home.

The Guru's Word is the Sound-current of the Naad; the Guru's Word is the Wisdom of the Vedas; the Guru's Word is all-pervading.

The Guru is Shiva, the Guru is Vishnu and Brahma; the Guru is Paarvati and Lakhshmi.

Even knowing God, I cannot describe Him; He cannot be described in words.

The Guru has given me this one understanding:

there is only the One, the Giver of all souls. May I never forget Him!

If I am pleasing to Him, then that is my pilgrimage and cleansing bath. Without pleasing Him, what good are ritual cleansings?

I gaze upon all the created beings: without the karma of good actions, what are they given to receive?

Within the mind are gems, jewels and rubies, if you listen to the Guru's Teachings, even once.

The Guru has given me this one understanding:

there is only the One, the Giver of all souls. May I never forget Him!

Even if you could live throughout the four ages, or even ten times more,

and even if you were known throughout the nine continents and followed by all,

with a good name and reputation, with praise and fame throughout the world—

still, if the Lord does not bless you with His Glance of Grace, then who cares? What is the use?

Among worms, you would be considered a lowly worm, and even contemptible sinners would hold you in contempt.

O Nanak, God blesses the unworthy with virtue, and bestows virtue on the virtuous.

No one can even imagine anyone who can bestow virtue upon Him.

Listening—the Siddhas, the spiritual teachers, the heroic warriors, the yogic masters.

Listening—the earth, its support and the Akaashic ethers.

Listening—the oceans, the lands of the world and the nether regions of the underworld.

Listening—Death cannot even touch you.

O Nanak, the devotees are forever in bliss.

Listening—pain and sin are erased.

Listening—Shiva, Brahma and Indra.

Listening—even foul-mouthed people praise Him.

Listening—the technology of Yoga and the secrets of the body.

Listening—the Shaastras, the Simritees and the Vedas.

O Nanak, the devotees are forever in bliss.

SECTION 1, PART 3

Listening—pain and sin are erased.

Listening—truth, contentment and spiritual wisdom.

Listening—take your cleansing bath at the sixty-eight places of pilgrimage.

Listening—reading and reciting, honor is obtained.

Listening—intuitively grasp the essence of meditation.

O Nanak, the devotees are forever in bliss.

Listening—pain and sin are erased.

Listening—dive deep into the ocean of virtue.

Listening—the Shaykhs, religious scholars, spiritual teachers and emperors.

Listening—even the blind find the Path.

Listening—the Unreachable comes within your grasp.

O Nanak, the devotees are forever in bliss.

Listening—pain and sin are erased.

The state of the faithful cannot be described.

One who tries to describe this shall regret the attempt.

No paper, no pen, no scribe

can record the state of the faithful.

Such is the Name of the Immaculate Lord.

Only one who has faith comes to know such a state of mind.

The faithful have intuitive awareness and intelligence.

The faithful know about all worlds and realms.

The faithful shall never be struck across the face.

The faithful do not have to go with the Messenger of Death.

Such is the Name of the Immaculate Lord.

Only one who has faith comes to know such a state of mind.

The path of the faithful shall never be blocked.

The faithful shall depart with honor and fame.

The faithful do not follow empty religious rituals.

The faithful are firmly bound to the Dharma.

Such is the Name of the Immaculate Lord.

Only one who has faith comes to know such a state of mind.

The faithful find the Door of Liberation.

The faithful uplift and redeem their family and relations.

The faithful are saved, and carried across with the Sikhs of the Guru.

The faithful, O Nanak, do not wander around begging.

Such is the Name of the Immaculate Lord.

Only one who has faith comes to know such a state of mind.

The chosen ones, the self-elect, are accepted and approved.

The chosen ones are honored in the Court of the Lord.

The chosen ones look beautiful in the courts of kings.

The chosen ones meditate single-mindedly on the Guru.

No matter how much anyone tries to explain and describe them,

the actions of the Creator cannot be counted.

The mythical bull is Dharma, the son of compassion;

this is what patiently holds the earth in its place.

One who understands this becomes truthful.

What a great load there is on the bull!

So many worlds beyond this world—so very many!

What power holds them, and supports their weight?

The names and the colors of the assorted species of beings

were all inscribed by the Ever-flowing Pen of God.

Who knows how to write this account?

Just imagine what a huge scroll it would take!

What power! What fascinating beauty!

And what gifts! Who can know their extent?

You created the vast expanse of the Universe with One Word!

Hundreds of thousands of rivers began to flow.

How can Your Creative Potency be described?

I cannot even once be a sacrifice to You.

Whatever pleases You is the only good done,

You, Eternal and Formless One!

Countless meditations, countless loves.

Countless worship services, countless austere disciplines.

Countless scriptures, and ritual recitations of the Vedas.

Countless Yogis, whose minds remain detached from the world.

SECTION 1, PART 4

Countless devotees contemplate the Wisdom and Virtues of the Lord.

Countless the holy, countless the givers.

Countless heroic spiritual warriors, who bear the brunt of the attack in battle (who with their mouths eat steel).

Countless silent sages, vibrating the String of His Love.

How can Your Creative Potency be described?

I cannot even once be a sacrifice to You.

Whatever pleases You is the only good done,

You, Eternal and Formless One.

Countless fools, blinded by ignorance.

Countless thieves and embezzlers.

Countless impose their will by force.

Countless cut-throats and ruthless killers.

Countless sinners who keep on sinning.

Countless liars, wandering lost in their lies.

Countless wretches, eating filth as their ration.

Countless slanderers, carrying the weight of their stupid mistakes on their heads.

Nanak describes the state of the lowly.

I cannot even once be a sacrifice to You.

Whatever pleases You is the only good done,

You, Eternal and Formless One.

Countless names, countless places.

Inaccessible, unapproachable, countless celestial realms.

Even to call them countless is to carry the weight on your head.

From the Word, comes the Naam; from the Word, comes Your Praise.

From the Word, comes spiritual wisdom, singing the Songs of Your Glory.

From the Word, come the written and spoken words and hymns.

From the Word, comes destiny, written on one's forehead.

But the One who wrote these Words of Destiny—no words are written on His Forehead.

As He ordains, so do we receive.

The created universe is the manifestation of Your Name.

Without Your Name, there is no place at all.

How can I describe Your Creative Power?

I cannot even once be a sacrifice to You.

Whatever pleases You is the only good done,

You, Eternal and Formless One.

When the hands and the feet and the body are dirty,

water can wash away the dirt.

When the clothes are soiled and stained by urine,

soap can wash them clean.

But when the intellect is stained and polluted by sin,

it can only be cleansed by the Love of the Name.

Virtue and vice do not come by mere words;

actions repeated, over and over again, are engraved on the soul.

You shall harvest what you plant.

O Nanak, by the Hukam of God's Command, we come and go in reincarnation.

Pilgrimages, austere discipline, compassion and charity

—these, by themselves, bring only an iota of merit.

Listening and believing with love and humility in your mind,

cleanse yourself with the Name, at the sacred shrine deep within.

All virtues are Yours, Lord, I have none at all.

Without virtue, there is no devotional worship.

I bow to the Lord of the World, to His Word, to Brahma the Creator.

He is Beautiful, True and Eternally Joyful.

What was that time, and what was that moment? What was that day, and what was that date?

What was that season, and what was that month, when the Universe was created?

The Pandits, the religious scholars, cannot find that time, even if it is written in the Puraanas.

That time is not known to the Qazis, who study the Koran.

The day and the date are not known to the Yogis, nor is the month or the season.

The Creator who created this creation—only He Himself knows.

How can we speak of Him? How can we praise Him? How can we describe Him? How can we know Him?

SECTION 1, PART 5

O Nanak, everyone speaks of Him, each one wiser than the rest.

Great is the Master, Great is His Name. Whatever happens is according to His Will.

O Nanak, one who claims to know everything shall not be decorated in the world hereafter.

There are nether worlds beneath nether worlds, and hundreds of thousands of heavenly worlds above.

The Vedas say that you can search and search for them all, until you grow weary.

The scriptures say that there are 18,000 worlds, but in reality, there is only One Universe.

If you try to write an account of this, you will surely finish yourself before you finish writing it.

O Nanak, call Him Great! He Himself knows Himself.

The praisers praise the Lord, but they do not obtain intuitive understanding

—the streams and rivers flowing into the ocean do not know its vastness.

Even kings and emperors, with mountains of property and oceans of wealth

—these are not even equal to an ant, who does not forget God.

Endless are His Praises, endless are those who speak them.

Endless are His Actions, endless are His Gifts.

Endless is His Vision, endless is His Hearing.

His limits cannot be perceived. What is the Mystery of His Mind?

The limits of the created universe cannot be perceived.

Its limits here and beyond cannot be perceived.

Many struggle to know His limits,

but His limits cannot be found.

No one can know these limits.

The more you say about them, the more there still remains to be said.

Great is the Master, High is His Heavenly Home.

Highest of the High, above all is His Name.

Only one as Great and as High as God

can know His Lofty and Exalted State.

Only He Himself is that Great. He Himself knows Himself.

O Nanak, by His Glance of Grace, He bestows His Blessings.

His Blessings are so abundant that there can be no written account of them.

The Great Giver does not hold back anything.

There are so many great, heroic warriors begging at the Door of the Infinite Lord.

So many contemplate and dwell upon Him, that they cannot be counted.

So many waste away to death engaged in corruption.

So many take and take again, and then deny receiving.

So many foolish consumers keep on consuming.

So many endure distress, deprivation and constant abuse.

Even these are Your Gifts, O Great Giver!

Liberation from bondage comes only by Your Will.

No one else has any say in this.

If some fool should presume to say that he does,

he shall learn, and feel the effects of his folly.

He Himself knows, He Himself gives.

Few, very few are those who acknowledge this.

One who is blessed to sing the Praises of the Lord,

O Nanak, is the king of kings.

Priceless are His Virtues, Priceless are His Dealings.

Priceless are His Dealers, Priceless are His Treasures.

Priceless are those who come to Him, Priceless are those who buy from Him.

Priceless is Love for Him, Priceless is absorption into Him.

Priceless is the Divine Law of Dharma, Priceless is the Divine Court of Justice.

Priceless are the scales, priceless are the weights.

Priceless are His Blessings, Priceless is His Banner and Insignia.

Priceless is His Mercy, Priceless is His Royal Command.

Priceless, O Priceless beyond expression!

Speak of Him continually, and remain absorbed in His Love.

The Vedas and the Puraanas speak.

The scholars speak and lecture.

Brahma speaks, Indra speaks.

SECTION 1, PART 6

The Gopis and Krishna speak.

Shiva speaks, the Siddhas speak.

The many created Buddhas speak.

The demons speak, the demi-gods speak.

The spiritual warriors, the heavenly beings, the silent sages, the humble and serviceful speak.

Many speak and try to describe Him.

Many have spoken of Him over and over again, and have then arisen and departed.

If He were to create as many again as there already are,

even then, they could not describe Him.

He is as Great as He wishes to be.

O Nanak, the True Lord knows.

If anyone presumes to describe God,

he shall be known as the greatest fool of fools!

Where is that Gate, and where is that Dwelling, in which You sit and take care of all?

The Sound-current of the Naad vibrates there, and countless musicians play on all sorts of instruments there.

So many Ragas, so many musicians singing there.

The praanic wind, water and fire sing; the Righteous Judge of Dharma sings at Your Door.

Chitr and Gupt, the angels of the conscious and the subconscious who record actions, and the Righteous Judge of Dharma who judges this record sing.

Shiva, Brahma and the Goddess of Beauty, ever adorned, sing.

Indra, seated upon His Throne, sings with the deities at Your Door.

The Siddhas in Samaadhi sing; the Saadhus sing in contemplation.

The celibates, the fanatics, the peacefully accepting and the fearless warriors sing.

The Pandits, the religious scholars who recite the Vedas, with the supreme sages of all the ages, sing.

The Mohinis, the enchanting heavenly beauties who entice hearts in this world, in paradise, and in the underworld of the subconscious sing.

The celestial jewels created by You, and the sixty-eight holy places of pilgrimage sing.

The brave and mighty warriors sing; the spiritual heroes and the four sources of creation sing.

The planets, solar systems and galaxies, created and arranged by Your Hand, sing.

They alone sing, who are pleasing to Your Will. Your devotees are imbued with the Nectar of Your Essence.

So many others sing, they do not come to mind. O Nanak, how can I consider them all?

That True Lord is True, Forever True, and True is His Name.

He is, and shall always be. He shall not depart, even when this Universe which He has created departs.

He created the world, with its various colors, species of beings, and the variety of Maya.

Having created the creation, He watches over it Himself, by His Greatness.

He does whatever He pleases. No order can be issued to Him.

He is the King, the King of kings, the Supreme Lord and Master of kings. Nanak remains subject to His Will.

Make contentment your ear-rings, humility your begging bowl, and meditation the ashes you apply to your body.

Let the remembrance of death be the patched coat you wear, let the purity of virginity be your way in the world, and let faith in the Lord be your walking stick.

See the brotherhood of all mankind as the highest order of Yogis; conquer your own mind, and conquer the world.

I bow to Him, I humbly bow.

The Primal One, the Pure Light, without beginning, without end. Throughout all the ages, He is One and the Same.

Let spiritual wisdom be your food, and compassion your attendant. The Sound-current of the Naad vibrates in each and every heart.

He Himself is the Supreme Master of all; wealth and miraculous spiritual powers, and all other external tastes and pleasures, are all like beads on a string.

Union with Him, and separation from Him, come by His Will. We come to receive what is written in our destiny.

Section 1, Part 7

I bow to Him, I humbly bow.

The Primal One, the Pure Light, without beginning, without end. Throughout all the ages, He is One and the Same.

The One Divine Mother conceived and gave birth to the three deities.

One, the Creator of the World; One, the Sustainer; and One, the Destroyer.

He makes things happen according to the Pleasure of His Will. Such is His Celestial Order.

He watches over all, but none see Him. How wonderful this is!

I bow to Him, I humbly bow.

The Primal One, the Pure Light, without beginning, without end. Throughout all the ages, He is One and the Same.

On world after world are His Seats of Authority and His Storehouses.

Whatever was put into them, was put there once and for all.

Having created the creation, the Creator Lord watches over it.

O Nanak, True is the Creation of the True Lord.

I bow to Him, I humbly bow.

The Primal One, the Pure Light, without beginning, without end. Throughout all the ages, He is One and the Same.

If I had 100,000 tongues, and these were then multiplied twenty times more, with each tongue,

I would repeat, hundreds of thousands of times, the Name of the One, the Lord of the Universe.

Along this path to our Husband Lord, we climb the steps of the ladder, and come to merge with Him.

Hearing of the etheric realms, even worms long to come back home.

O Nanak, by His Grace He is obtained. False are the boastings of the false. ||32||

No power to speak, no power to keep silent.

No power to beg, no power to give.

No power to live, no power to die.

No power to rule, with wealth and occult mental powers.

No power to gain intuitive understanding, spiritual wisdom and meditation.

No power to find the way to escape from the world.

He alone has the Power in His Hands. He watches over all.

O Nanak, no one is high or low.

Nights, days, weeks and seasons;

wind, water, fire and the nether regions

—in the midst of these, He established the earth as a home for Dharma.

Upon it, He placed the various species of beings.

Their names are uncounted and endless.

By their deeds and their actions, they shall be judged.

God Himself is True, and True is His Court.

There, in perfect grace and ease, sit the self-elect, the self-realized Saints.

They receive the Mark of Grace from the Merciful Lord.

The ripe and the unripe, the good and the bad, shall there be judged.

O Nanak, when you go home, you will see this.

This is righteous living in the realm of Dharma.

And now we speak of the realm of spiritual wisdom.

So many winds, waters and fires; so many Krishnas and Shivas.

So many Brahmas, fashioning forms of great beauty, adorned and dressed in many colors.

So many worlds and lands for working out karma. So very many lessons to be learned!

So many Indras, so many moons and suns, so many worlds and lands.

So many Siddhas and Buddhas, so many Yogic masters. So many goddesses of various kinds.

So many demi-gods and demons, so many silent sages. So many oceans of jewels.

So many ways of life, so many languages. So many dynasties of rulers.

So many intuitive people, so many selfless servants. O Nanak, His limit has no limit!

In the realm of wisdom, spiritual wisdom reigns supreme.

The Sound-current of the Naad vibrates there, amidst the sounds and the sights of bliss.

In the realm of humility, the Word is Beauty.

Forms of incomparable beauty are fashioned there.

These things cannot be described.

One who tries to speak of these shall regret the attempt.

The intuitive consciousness, intellect and understanding of the mind are shaped there.

The consciousness of the spiritual warriors and the Siddhas, the beings of spiritual perfection, are shaped there.

In the realm of karma, the Word is Power.

No one else dwells there,

except the warriors of great power, the spiritual heroes.

They are totally fulfilled, imbued with the Lord's Essence.

Myriads of Sitas are there, cool and calm in their majestic glory.

Their beauty cannot be described.

Neither death nor deception comes to those,

within whose minds the Lord abides.

The devotees of many worlds dwell there.

They celebrate; their minds are imbued with the True Lord.

In the realm of Truth, the Formless Lord abides.

Having created the creation, He watches over it. By His Glance of Grace, He bestows happiness.

There are planets, solar systems and galaxies.

If one speaks of them, there is no limit, no end.

There are worlds upon worlds of His Creation.

As He commands, so they exist.

He watches over all, and contemplating the creation, He rejoices.

O Nanak, to describe this is as hard as steel!

Let self-control be the furnace, and patience the goldsmith.

Let understanding be the anvil, and spiritual wisdom the tools.

With the Fear of God as the bellows, fan the flames of tapa, the body's inner heat.

In the crucible of love, melt the Nectar of the Name,

and mint the True Coin of the Shabad, the Word of God.

Such is the karma of those upon whom He has cast His Glance of Grace.

O Nanak, the Merciful Lord, by His Grace, uplifts and exalts them. ||38||

Shalok:

Air is the Guru, Water is the Father, and Earth is the Great Mother of all.

Day and night are the two nurses, in whose lap all the world is at play.

Good deeds and bad deeds-the record is read out in the Presence of the Lord of Dharma.

According to their own actions, some are drawn closer, and some are driven farther away.

Those who have meditated on the Naam, the Name of the Lord, and departed after having worked by the sweat of their brows

—O Nanak, their faces are radiant in the Court of the Lord, and many are saved along with them!

XII.2 The Mūl Mantra (The Ādi Granth): The Basic Sikh Statement of Faith

There is one supreme God, known by grace by the true Gurū.

The True Name, the Creator, fearless and formless;

Timeless, never incarnated, self-existent.

Key Terms

Adi Granth   Sacred book of Sikhism. It is regarded as the eternal guru for the Sikh community. It is the central focus of the Sikh home and of the Gurdwara.

Diwali   Festival of light celebrated by Hindus, Jains, and Sikhs. For Sikhs it is a commemoration of the release from prison of the sixth guru and his return to the city of Amritsar.

gurdwara   Sikh temple and meeting place, consisting of a worship area which houses the Adi Granth, and a cooking and eating area for the symbolic meal which ends Sikh worship.

karma   The belief every action has inevitable consequences which attach themselves to the doer requiring reward or punishment. Karma is thus the moral law of cause and effect. It explains the inequalities of life as the consequences of actions in previous lives. The notion of karma probably developed among the Dravidian people of India. In Mahayana Buddhism the concept is transformed by the idea of the bodhisattva. Merit can be transferred by grace or faith, thus changing the person's karma.

Khalsa   Originally the militant community of Sikhs organized by Guru Gobind Singh in 1699. Now it is the society of fully committed adult members of the Sikh community. Traditional marks of membership are uncut hair, a comb worn in the hair, a sword, knee-length breeches and a steel bracelet.

moksha   Sanskrit word meaning liberation from the cycle of birth, death and rebirth. Permanent spiritual perfection experienced by an enlightened soul after the physical body has died. No further incarnations will be endured.

Questions for Study and Discussion

1.   Briefly explain Sikhism's concept of *Ek Onkar*.
2.   Identify evidence in the traditional core beliefs of Sikhism of the influence of Hinduism.
3.   Explain how a "*jivan-mukta* Sikh is like a lotus which remains clean despite living in muddy water" (p. 440).
4.   Why do Sikhs believe that religious asceticism, such as that of yogis, is wrong?
5.   How does the physical structure of the Golden Temple at Amritsar (see p. 444) reflect the basic principles of Sikhism?
6.   Describe the affect the Sikh reform movement has had on contemporary Sikh practice and community.
7.   Compare the Sikh diaspora's relationship to the Sikh community of the Punjab with the Jain diaspora's relationship to its home community.

Questions for Reflection

Write your personal reflections to each of these questions in the space provided.

1.   What was central the idea of Guru Nanak? (See pp. 430–31.)

2.   Discuss the social importance of the *Khalsa*. (See p. 434.)

3.   How do Sikhs think about their scriptures? Is there a similar view of scripture in your own tradition or other world religion you are familiar with? (See pp. 436–37.)

4.   Can you identify any similarities between Sikh worship and Hindu *puja*? (See pp. 442–43.)

5. Think about the similarities among Hinduism, Islam, and Sikhism, and indicate what they tell us about the historical relationship of religions.

Selected Online Resources

▶ The Sikhism Home Page—information on Sikhism's history and beliefs with additional resources, such as recommended reading and a glossary of terms
http://www.sikhs.org/topics.htm

▶ Eternal Glory of Baba Nand Singh Ji Maharaj—with quotations from the Sikh leader, illustrations, audio clips, etc.
http://www.babanandsinghsahib.org/main.htm

▶ Audio/Video Sikhnet—a collection of videos related to Sikhism and contemporary Sikhs around the world
http://www.sikhnet.com/news/audio-video

Part 13: Religions in Today's World

Chapter Summaries

83. From Existentialism to Postmodernism

Important philosophical ideas from Immanuel Kant, Georg W. F. Hegel, and Søren Kierkegaard influenced the development of religious thought in the West. Existentialism in its various forms features a deep suspicion of human reason and emphasizes the limits of the individual perspective. The personal is prioritized over the abstract, and firsthand involvement over objectivity. Existentialism can be Christian in orientation—God is beyond human reason and must be accepted by faith—or atheistic—God is a human construct, and all claims to objective truth are illusory. Postmodernism, involving the belief that all claims to truth serve the interests of the claimants, evolved through the work of Roland Barthes and Jacques Derrida. Some postmodern perspectives are more optimistic than others; for example, Richard Rorty argued a pragmatic philosophy based on the concept of ethnocentric values being true for specific communities. Postmodernity can be seen as promoting the tolerance of all beliefs because of the denial of objective truth and of the right to impose values on another. Some believe it offers only a means to blame the power interests of competing groups for all ills in society.

84. New Religious Movements

NRMs tend to fall outside mainstream religion but typically have their roots in one or major faiths. Christian-related NRMs include the Seventh-Day Adventists, the Jehovah's Witnesses, the Church of Jesus Christ of the Latter-Day Saints (the Mormons), and the Church of Christian Science. A later wave of NRMs in the 1960s and '70s includes the Family International and the Unification Church, led by Reverend Moon. NRMs from India include groups led by Hindu *swamis* (world renouncers); the Maharishi Mahesh Yogi was responsible for developing Transcendental Meditation, which became popular in the West. Other NRMs include Buddhist-based movements; Black Power movements, including the Nation of Islam; and Scientology.

85. The Bahá'í Faith

The Bahá'í faith has its origins in nineteenth-century Persia, where Sayyid 'Ali Muhammad claimed to be a Messenger of God. His successor, Bahá'u'lláh, was exiled and moved to Baghdad, where he claimed to bear a new message from God that would take humanity to the next stage of development: world unity. The Bahá'í scripture includes the writings of Bahá'u'lláh: laws, theological treatises, and letters. The Universal House of Justice legislates in areas not covered by scripture.

Bahá'ís believe the purpose of life is to demonstrate such spiritually valuable qualities as love, justice, compassion, and wisdom, which draw people closer to God. Human beings can only know something of the supreme being through intermediaries—the founders of the world's great religions. The human soul survives after death and continues to progress toward the goal of reunion with God.

Bahá'í worship features prayers and the recitation of scripture. They observe an annual fast and a communal feast every nineteen days. Those who are able go on pilgrimage to Bahá'í holy places.

The family is fundamental to a person's spiritual development, and Bahá'ís are encouraged to work toward peace by acting as a citizen of the world rather than thinking of themselves in racial, religious, ethnic, or class terms. True happiness comes from being detached from wealth and serving others.

86. Secularization and Sacralization

Generally the West has experienced secularization since the late nineteenth century, although religious belief and self-identification remain at high levels. There has been a recent shift toward spirituality and away from specific commitment to a religion. Outside the West many societies have seen a resurgence in traditional religions, especially postcolonial regions. Theories about the causes of secularization focus on the rise in rationalization and pluralism in society. Sacralization can be explained in some places by the connections made between religion and dominant political movements.

87. Religion and Globalization

Religious activity is both a cause and an effect of globalization. Missionary movements were part of an early globalization trend. Religions can more easily have a global reach through technological means, allowing the diaspora to stay more closely tied to its origins and also providing a way to spread a religion's message to more people far away. Yet what forces may bring people together can also divide them. Today's fundamentalisms are influenced by globalization and other cultural forces; religious renewal can be a response to what is seen as the negative effects of globalization, such as capitalist greed and economic injustice.

88. Religion and Politics

Religion tends to influence politics through its leaders and their teachings and through individuals in political life. Different world religions interact with political systems in various ways: Israel is a Jewish state that justifies its existence through interpretation of tradition and history; Christianity has typically acknowledged a separation between sacred concerns and secular life but has also had strong ties to power; in Islam there is no separation between sacred and secular, and therefore all political action must be tied to religious belief. Around the world since the mid-twentieth century a renewal of ties between religion and politics has developed. Hindu nationalism is a strong force in India. Sikhism gained power through its statehood, declared in 1986. Fundamentalist and other conservative Christians have strongly influenced state and federal law and policy in the United States. The association of religion and politics continues to have both beneficial effects and harmful results around the world.

Key Personalities

Ellen G. White (1827–1915)

American founder of the Church of the Seventh-Day Adventists.

"Godly mothers will inquire, with the deepest concern, Will our children continue to practice habits which will unfit them for any responsible position in this life? Will they sacrifice comeliness, health, intellect, and all hope of Heaven, everything worth possessing, here and hereafter, to the demon passion? May God grant that it may be otherwise, and that our children who are so dear to us, may listen to the voice of warning, and choose the path of purity and holiness."

(Ellen G. White Writings, *An Appeal to Mothers*, 1864, http://egwwritings.org)

Joseph Smith (1805–44)

Founder of Mormonism. He claimed to be the recipient of a divine revelation to the former inhabitants of America in the form of golden plates inscribed in ancient languages. With the help of the Angel Moroni, he translated these and they became the basis of the Book of Mormon. Ordained priest by the heavenly messenger, he founded the Church of Jesus Christ of Latter-day Saints in 1830. He died at the hands of a mob.

"'And it came to pass when I was seventeen years of age, I called again upon the Lord and he shewed unto me a heavenly vision. For behold an angel of the Lord came and stood before me. It was by night and he called me by name and he said the Lord had forgiven me my sins. He revealed unto me that in the Town of Manchester, Ontario County, New York, there was plates of gold upon which there was engravings which was engraven by Maroni and his fathers, the servants of the living God in Ancient days, deposited by the commandments of God and kept by the power thereof and that I should go and get them. He revealed unto me many things concerning the inhabitants of the earth which

since have been revealed in commandments and revelations.'"

(Joseph Smith, quoted in "Joseph Smith and the Book of Mormon," American Studies Department, University of Virginia, n.d., http://xroads.virginia.edu/~hyper/hns/mormons/smith.html)

Mary Baker Eddy (1821–1910)

American spiritual teacher and founder of Christian Science. She believed that orthodox Christianity had repressed Christ's teaching and practice of spiritual healing and that healing was not miraculous but a natural expression of the divine will. She founded the First Church of Christ Scientist in Boston in 1879; it remains the mother church of Christian Science. She wrote the authoritative work of the movement: *Science and Health* (with *Key to the Scriptures*) and founded the newspaper the *Christian Science Monitor*.

Helena P. Blavatsky (1831–91)

Founder in 1875 of the Theosophical Society, who claimed to have received the "ancient wisdom" after seven years in Tibet being taught by various mahatmas. She wrote books defending spiritualism and various occult teachings.

Bhagavan Shri Rajneesh (1931–90)

Indian spiritual teacher and philosopher who founded his own ashram at Pune (Poona) in India. His daily talks and reflections have been transcribed and widely published in the West.

Sayyid 'Ali Muhammad (1819–50)

Persian religious leader who called himself the Messenger of God and the Gate (Báb). Executed as an Islamic heretic.

"Whosoever says: 'God, God is my Lord, and I associate no-one with my Lord. The Essence of the Letters of the Seven is the Gate of God [bab Allah], and I do not believe in any gate other than him'; (whoever says this) and believes in the one God shall manifest, such a man has attained to this first gate of the first unity. Blessed be they who have attained to the bounty of a mighty day, the day on which all shall bring themselves into the presence of God, their Lord."

(Sayyid 'Ali Muhammad Shirazi, *The Persian Bayan*, trans. Denis MacEoin, http://www.h-net.org/~bahai/trans/bayan /bay1-1.htm)

Bahá'u'lláh (Mirza Husayn 'Ali Nuri) (1817–92)

A follower of Báb who became the founder of the Bahá'í faith. In Baghdad in 1863 he claimed to be the bearer of a new message from God that built on previous religions and was destined to take humanity to the next stage of social development.

"O children of men! Know ye not why We created you all from the same dust? That no one should exalt himself over the other. Ponder at all times in your hearts how ye were created. Since We have created you all from one same substance it is incumbent on you to be even as one soul, to walk with the same feet, eat with the same mouth and dwell in the same land, that from your inmost being, by your deeds and actions, the signs of oneness and the essence of detachment may be made manifest. Such is My counsel to you, O concourse of light! Heed ye this counsel that ye may obtain the fruit of holiness from the tree of wondrous glory."

("Writings of Bahá'u'lláh in His Own Hand," *The Life of Bahá'u'lláh: A Photographic Narrative*, http://www.bahaullah .org/tablets/)

'Abdu'l-Bahá ('Abbas Effendi) (1844–1921)

The son of Bahá'u'lláh, his successor as head of the Bahá'í faith, and the authorized interpreter of Bahá'u'lláh's writings.

"Note thou carefully that in this world of being, all things must ever be made new. Look at the material world about thee, see how it hath now been renewed. The thoughts have changed, the ways of life have been revised, the sciences and arts show

a new vigour, discoveries and inventions are new, perceptions are new. How then could such a vital power as religion—the guarantor of mankind's great advances, the very means of attaining everlasting life, the fosterer of infinite excellence, the light of both worlds—not be made new? This would be incompatible with the grace and loving-kindness of the Lord."

('Abdu'l-Bahá, *Selections from the Writings of 'Abdu'l-Bahá*, Bahá'í World Center, 1982, http://reference.bahai .org/en/t/ab/SAB/sab-24.html)

Shoghi Effendi (Rabbani) (1897–1957)

Grandson of 'Abbas Effendi, his successor as head of the Bahá'í faith, and the authorized interpreter of Bahá'í scriptures.

D. T. Suzuki (1870–1966)

Japanese Zen scholar who played a major part in introducing Zen Buddhism to the Western world. He was a member of the Rinzai sect and was sympathetic to Christianity.

"Nature is sometimes treaded by Western people as something already 'there' into which Man comes, and which he finds himself confronting, with hostility, because he feels he does not belong in it. . . . There is, however, another way of considering Nature and Man. . . . The very fact that Man finds himself encountering Nature demonstrates that the two are not unknown to each other. To this extent, then, Nature is already telling Man something of itself and Man is to that extent understanding Nature. . . .

"Here there is room for Zen Buddhism to enter, and to give its own views on the relationship of Nature and Man. . . . Man is still a part of Nature, for the fact of separation itself shows that Man is dependent on Nature. . . . Man came from Nature in order to see Nature in himself; that is, Nature came to itself in order to see itself in Man."

(D. T. Suzuki, *Studies in Zen*, ed. Christmas Humphreys [New York: Dell, 1955], 182–83)

Elijah Muhammad (Elijah Poole) (1897–1975)

Leader of the Nation of Islam and an advocate of independent, black-led institutions, including businesses and religious organizations.

"Slowly but surely the Spirit of Allah is making manifest to the Black Man that the church and its religion called Christianity is the chain that binds the Black Man in mental slavery (seeking salvation where there is none) and thinking that he must die first to get to heaven. This is really a misunderstanding because heaven is a condition of life and not a special place. Heaven is enjoying peace of mind and contentment with the God of the righteous and the Nation of the righteous."

(Elijah Muhammad, *Our Savior Has Arrived* [Chicago: Muhammad's Temple of Islam no. 2, 1974])

Primary Source Reading

Additional primary sources are available both in print and online, and students are encouraged to contact their instructors for further information.

XIII.1 Abdul Baha: "The Servant of God"

Source: Eric Hammond, *The Splendour of God*, 1909, http://www.sacred-texts.com/bhi/sog/sog07.htm

ABBAS EFFENDI

That the Bahais should not be left unshepherded was fore-ordained.

Baha'u'llah, with unerring insight, recognised the undoubted fitness of his eldest son for the leadership of his fast-increasing flock.

This son, known now as Abbas Effendi, was born on May 23, 1844; "the day on which The Bab began his ministry."

Not only had he eagerly assimilated the instructions of The Bab; he had also perceived and rejoiced in the fulfilment, in his Father's person, of The Bab's prophecy that "God would become Manifest."

His acquiescence in, and joyous acceptance of Baha'u'llah was complete. He called him "Lord" as well as "Father."

Used to the existence of the exiled; accustomed to all the details and requirements of the position; filled with unalterable faith in The Bab's message;—his Father's mission;—his own standing as "The Chosen One"; he took upon himself the burdensome yoke, the onerous duties, of "The Servant of God."

His knowledge of the sufferings of his people was personal and profound; he had shared in their sacrifice. His conviction that, through Bahaism, East and West would be, in God's good time, brought together in the Divine Unity, enabled him to take up bravely the burden imposed upon him by his Father.

Very wisely, as well as very bravely, has he borne that burden.

Abdul Baha, Abbas Effendi, exhibits to perfection the force and sweetness of what we call personality. We have noticed that he addressed his parent sometimes as "Father," sometimes as "Lord." This beautiful appreciation of a beautiful character is repeated in the home of Abbas Effendi, whose daughters employ the same expressions. He who is their Father according to the flesh, is also their Lord according to the spirit. They recognise in him the ideal blending of attributes human and divine; and, in this connection, it must be remembered that it is a man's family who know him most intimately. He who is both loved and reverenced by his own children has a "personality" which survives, and is exalted by, criticism.

Men of various nationalities, rightly proud of intimate acquaintance with him, speak enthusiastically of him as a living example of the practice in everyday life of the highest and, at the same time, most endearing qualities. An Englishwoman, after eight months' residence under his roof, expressed herself as having found her esteem and admiration of Abbas Effendi increase day by day. Known as "The Servant of God," the fitness of that description is proved and recognised by his service to man. His method of life has been, and continues to be, a luminous example of the fact that, here and now, despite all the surroundings of struggle for fame and wealth and material mastery, an existence guided and guarded by the Light of the Spirit is a possible, actual thing. Those who pray for the coming of the Kingdom of God on earth, may see in Abbas Effendi one who dwells in that kingdom consciously, and creates an environment pulsating with the Peace that passeth ordinary understanding.

Heeding, obeying the Supreme Voice of God sounding within, he conveys to those who come in contact with him the sense of the nearness of God. He inspires them so completely with that immanence that they are impelled to imitate him in accepting the dictates of that divine being. He who becomes assured of the indwelling God, cannot be perverted from living in the light of God, Their light, too, must be seen of men.

Is there, then, any wonder that the kindliness of heart and head and hand shown by Abbas Effendi creates corresponding kindliness in his adherents? Is there any wonder that his vast love, for humanity obliges man to love man? To those whose inner eyes are opened, the kingdom of God is on earth, for "the Kingdom of Heaven is within" them.

In himself, his everyday bearing, his ways and words, Abbas Effendi furnishes the modern world with a living object-lesson of the transforming energy of The Light of Love. He has said, "All beside love is but words." In his own person he conveys the proof of his own prophecy that the religion of Bahaism is a religion of deeds, vocalising itself not in syllables but in active signs of The Light in the life. The author of the Fourth Gospel wrote, "The life was the light of men."

He bids his followers to recognise the rays of The Light wherever they may appear; in any country; in the professors of any creed. The Light, the unifying influence, should draw men of all classes and conditions together, by dissolving clouds of difference that tend to separation.

He assures his people that the world has received enlightenment through divinely inspired seers who, from time to time, have appeared. Every religion that has arisen in the world owed its rise to these. Thus every religion is of divine origin. Prophets have proclaimed truth, teachers have unfolded the will of the Highest; each prophet, each teacher, of any religious school, has fulfilled the function of a lamp through which The Light has shone upon men.

The history of belief has in it many chapters concerning the rise and progress of religions and has been compelled to add many other chapters bearing upon the fact that the value of each religion, from a spiritual point of view, has lessened and dwindled because of the growth around it of the fungi of superstition and the frequently deadening effect of reverence for ritual. These inevitably shade the shining of The Light and prevent its irradiance. Thus life, created and moved by light, becomes dull in sympathy with the dimness of The Light. Then, at such periods, a new lamp is necessary; a new prophet passes into being, and the world once again rejoices in One who is made manifest by reason of the luminosity of The Light with which He is privileged to move among men.

By virtue of the light borne by himself, he would lead men on the Path of Peace. His light shines full upon the oneness of man with God.

If climatic and geographical considerations have produced antagonism, it is certain that a creed in one quarter has created a crux in another. Men's vision, obscured by films that have imposed themselves upon faith, could not descry hope in one another's outlook. Spiritual perception required, in these latter days, a fresh and lustrous exposition of The Eternal Light. Hence the coming of The Bab, the succession of Baha'u'llah, the culminating influence of Abbas Effendi, who spends himself making clear to men the solidarity of the race as one with each other and with God. His life is his lesson. He lops off no limb of religion from the body of mankind. He urges men to be true to that aspect of the highest that appeals to them; for the core of each creed is truth; the seed of each religion was sown by the Lord.

That Baha'u'llah acted wisely and well in proclaiming his son Abbas Effendi his successor, events have plentifully proved.

Courteous, kindly, dignified, his personality fascinates and compels towards goodness.

Honourable and just, he so disarms prejudice that "his jailers have become his friends." That the people of Acca esteem him and look to him for sympathy and justice might be supposed, but it is a remarkable and noteworthy fact to record that equal esteem is evinced for him by successive governors of the city and by military officers in authority there.

Nearly forty years he has dwelt, imprisoned, in that little city of Acca, a familiar figure, a marked man. Familiarity has not bred contempt, but sincerest admiration and reverence.

Those who have visited him—when the powers that were permitted such visits—have found their love and respect for him increase day by day, even month by month. Prolonged intimacy is the severest of all tests, but, tried by this test, Abbas Effendi is, throughout, the gainer.

Always under surveillance, frequently under suspicion (of political or other inimical intent), his courage has disarmed espionage, and his untiring faculty for forgiving has rendered suspicion foolish.

His devotion and attention to his people have increased rather than lessened during the years of a busy, harassed life. Through persecution, misapprehension, and many misrepresentations, he has proved true to his ideal; unswerving in the pursuance of his purpose.

His liberality relative to varying creeds is equalled by his generosity to friends and foes. Poverty and suffering exist, he considers, in order to be relieved at any personal cost and inconvenience. Those who

have vehemently opposed and strenuously fought to hinder him, have participated in much material benefit at his hands. Intolerance is, in the rule of the Bahai, the one impossible word.

In dealing with conflicting opinions and rituals, Abbas Effendi's method is that of acute intelligence and spiritual perception. He exercises his fine insight into the minds of others; an insight as sympathetic as it is immediate. Thus he treats any theme under discussion from the point of view of the religion professed by the enquirer, selecting, as arguments, texts from the Scripture sacred to that religion.

All that is evil or untoward in a man's or a country's condition, he comprehends, deplores, forthwith strives to remedy.

His advanced scientific and hygienic principles have aided him, prisoner and poor, to redeem Acca, at least in part, from its notorious insalubrity.

In signs and miracles he deals not at all. Gifted to no small extent with healing powers—largely the result of education and experience in suffering—he firmly deprecates any imputation of the supernatural.

"If men's minds are fixed on miracles, which prove nothing in themselves, they will be less open to the reception of truth, or be closed entirely to the Divine Message."

How far the sweetness and light of that message as delivered by The Bab, the enlightening revelations of Baha'u'llah, and the Gospel according to Abbas Effendi, have permeated the Persian conscience or penetrated into other Oriental castes, concerns our present purpose but little. The last named of these, however, rejoices with exceeding joy in the promised, and promising, Constitutions of Eastern countries. "For the first time during seven years," writes a devoted friend from Acca in the autumn of 1908, "our Lord has been allowed to visit the tomb of Baha'u'llah. With him I saw the tomb and was permitted to share in his freedom and that of his people."

The chains of the captivity are released. Freedom, to live here or to live there; Freedom, to speak and write tidings of goodwill; Freedom—the word, the thing—cannot be entered into by men who have been born and who have lived, free. It cannot be adequately put into any language. It can only be enjoyed to the uttermost by those to whom liberty has been a lifelong hope, a lifelong sacred dream which the Infinite One in His infinite goodness might make real. It can only become real to those who, like the Bahais, have "suffered and are strong," because of a supreme faith in a supreme cause.

Freedom, liberty, light;—not for one tribe or worshippers in one temple, but for all the sons of men and of God;—these are the one desire of Abdul Baha, Abbas Effendi. His acute apprehension of man's soul urges him to preach that no people are so distrustful of others as those who, isolated and self-contained, know little, and care less, of contact with other folk. It is their natural tendency to become more and more satisfied with their limitations and indeed to believe at last that material and spiritual salvation can only be acquired within those limits. Upheavals are essential. The advent of a prophet is a necessity; first, perhaps, to be despised, doubted; but, in the end, to cause a vital current of opinion to flow in the direction of charitable speculation. It is true that the parochialist in religion usually uplifts his voice clamorously against the prophet and the prophecy. It is true, too, that when a master-mind frames truth in a new setting, or boldly breaks away incrustations which have longtime concealed truth, and been adored in mistake for truth, a storm of disapproval attempts to drown the missioner's voice and mar his message. Limitations, too frequently the accumulation of custom, convention, or superstition, have, on requisite occasion, to be shattered; with all courtesy,

with all generosity, but with unyielding decision. It is essential to the welfare of the world that seers should arise to utter the truth that has existed from the beginning; the truth that has always, to less extent or more, been uttered in the East.

Out of the East, Abbas Effendi's humanising, spiritualising influence is spreading near and far. In the Eastern firmament a Star has again arisen and its beams are shedding light upon the dark places of the earth.

Each philosophy has many facets. Diamondwise, the philosophy of Bahaism has been skilfully wrought by experts in prayer and practice.

For example;—Abbas Effendi has been entitled "His Highness the Master"; he prefers to be known as "The Servant," and, day by day, holds himself in readiness to serve. Customary Mohammedan observances are maintained "for the sake of peace and to avoid the imputation of social innovation." Constant generosity is enjoined. These are facets of jewels shining in the Bahai crown.

Monogamy is advised, and Abbas Effendi's example is respected and admired.

Differences of religious opinion should be disregarded; most of all when charity (alms-giving) is concerned.

Each Bahai should have good working knowledge of some useful trade or profession. Industry is expected of all. The emancipation of woman and the equal education of girls and boys is Abbas Effendi's desire and prophecy. Cleanliness of body and mind; practical thrift; personal action towards universal Brotherhood;—these are parts of the clauses in the holy ordinance.

Key Terms

The Book of Mormon Sacred scripture of Mormonism which was revealed to Joseph Smith. It describes a conflict between two branches of a family that had emigrated under divine guidance from Jerusalem to America in 600 BCE. The Mormons regard it as the completion of the biblical revelation.

fundamentalism The doctrine that the Bible is verbally inspired and therefore inerrant and infallible on all matters of doctrine and history; from *The Fundamentals*, published in 1909.

Kitab-I-Aqdas Meaning "the most holy book," this is one of the most important works of Bahá'u'lláh. It contains most of the laws and many social ordinances of Bahá'u'lláh.

Kiab-I-Iqan Meaning "the book of certitude," this is one of the most important works of Bahá'u'lláh. It addresses a range of theological questions and provides interpretations of the Bible and the Qur'an.

Nation of Islam African American religious movement founded by Wallace D. Fard in Detroit in 1930 and influenced by Black Power.

New Age With roots in particularly Theosophy, the term refers to alternative spiritualities, which emerged in the mid-1960s principally on the west coast of the United States and spread throughout North America and Europe. The movements are characterized by a concern to realize the spiritual potential of the individual self, which is often believed to be divine. Also common is the belief that, as we move from the astrological age of Pisces into the age of Aquarius, we are witnessing a spiritual renaissance, a New Age of nonhierarchical, non-patriarchal, eco-friendly spirituality. Drawing from discoveries in physics and cosmology, their teachings claim to revive ancient mystical traditions of East and West. They emphasize healing, a healthy and balanced lifestyle and expansion of self-awareness through meditation and personal counseling.

Nineteen Day Feast Bahá'í communal meal held once every nineteen days; has three portions: devotional, consultative, and social.

Rastafarians Religious and political movement centered in the Caribbean. It is a cult of Ras Tafari, better known as Haile Selassie (1892–1975), emperor of Ethiopia (1930–74). Many Rastafarians (not all) are distinguished by keeping their hair in dreadlocks and by their use of cannabis in worship. They helped develop the reggae style of music, which they use to express their political and religious aspirations. The singer Bob Marley has become one of the heroes of the movement.

swami General term for a Hindu holy man or member of a religious order.

Tablets Letters written by Bahá'u'lláh responding to questions from his followers and others and considered part of the Bahá'í scriptures.

Transcendental Meditation (TM) Meditation technique taught by Maharishi Mahesh Yogi which has flourished in the West since the 1960s. Practitioners need no religious beliefs. They are taught to meditate for fifteen to twenty minutes twice a day; this reduces stress and aids relaxation. In some states in the United States it has been ruled that Transcendental Meditation is a religion of Hindu origin.

Universal House of Justice Ordained in the writings of Bahá'u'lláh but not founded until 1963, this is now the supreme administrative body of the Bahá'í faith.

Questions for Study and Discussion

1. What is existentialism? Explain how an existentialist could be of any religious faith or none at all.
2. The author Anthony C. Thiselton writes, "Postmodernism is finally unmasked as offering not the freedom which it claims, but conflict and uncertainty, and an invitation to blame the power interests of competing groups for all ills" (p. 462). Do you agree or disagree? Explain.
3. Choose two Christian-related NRMs mentioned in the chapter (see pp. 463–67) and describe their main distinguishing features. How did each movement change a fundamental Christian value, belief, or practice? What aspects of Christianity seem to have remained in some version in these movements?
4. Briefly describe Benjamin Zephaniah's faith as he reports it ("I am a Rastafarian," pp. 474–75). What of his values are similar to other religious traditions? Name two or three features of his spiritual views or practices that seem to be unique to Rastafarianism.
5. What are the five theories of secularization?
6. David Lyon argues that "religious activity is both a cause and effect of globalization" (p. 476). How does the Internet play a role in this relationship?
7. What role do you believe religions should play, if any, in politics in the country in which you live? What role do you think they should play, if any, in international politics?

Questions for Reflection

Write your personal reflections to each of these questions in the space provided.

1. How has philosophy influenced religion? (See pp. 458–62.)

2. Note which New Religious Movements (NRMs) come from which world religions or have been influenced by indigenous religions. (See pp. 463–67.)

3. Compare a UFO religion with a traditional religion and draw similarities using the theories discussed in Part 1. Are there rituals, sacred calendars, etc.? (See p. 466–67.)

4. Describe the core principles of the Bahá'í faith. (See pp. 469–70.)

5. How has globalization affected religion? Have you witnessed religions meeting in a "globalized" manner? (See pp. 476–79.)

Selected Online Resources

▶ The World Religions & Spirituality Project—an extensive archive of articles and resources related to the world's religions, with a focus on those found in North America
http://www.has.vcu.edu/wrs/index.html

▶ "A Protestant View of Globalization"—five-part essay on the ability of Christianity to address globalization, published on *The Globalist*, an online magazine, April 2010
http://www.theglobalist.com/storyid.aspx?StoryId=8381

▶ Online Texts about Cults and New Religious Movements—links to scholarly essays and book chapters on various topics related to NRMs
http://www.skepsis.nl/onlinetexts.html

A SHORT GUIDE TO WRITING RESEARCH PAPERS ON WORLD RELIGIONS

This guide is meant to help you organize and compose a traditional academic research paper on world religions. You may find the basic sequence and resources helpful in other disciplines, too.

Short or long, your research paper can be crafted in five steps: (1) choose a topic, (2) research your topic, (3) outline your argument, (4) write the first draft, and (5) refine the final paper.

1. Choose a Topic

If your topic is not chosen for you, you should aim to choose one that is (1) interesting to you, (2) manageable (with readily available sources) and malleable (so you can narrow in on an especially interesting or important aspect), and (3) arguable. Your research paper will essentially be an argument based in the available primary and secondary sources and authorities.

A good place to start is the chapters of *Introduction to World Religions*. Perhaps there was a topic in one of the chapters (such as an ascetic tradition or the history of a religion's sacred writings) that caught your interest. Also, look over this study guide. Is there a particular question or idea that sparks your interest? Check out the Selected Online Resources; perhaps a website will lead you to a good research topic. Below are some additional suggestions:

Methodological Topics

What do the concepts of "cult" and "sect" mean from the perspective of the sociology of religion? How have these concepts changed during the development of the field?

How did C. G. Jung's and Sigmund Freud's theories affect the study of religion in the twentieth century?

How was Søren Kierkegaard able to integrate existentialism into his critique of Christianity and his concept of Christian theology?

What benefits and drawbacks do postmodernist theories have to offer the study of religion?

Historical Topics

What do the Vedas tell us about the Aryans' culture and worldview?

How did the Jews fare under the Ottoman Empire?

How did the Christian biblical canon come about? Was it universally adopted?

How has the role of the *Shari'a* in Muslim governments changed over time?

Interpretive or Comparative Topics

How do the religious role of the ancient Egyptian kings and that of the ancient Roman emperors compare?

How did the worship forms and styles of the Norse and the Celts reflect their views of nature?

How does the encounter between colonial powers and an indigenous people affect both the indigenous religion and that of the colonizing people?

How has Hinduism influenced the religious beliefs and structures of Jainism and Sikhism?

Resources for Choosing a Topic and Beginning a Research Paper

Booth, Wayne C., Gregory G. Colomb, and Joseph M. Williams. *The Craft of Research*. 3rd ed. Chicago: University of Chicago Press, 2008.

Mann, Thomas. *The Oxford Guide to Library Research*. 3rd ed. New York: Oxford University Press, 2005.

Vyhmeister, Nancy Jean. *Quality Research Papers: For Students of Religion and Theology*. Grand Rapids, MI: Zondervan, 2001.

2. Research Your Topic

Material about your topic may reside in a single text or an array of historical texts by one or many authors or in the conflicting opinions of contemporary scholars. In most cases, you can build your research by moving from general to specific treatments of your topic.

One caution: In your research, it is vital that you not allow your expanding knowledge of what others think about your topic to drown your own curiosities, sensibilities, and insights. Instead, as your initial questions expand and then diminish with increased knowledge from your research, your ideas, theories, and point of view should emerge and grow.

Encyclopedia articles, scholarly books, dictionaries of religions, journal articles, and other standard reference tools contain a wealth of material and helpful bibliographies to orient you to your topic and its historical context. Look for the most authoritative and up-to-date sources. Checking cross-references will deepen your knowledge.

General Reference Works

Black, Jeremy, and Anthony Green. *Gods, Demons, and Symbols of Ancient Mesopotamia: An Illustrated Dictionary*. Austin: University of Texas Press, 1992.

Coogan, Michael D. *Eastern Religions: Hinduism, Buddhism, Taoism, Confucianism, Shinto*. New York: Oxford University Press, 2005.

Encyclopedia of Early Christianity. Ed. Everett Ferguson. 2nd ed. New York: Garland, 1998.

Encyclopedia of Islam and the Muslim World. 2 vols. Edited by Richard C. Martin. New York: Macmillan Reference, 2004.

Encyclopedia of Religion. Edited by Lindsay Jones. 15 vols. 2nd ed. New York: Macmillan Reference, 2005.

Encyclopedia of Religion and Nature. Edited by Bron R. Taylor et al. New York: Continuum, 2008.

Encyclopedia of Religion in America. Edited by Charles H. Lippy and Peter W. Williams. Washington, DC: CQ Press, 2010.

Encyclopedia of Religion in Australia. Edited by James Jupp. Cambridge, UK: Cambridge University Press, 2009.

Encyclopedia of Religious Rites, Rituals, and Festivals. Ed. Frank A. Salamone. New York: Routledge, 2004.

The Encyclopedic Sourcebook of New Age Religions. Edited by James R. Lewis. Amherst, NY: Prometheus Books, 2004.

Flood, Gavin. *An Introduction to Hinduism*. Cambridge, UK: Cambridge University Press, 1996.

Irons, Edward A. *Encyclopedia of Buddhism*. Encyclopedia of World Religions / Facts on File Library of Religion and Mythology. New York: Facts on File, 2008.

Mazur, Eric Michael. *Encyclopedia of Religion and Film*. Santa Barbara, CA: ABC-CLIO, 2011.

Muesse, Mark W. *The Hindu Traditions: A Concise Introduction*. Minneapolis: Fortress Press, 2011.

New Encyclopedia of Judaism. Edited by Geoffrey Wigoder et al. New York: New York University Press, 2002.

Oxford Dictionary of the Christian Church. Edited by F. L. Cross and E. A. Livingstone. 3rd ed. rev. Oxford, UK: Oxford University Press, 2005.

Sullivan, Lawrence E. *Religions of the World: An Introduction to Culture and Meaning.* Minneapolis: Fortress Press, 2012.

Online Resources

Although not all Internet sources meet scholarly standards, some very good reference tools do appear online. Some of them are listed here. When researching online, be sure to check on the source of a piece of information presented as fact or theory: the citation should be clear and verifiable, or the original author should be listed and should be a trusted source (e.g., a scholar who has published in a peer-reviewed journal).

Note: All URLs were current when this book was published.

▶ The Wabash Center's Internet Guide to Religion—"A selective, annotated guide to a wide variety of electronic resources of interest to those who are involved in the study and practice of religion: syllabi, electronic texts, electronic journals, web sites, bibliographies, liturgies, reference resources, software, etc." http://www.wabashcenter.wabash.edu/resources /guide_headings.aspx

▶ Sacred Texts: World Religions—lists pages for all major world religions, which feature links to full texts of scriptures and other sacred writings (translated into English where relevant) http://www.sacred-texts.com/world.htm

▶ Virtual Religion Index—covers many categories of ancient and contemporary world religions; provides links to assist in academic research and study of religion http://virtualreligion.net/vri

▶ Religious Studies Web Guide—offers resources arranged by format and topic http://people.ucalgary.ca/~lipton/catalogues .html

▶ The World Religions & Spirituality Project— an extensive archive of articles and resources related to the world's religions, with a focus on those found in North America http://www.has.vcu.edu/wrs/index.html

It's best to start listing the sources you've consulted right away in standard bibliographical format (see section 5, below, for examples of usual formats). You'll want to assign a number or code to each one so you'll be able to reference them easily when you're writing the paper.

Periodical Literature

Even if you are writing on a single text (e.g., an excerpt from the *Upanishads*, the Gospel of Mark, the Tao Te Ching), you'll be able to place your interpretation in contemporary context only by referring to what other scholars today are saying. Their work is largely published in academic journals and periodicals. In consulting the chief articles dealing with your topic, you'll learn where agreements, disagreements, and open questions stand; how older theories have fared; and the latest relevant tools and insights. Since you cannot consult them all, start with the most recent, looking for the best and most directly relevant articles from the last five years and then going back ten or twenty years, as ambition and time allow.

A good place to start is the ATLA Religion Database (www.atla.com), which indexes articles, essays, book reviews, dissertations, theses, and even essays in collections. You can search by keywords, subjects, persons, or scripture references. Below are other standard indexes to periodical literature. Check with your institution's library to learn which ones it subscribes to.

Guide to Social Science and Religion in Periodical Literature (http://www.nplguide.com)

Readers' Guide to Periodical Literature

Dissertation Abstracts International

ATLA Catholic Periodical and Literature Index

Humanities International Index

Research the Most Important Books and Primary Sources

By now you can identify the most important sources for your topic, both primary and secondary. *Primary sources* are actual historical documents or artifacts that provide data for interpretation: sacred writings (such as the Vedas, the Bible, the Qur'an, prayers, hymns, poems), interviews, and memoirs, for example. *Secondary sources* are all the articles or books that analyze or interpret primary sources.

Your research topic might be in a single primary source—for example, the notion of enlightenment in the Lotus Sutra—with many secondary commentaries, analyses, or interpretations. Or your primary resources may be large—the polled opinions of thousands of people, the mystical writings of a tradition, or a body of religious law created over centuries—and may or may not have many associated secondary sources.

Apart from books you've identified through the sources you've consulted, you can find the chief works on any topic readily listed in your school library's catalog, the Library of Congress subject index (http://catalog2.loc.gov), and other online library catalog sites. Many theological libraries and archives are linked at the "Religious Studies Web Guide": http://people.ucalgary.ca/~lipton/catalogues.html.

The eventual quality of your research paper rests entirely on the quality or *critical character* of your sources. The best research uses academically sound treatments by recognized authorities arguing rigorously from primary sources.

Taking Notes

With these sources on hand—whether primary or secondary, whether in books or articles or websites or polling data—you can review each source, noting down its most important or relevant facts, observations, or opinions.

One method is to create a document for each main source that includes its bibliographical (publication) information and its key points. You'll need each notable point to identify the subtopic, the main idea or direct quotation, and the page number(s).

This practice will allow you to redistribute each point to wherever it is needed in your eventual outline.

While most of the notes you take will simply summarize points made in primary or secondary sources, direct quotes are used for (1) word-for-word transcriptions, (2) key words or phrases coined by the author, or (3) especially clear or summary formulations of an author's point of view. Remember, re-presenting another's insight or formulation without attribution is plagiarism. You should also be sure to keep separate notes about your own ideas or insights into the topic as they evolve.

When Can I Stop?

As you research your topic in books, articles, or reference works, you will find it coalescing into a unified body of knowledge or at least into a set of interrelated questions. Your topic will become more and more focused, partly because that is where the open question or key insight or most illuminating instance resides and partly for sheer manageability. The vast range of scholarly methods and opinions and sharply differing points of view about most religious topics (especially in the contemporary period) may force you to settle for laying out a more circumscribed topic carefully. While the sources may never dry up, your increased knowledge gradually gives you confidence that you have the most informed, authoritative, and critical sources covered in your notes.

3. Outline Your Argument

On the basis of your research findings, in this crucial step you refine or reformulate your general topic and question into a specific question answered by a defensible thesis. You then arrange or rework your supporting materials into a clear outline that will coherently and convincingly present your thesis to your reader.

First, review your research notes carefully. Some of what you initially read may now seem obvious or irrelevant, or perhaps the whole topic is simply too massive. But as your reading and note taking progressed, you might also have found a piece of your topic, from which a key question or problem has emerged and around which your research has gelled. Ask yourself:

- What is the subtopic or subquestion that is most interesting, enlightening, and manageable?
- What have been the most clarifying and illuminating insights I have found into the topic?
- In what ways have my findings contradicted my initial expectations? Can this serve as a clue to a new and different approach to my question?
- Can I frame my question in a clear way, and, in light of my research, do I have something new to say and defend—my thesis—that will answer my question and clarify my materials?

In this way you will advance from topic and initial question to specific question and thesis. For example, as you research primary and secondary sources on the role of the apocryphal scriptures in the early development of Buddhism. You might then find evidence that the Tantras were a particularly important factor in the spread of Buddhism in Southeast Asia. You might then advance a thesis that the elements of secrecy and magical rituals had significant appeal for non-Mahayana Buddhist cultures. So you have:

Topic: Apocryphal scriptures and Buddhism's development

Specific topic: The role of the Tantras in the spread of Buddhism in Southeast Asia

Specific question: What made the Tantras appealing to Buddhists outside the Mahayana tradition?

Thesis: The Tantras' focus on secrecy and magic were key factors in their spread beyond Mahayana Buddhist cultures in Southeast Asia.

You can then outline a presentation of your thesis that organizes your research materials into an orderly and convincing argument. Functionally your outline might look like this:

Introduction: Raise the key question, and announce your thesis.

Background: Present the necessary literary or historical or theological context of the question. Note the state of the question—the main agreements and disagreements about it.

Development: Present your own insight in a clear and logical way. Present evidence to support your thesis, and develop it further by:

- offering examples from your primary sources
- citing or discussing authorities to bolster your argument
- contrasting your thesis with other treatments, either historical or contemporary
- confirming it by showing how it makes good sense of the data, answers related questions, or solves previous puzzles.

Conclusion: Restate the thesis in a way that recapitulates your argument and its consequences for the field or the contemporary religious horizon.

The more detailed your outline, the easier will be your writing. Go through your note files, reorganizing them according to your outline. Fill in the outline with the specifics from your research, right down to the topic sentences of your paragraphs. Don't hesitate to set aside any materials that now seem off-point, extraneous, or superfluous to the development of your argument.

4. Write the First Draft

You are now ready to draft your paper, essentially by putting your outline into sentence form while incorporating specifics from your research notes.

Your main task, initially, is just to set your ideas down in as straightforward a way as possible. Assume your reader is intelligent but knows little or nothing about your particular topic. You can follow your outline closely, but you may find that logical presentation of your argument requires making some adjustments to the outline. As you write, weave in quotes judiciously from primary or secondary literature to clarify or punch your points. Add brief, strong headings at major junctures. Add footnotes to acknowledge ideas, attribute quotations, reinforce your key points through authorities, or refer the reader to further discussion or resources. Your draft footnotes will refer to your sources in abbreviated form based on your files; be sure to include page numbers. You can add full publishing data once your text is firm.

5. Refine the Final Paper

Your first draft puts you within sight of your goal, but your project's real strength emerges from reworking your initial text in a series of revisions and refinements.

In this final phase, be sure to refer to the style manual preferred by your instructor or institution, or use one listed below:

The Chicago Manual of Style. 16th ed. Chicago: University of Chicago Press, 2010.

MLA Handbook for Writers of Research Papers. 7th ed. New York: Modern Language Association, 2009.

Turabian, Kate L. *A Manual for Writers of Research Papers, Theses, and Dissertations: Chicago Style for Students and Researches.* 8th ed. Revised by Wayne C. Booth, Gregory G. Colomb, Joseph M. Williams, et al. Chicago: University of Chicago Press, 2013.

Williams, Joseph M. *Style: Toward Clarity and Grace.* Chicago Guides to Writing, Editing, and Publishing. Chicago: University of Chicago Press, 1995.

Online, see the searchable website Guide to Grammar and Writing: http://grammar.ccc .commnet.edu/grammar.

Polishing the Prose

To check spelling and meaning of words or to help vary your prose, try Merriam-Webster Online, which contains both the Collegiate Dictionary and the Thesaurus: http://www.m-w.com.

Closely examine your work several times, paying attention to:

▶ Structure and Argument. Ask yourself, Do I state my question and thesis accurately? Does my paper do what my introduction promised? (If not, adjust one or the other.) Do I argue my thesis well? Do the headings clearly guide the reader through my outline and argument? Does this sequence of topics orchestrate the insights my reader needs to understand my thesis?

▶ Style. "Style" here refers to writing patterns that enliven prose and engage the reader. Three simple ways to strengthen your academic prose are:

— Topic sentences: Be sure each paragraph clearly states its main assertion.

— Active verbs: As much as possible, avoid using the linking verb "to be," and instead rephrase using active verbs.

— Sentence flow: Above all, look for awkward sentences in your draft. Disentangle and rework them into smooth, clear sequences. To avoid boring the reader, vary the length and form of your sentences. Check to see if your paragraphs unfold with questions and simple declarative sentences, in addition to longer descriptive phrases.

Likewise, tackle some barbarisms that frequently invade academic prose:

▶ Repetition: Unless you need the word count, this can go.

▶ Unnecessary words: Such filler phrases as "The fact that" and "in order to" and "There is/are" numb your reader. Similarly, such qualifiers as "somewhat," "fairly," and "very" should be avoided unless they are part of a clearly defined comparison.

▶ Jargon: Avoid technical terms when possible. Explain all technical terms that you do use. Avoid or translate foreign-language terms.

▶ Overly complex sentences: Short sentences are best. Avoid run-on sentences. Avoid "etc."

Along with typographical errors, look for stealth errors—the common but overlooked grammatical gaffes: subject-verb disagreement, dangling participles, mixed verb tenses, overuse and underuse of commas, misuse of semicolons, and inconsistency in capitalization, hyphenation, italicization, and treatment of numbers.

Footnotes

Your footnotes credit your sources for every direct quotation and for other people's ideas you have used. Below are samples of typical citation formats in Modern Language Association style. (For more information on citing online sources, see Robert Harris's "Citing Web Sources MLA Style": http://www.virtualsalt.com/mla.htm.)

▶ Basic order
  Author's full name, *Book Title,* ed., trans., series, edition, vol. number (Place: Publisher, year), pages.
▶ Book
  Bell, Diane. *Daughters of the Dreaming*, 2nd ed. (Minneapolis: University of Minnesota Press, 1993), 27.
▶ Book in a series
  Westerkamp, Marilyn J. "Gendering Christianity." In *Modern Christianity to 1900*, ed. Amanda Porterfield, 261–90. A People's History of Christianity, vol. 6. Minneapolis: Fortress Press, 2007.
▶ Essay or chapter in an edited book
  Sallie B. King, "Human Rights in Contemporary Engaged Buddhism," in *Buddhist Theology: Critical Reflections by Contemporary Buddhist Scholars*, ed. Roger Jackson and John Makransky (London: Curzon Press, 2000), 294.
▶ Multivolume work
  B. McGinn, J. J. Collins, and S. Stein, eds., *The Encyclopedia of Apocalypticism* (New York: Continuum, 1998), 1:85.
▶ Journal article
  Philip J. Ivanhoe, "Thinking and Learning in Early Confucianism," *Journal of Chinese Philosophy* 17 (December 1990): 473–93.

▶ Online journal article
  Jon R. Norman, "Congregational Culture and Identity Politics in a Lesbian, Gay, Bisexual, and Transgender Synagogue: Making Inclusiveness and Religious Practice One and the Same," *Journal of Religion and Society* 13 (2011), http://moses.creighton.edu/JRS/2011/2011-2.html.
▶ Bible
  Cite in your text (not in your footnotes) by book, chapter, and verse: Gen. 1:1-2; Exod. 7:13; Rom. 5:1-8. In your bibliography list the version of the Bible you have used.
▶ Qur'an
  Cite in your text (not in your footnotes) by *surah*, e.g., *surah* 2:106. In your bibliography list the published translation you have used.

If a footnote cites the immediately preceding source, use "Ibid." (from the Latin *ibidem*, meaning "there"). For example:

61. Ibid., 39.
Sources cited earlier can be referred to by author or editor's last name(s), a shorter title, and page number. For example: Koester, *Introduction,* 42.

Bibliography

Your bibliography can be any of several types:

▶ Works Cited: just the works—books, articles, etc.—that appear in your footnotes;
▶ Works Consulted: all the works you checked in your research, whether they were cited or not in the final draft; or
▶ Select Bibliography: primary and secondary works that, in your judgment, are the most important source materials on this topic, whether cited or not in your footnotes.
  Some instructors might ask for your bibliographic entries to be annotated, that is, including a comment from you on the content, import, approach, and helpfulness of each work.

Bibliographic style differs somewhat from footnote style. Here are samples of typical bibliographic formats in MLA style:

▶ Basic order
Author's last name, first name and initial. *Book Title.* Editor. Translator. Series. Edition. Number of volumes. Place: Publisher, Year.

▶ Book
Bell, Diane. *Daughters of the Dreaming.* Second edition. Minneapolis: University of Minnesota Press, 1993.

▶ Book in a series
Westerkamp, Marilyn J. "Gendering Christianity." In *Modern Christianity to 1900,* ed. Amanda Porterfield, 261–90. A People's History of Christianity, vol. 6. Minneapolis: Fortress Press, 2007.

▶ Edited book
Kwam, Kristen E., Linda S. Schearing, and Valarie H. Ziegler, eds. *Eve and Adam: Jewish, Christian, and Muslim Readings on Genesis and Gender.* Bloomington: Indiana University Press, 1999.

▶ Essay or chapter in an edited book
King, Sallie B. "Human Rights in Contemporary Engaged Buddhism." In *Buddhist Theology: Critical Reflections by Contemporary Buddhist Scholars,* ed. Roger Jackson and John Makransky, 293–311. London: Curzon, 2000.

▶ Multivolume work
McGinn, B., J. J. Collins, and S. Stein, eds. *The Encyclopedia of Apocalypticism.* 3 vols. New York: Continuum, 1998.

▶ Journal article
Ivanhoe, Philip J. "Thinking and Learning in Early Confucianism." *Journal of Chinese Philosophy* 17 (December 1990): 473–93.

▶ Online journal article
Norman, Jon R. "Congregational Culture and Identity Politics in a Lesbian, Gay, Bisexual, and Transgender Synagogue: Making Inclusiveness and Religious Practice One and the Same." *Journal of Religion and Society* 13 (2011). http://moses.creighton.edu /JRS/2011/2011-2.html.

▶ Bible
The Holy Bible: Revised Standard Version. New York: Oxford University Press, 1973.

Final Steps

After incorporating the revisions and refinements into your paper, print out a fresh copy, proofread it carefully, make your last corrections to the electronic file, format it to your instructor's or school's specifications, and print your final paper.